WHERE ARE THE WOMEN?

WHERE ARE THE WOMEN?

WHY EXPANDING THE ARCHIVE MAKES PHILOSOPHY BETTER

SARAH TYSON

Columbia University Press *New York*

Columbia University Press
Publishers Since 1893
New York Chichester, West Sussex
cup.columbia.edu

Library of Congress Cataloging-in-Publication Data
Names: Tyson, Sarah, author.
Title: Where are the women? : why expanding the archive makes philosophy better / Sarah Tyson.
Description: New York : Columbia University Press, 2018. |
Includes bibliographical references and index.
Identifiers: LCCN 2018002866| ISBN 9780231183963 (cloth : alk. paper) |
ISBN 9780231183970 (pbk. : alk. paper) | ISBN 9780231545259 (ebook)
Subjects: LCSH: Women philosophers.
Classification: LCC B105.W6 T97 2018 | DDC 108.2—dc23
LC record available at https://lccn.loc.gov/2018002866

Columbia University Press books are printed on permanent
and durable acid-free paper.
Printed in the United States of America

Cover design: Elliott S. Cairns
Cover image: Judy Chicago, The Dinner Party, Elizabeth A. Sackler
Center for Feminist Art, Brooklyn Museum. © 2018 Judy Chicago /
Artists Rights Society (ARS), New York. Photo: © Donald Woodman.

For Josh and Iris

CONTENTS

ACKNOWLEDGMENTS

Having done both, I do not know which is harder, writing a book or gestating and giving birth to a baby. They are mostly incomparable, but for me these experiences shared an important feature: they required the support, encouragement, and critical feedback of many, many people. Books give one the opportunity to thank the people who helped, and thus could begin an extensive list of the differences in these activities. Instead, I would like to thank as many people as I can for making this book possible.

First, thanks to all the people who supported my work on this project from its very early stages to right now. It's hard for me to separate out who gave me support as a friend, a colleague, or a mentor, and I think that is a sign of my great good fortune. My enormous thanks to Buick Audra, Carolyn Benedict, Valri Bromfield, Amy Bryant, Edward Burger, Julie Carr, Polly Case, Amanda Chiampi, Natalie Cisneros, Stacy Clifford, Elizabeth Covington, Kate Cox, Carolyn Cusick, Rebecca Davenport, Christina Dickerson, Idit Dobbs-Weinstein, Amanda Dort, Nate Dort, Michael Eck, Sarah Kate Edwards, Teddy Edwards, Pete Emerson, Jennifer Foley, Mona Frederick, Edward Friedman,

Gesa Frömming, Kent Fuka, Karla Gudino, Omar Gudino, Sarah Glynn, Colleen Hackett, Sarah Hansen, Mike Heigemann, Clive Hunter, Billy Husher, Patrick Jackson, Gary Jaeger, Megan Jones, Jessica Justice-Eck, Chad Kautzer, Sheila Keller, Prafull Kotecha, Libor Koudelka, Helen Koudelkova, Amanda Knudsen, Elliotte Krier, Nick Lerman, Adam McAboy, Gail McConnell, Joanna Matocha, José Medina, Brandon Mills, Karen Mills, Elena Mirabal, Lucius T. Outlaw, Nomad Ovunc, Jason Parker, Kate Rattner, Emily Rodriguez, Kimberly Rogers, Camisha Russell, Francey Russell, Misty Saribal, Rebecca Saxon, Mark Schnug, Matt Schreiber, Melita Schwartz, CJ Sentell, Maria Talero, Robert Talisse, Allison Thompson, Jeffrey Tlumak, Danielle Vance, Mare Wakefield, Sam Webber, Mark Whitaker, Matt Whitt, Elizabeth Zagatta, and Sara Zimmerman. Thanks to Jonathan Neufeld, who was the first person to think I might be on to something. Thanks to Kelly Oliver, who has unflaggingly supported my work on this project, and in philosophy, through every stage of its development. Lisa Guenther, Gregg Horowitz, and Penelope Deutscher all offered critical feedback and guidance at early stages of this project, for which I am so thankful.

I am grateful to many people at the University of Colorado Denver, for their support and encouragement, not just of this book, but also of me as a scholar and a person. My thanks to Andres Ayala-Patlan, Mark Bauer, Nicky Beer, Jeffrey Golub, Sarah Hagelin, David Hildebrand, Boram Jeong, Pamela Laird, Brian Lisle, Joanna Luloff, Robert Metcalf, Elizabeth Puente-Calderón, Donna Reeves, Candice Shelby, Mark Tanzer, Sam Walker, Melinda Wilding, and Gabriel Zamosc-Regueros. I owe a special thanks to Andres for help with research. And another special thanks to David for reading parts of this project and offering feedback.

My writing group at University of Colorado Denver has read parts of this project, given me invaluable feedback, and made my life better with their humor, understanding, and guidance. Many thanks to Michelle Comstock, Sarah Fields, Amy Hasinoff, Marjorie Levine-Clark, Lucy McGuffey, Gillian Silverman, and Margaret Woodhull. A special thanks to Amy for closely reading a chapter and marking every single place she had a question. And another special thanks to Gillian for reading multiple drafts of multiple parts, sometimes out loud to me, despite my cringing.

Thanks to Perry Zurn for reading, giving comments, and talking poetry. Thanks to Brady Heiner for reading, giving comments, and writing with me. Thanks to Andrew Dilts, who read some parts multiple times, always had a new reference for me, and was always willing to talk seriously about all the stuff. Thanks to Geoffrey Adelsberg, who also generously read multiple drafts of multiple parts and always expressed a skepticism that ought to have been cutting, but was said with such genuine goodwill that it always motivated me instead. I am also grateful to Geoff for taking a long look at his bookshelf one day before saying, "I need your book there." Nicole A. Spigner has read, and read, and read. And talked. And challenged. And encouraged me. And then fed me and my family. And then read, again. For this, and much more, I am so grateful.

Sina Kramer read the whole damn thing and gave me extensive comments on the whole damn thing. It is hard to know how to thank the person who has been setting the bar high since you were new philosophy students together. I am so grateful for the enormous luck of place and time and opportunity. But I am even more grateful for what you have made of all that, Sina.

I am grateful to the team at Columbia University Press. I was always treated with a warmth and professionalism that made this process a pleasure. Two anonymous reviewers gave me helpful critical feedback that made this book better. Thanks to Robert Demke for his editing of the manuscript. I owe a special thanks to my editor, Wendy Lochner, who never failed to get what I was up to.

Eloisa Palacio's friendship, good humor, and many trips to the park and library made this book possible.

I am so grateful to my family who has fed me, encouraged me, held my hand in difficult times, and celebrated many of the small and big joys of our lives. Special thanks to Donna Dunaway, Mary Gentry, Gretchen Kopp, Kristi and Scott Robertson, Amy, Brett, Erin, Jill, and Robin Steinbrink, and Ruth and Carla Whiteside, Jon and Christian Wilcheck, and Tina Woodward.

My life has changed quite a lot in the course of writing this book, but the goodwill and benign condescension of Addy and Fern have never wavered—thanks, you two. My parents have each read the whole thing several times and always thought it was good! Thanks to Carl Tyson for talking history, philosophy, politics, and everything else. Thanks to Toni Tyson for always supporting my choices, regardless of how ill advised, and for your merciless sense of humor. Thanks to the Fusons, especially Gabe, Jeff, and Lisl, for thinking this was a good way to spend my time, without question. I am grateful to Iris Tyson, who has never once thought my work was more important than spending time together. And I am more grateful than I can ever say to Josh Fuson, who, among one million other wonderful things, always shows me that he values my work.

INTRODUCTION

I want to find it interesting, rather than depressing, when people with little formal exposure to philosophy, upon hearing about my research interests, ask: Were there women in the history of European and Anglophone philosophy? I want to politely laugh when people working in academic philosophy ask the same question, because usually they have the good manners to sound rueful as they ask it. They are making a joke, and I know what it is like to feel compelled to make a joke you know is not funny. How is it that people who do not really know much about European and Anglophone philosophy "know" there were not women in its history? How is it that people who probably were not required to read any historical women as part of their education in European and Anglophone philosophy feel uncomfortable enough (and, on good days I think, sympathetic enough) to joke about women in its history?

Somehow, it has become common knowledge, both within the formal discipline of European and Anglophone philosophy and outside of it, that historical women did not contribute to philosophy and they have little to contribute to it now. Consider this description from Alain de Botton's popular book on philosophy:

> In spite of the vast differences between the many thinkers described as philosophers across time (people in actuality so diverse that had they been gathered together at a giant cocktail party, they would not only have had nothing to say to one another, but would most probably have come to blows after a few drinks), it seemed possible to discern a small group of men, separated by centuries, sharing a loose allegiance to a vision of philosophy suggested by the Greek etymology of the word—*philo*, love; *sophia*, wisdom—a group bound together by a common interest in saying a few consoling and practical things about the causes of our greatest griefs.[1]

The description, compelling as it may be, has a fateful phrase: "a small group of men." Research, primarily by feminist philosophers, shows that de Botton's perception of the history of European and Anglophone philosophy reflects a widely shared belief even within the discipline of philosophy that women have not done and do not do philosophy, that women were not and are not philosophers.[2] The problem in the passage is not that de Botton has expressed a misogynist sentiment; rather he has not had to go to the trouble of saying anything about women at all. Women simply do not figure into the practice of philosophy. And that lack of figuring is a powerful mode of prohibition—philosophy is not a practice for women.

But not everyone questions whether there were women in the history of European and Anglophone philosophy. Some people "know" there have not been very many or very many of any quality. Sometimes this view is sympathetically rendered: women have been barred from European and Anglophone philosophy or the fundamental skills that make philosophy possible, such as literacy, so it is not surprising that there are so few (worthwhile) women in the history of philosophy. And it is easy to think that when someone names, or even discusses, a woman or two in the history of European and Anglophone philosophy progress has been made. Ah, Margaret Cavendish! Yes, she was a very important thinker in the seventeenth century.

Michèle Le Doeuff, attending to how conceptions of the relationship between women and philosophy have changed significantly through time, notes that the mid-eighteenth century marks the beginning of explicit theorization about a conflict between femininity and philosophy.[3] In her reflection on this change, Le Doeuff warns that acknowledging the philosophical work of a few women might not be progress (or even a salutary regression to the time of Diogenes Laertius or Descartes, neither of whom seemed to think there was a necessary conflict between women and philosophy). Rather, Le Doeuff writes: "The semi-clever argue that there really is a prohibition. As for the clever, they have a more subtle relationship with the prohibition: a relationship which can be described as permissive, as long as it is understood that permissiveness is a sly form of prohibition, and just the opposite of anything that might count as transgression or subversion."[4]

While de Botton simply excludes women from European and Anglophone philosophical history, Le Doeuff points to exclusion rendered through certain forms of inclusion. This latter mode of prohibition—permissive prohibition—acknowledges women's presence in the history of European and Anglophone philosophy while dismissing their authority, through attention to a woman's biography (particularly her romantic interests), for instance, rather than her work.

Feminist scholars have been aware of this problem of permissive prohibition for some time. As Linda Alcoff argued in the mid-1990s:

> The first response to a survey of the "blind spots"[5] on women in the canon should not be simply new work on women using previous methods but must be a self-reflective, self-critical one, on the part of philosophy itself, in order to answer *how* it could be the case that, as Le Doeuff puts it, "where women are concerned the learned utter, and institutions let them utter, words which fall clearly below their own usual standards of validation." How does this *licensing* of misogyny operate within canonical texts? What standards of validation permit the opportunist devolution of the usual standards when the subject is women?[6]

Alcoff warned that we should not expect old methods, which have licensed misogyny, to yield new results. Her critique was directed toward a canonical version of European and Anglophone philosophy's history, one that might admit a few women (Héloïse, Elizabeth of Bohemia, or Mary Wollstonecraft) only to deem their work beneath real philosophical inquiry. The lesson remains vital: simply trying to bring historical women's writing to philosophical attention without changing the practices by which we deem something worthy of philosophical attention can aid in the exclusion of women from philosophy, even in the guise of certain forms of permissiveness. So long as we "know" that "women" and "philosophy" are antithetical categories, reclaiming historical women's philosophical work risks reinforcing what it is meant to displace—women's exclusion from philosophy.

Before offering reassurances that there is much that can be done about women's exclusion, there is another set of problems

I need to acknowledge. Reading the history of European and Anglophone philosophy in relation to women's exclusion is tricky. The history of feminism is also a history of exclusion. Hortense Spillers, critiquing feminism's imbrication with white hetero-supremacy, points to the "duplicitous involvement of much of feminist thinking in the mythological fortunes (words and images) of patriarchal power."[7] Thus, in addition to pointing to the misogyny that structures the discipline of European and Anglophone philosophy, this project also troubles feminist approaches to misogyny. There is not a straightforward approach to claiming philosophical authority for women because philosophical authority has been established through women's exclusion, the focus of chapters 2, 3, and 4. But there is also not a straightforward approach because the category of "women" is itself a field of contestation.[8] The important work of what has come to be called reclamation has laid bare women's prohibition (and sometimes elimination) from European and Anglophone philosophy while often making the term "women" appear unified and homogenous.[9] We err if we accept that unified rendering in trying to reclaim women's philosophical authority, and we err in an all-too-common way. As Spillers has written in reference to the term "sexuality": "Feminist thinking often appropriates the term in its own will to discursive power in a sweeping, patriarchist, symbolic gesture that reduces the human universe of women to its own image. The process might be understood as a kind of deadly metonymic playfulness—a part of the universe of women speaks for the whole of it."[10]

Reclamation engages in such appropriation when it fails to interrogate the category of "women." The fact that the majority of women who have thus far been reclaimed in the history of European and Anglophone philosophy are white must be understood as an effect of geopolitical developments that have shaped European and Anglophone philosophy, and thus its interdictions, more broadly. These developments include, but are certainly not limited to, European genocidal colonialism and the Atlantic slave trade. To resist reproducing the epistemological effects of these violent exclusions in, as Spillers puts it, its own will to discursive power, feminist reclamation must recognize these apparently extraphilosophical forces for the way they have been enacted through and shaped by philosophical practices.

To be clear, the focus of this book is incredibly narrow, inasmuch as the exclusion of women is only one facet of European and Anglophone philosophy's exclusionary practices.[11] But through offering critical reflection on strategies for conceiving of and redressing this exclusionary practice, I hope to aid in the redress of other, imbricated practices. This redress can only be accomplished, however, if the ways we theorize women's exclusion do not engage in what Spillers called a "deadly metonymic playfulness." We cannot take the exclusion of some white, European and Anglophone women as the paradigm work of exclusion.

As a way of working against the deadly metonymic playfulness within the field of reclamation, I focus on how chattel slavery has formed not only the canons of European and Anglophone philosophy, but also the archives of European and Anglophone feminist reclamation. I seek reclamation practices that thematize and, where possible, transform the effects of those exclusions, rather than accepting dominant practices of constituting the traditions of European and Anglophone philosophy. Part of the work of chattel slavery was the violent erasure of the thoughts of the enslaved—indeed, of even acknowledging that those enslaved were capable of thought at all. Reclamation that works against this powerful history needs practices of critically excessive engagements with texts to which no philosophical authority has been granted, as they *seem* so far beyond philosophy's ambit. We must attend to how the thoughts of those enslaved have been made to seem outside the work of philosophy. And we must employ modes of engagement that do not reinforce such boundary setting. Such engagements cannot bring back the thoughts of the vast majority of those destroyed by rapacious European expansion. But we can do much more, philosophically, with the texts we have.

MEETING AT A DINNER PARTY

One of the origins of feminist reclamation of women in the history of European and Anglophone philosophy was Judy Chicago's *The Dinner Party* (presumably not the kind of gathering de Botton had in mind). This installation, first exhibited in 1979, is a banquet of thirty-nine place settings on a triangular table atop a raised dais. Each place setting honors a different woman, with an additional 999 names inscribed on the dais. Mary Ellen Waithe was provoked by seeing the installation with the label "philosopher" for several of the women who had a place setting, and that provocation is part of the reason she started the work that led to the four-volume *A History of Women Philosophers*, one of the earliest texts of reclamation and a focus of analysis in the first chapter. Thus, Waithe, like many who have seen *The Dinner Party*, was challenged by Chicago's version of history. But unlike many, Waithe took the challenge as an invitation to change history through attention to women thinkers in the history of European and Anglophone philosophy. She remains silent, however, about one of the women with a place setting who was not labeled a philosopher: Sojourner

FIGURE 1 Judy Chicago, *The Dinner Party*, 1974–79, mixed media: ceramic, porcelain, textile, 576 × 576 in. Brooklyn Museum. (Photo courtesy of Judy Chicago/Art Resource, NY.)

Truth. This silence is understandable at one level, because it was the label "philosopher" that Waithe sought to reclaim with her work. If Chicago had labeled Truth a philosopher, we have every reason to believe that Waithe would have investigated.

But the obstacles to Truth's inclusion in the history of European and Anglophone philosophy, to establishing her authority within that philosophical tradition, are complex and trouble not just the discipline of European and Anglophone philosophy, but that of U.S. feminism. At another level, then, Waithe's silence must be interrogated, rather than explained away. Truth, the only black woman at *The Dinner Party*, was also one of two guests not to be represented by a vulva.[12] Spillers's analysis of Chicago's decision reads into it "a range of symbolic behavior":[13]

FIGURE 2 Judy Chicago, *The Dinner Party* (Sojourner Truth place setting), 1974–79, porcelain with overglaze enamel (China paint), rainbow luster glaze, and paint, 14 × 14 × 1 in. Brooklyn Museum. (Photo courtesy of Judy Chicago/Art Resource, NY.)

"The excision of the female genitalia here is a symbolic castration. By effacing the genitals, Chicago not only abrogates the disturbing sexuality of her subject, but might as well suggest that her sexual being did not exist to be denied in the first place. Truth's 'femaleness,' then, sustains an element of drag."[14]

Spillers speaks not of "the black female in her historical apprenticeship as an inferior social subject, but, rather, the paradox of non-being."[15] An aim of this book is to make Truth's absence from European and Anglophone philosophy notable and troubling as it signals a range of symbolic behaviors that ascribe black women not just inferior status, but nonstatus. I seek to understand how dominant European and Anglophone philosophical practices of telling its history *and* feminism's critical work on that history have contributed to the paradox of nonbeing. The category of "women," as Spillers makes clear, is not the remedy to the exclusions of European and Anglophone philosophy, but rather a site of strategic maneuvering.[16] We need reclamation practices that recognize and account for this strategic maneuvering rather than ones that rely on, and thereby reproduce, these exclusions, as feminist reclamation has often done. My point is not to castigate Chicago or Waithe or the reclamationists I critique, but rather to understand where reclamation comes from "in order to be creative," as Audre Lorde writes, and to find "the courage and sustenance to act where there are no charters."[17]

DIOTIMA

To argue for new practices of critical reclamation, throughout the book, I track the fate of a character spoken about in Plato's *Symposium*, Diotima. Plato has Socrates claim that Diotima was a Manitean priestess who taught him about love; she reportedly laughs at the limitations of his thinking. Waithe's *A History of Woman Philosophers* framed Diotima's importance for feminist reclamation, but the latter's repute for having taught Socrates was always an idea that traditional European and Anglophone philosophy has tried to manage. Waithe's intervention thus came in the midst of long-established conversations about this woman in the history of European and Anglophone philosophy.

It is worth a quick review of this history to understand the situation into which Waithe launched her project.

After Plato let Diotima onto the scene of philosophy, many have tried to dismiss her through permissive prohibition. Indeed, Plato brings her to the scene of philosophy in a permissively prohibitory way. In the dialogue, Diotima does not appear, let alone speak; Socrates rather claims to relate her teachings at least a quarter century after receiving them. To complicate things further, this dialogue is the report of Aristodemus's reconstruction of the speeches, not from Artistodemus, but from Apollodorus, who heard it from Aristodemus and is now repeating it for the second time in three days. Not just Diotima is absent from the event at which the speeches were given—Socrates and Aristodemus, along with all the other speechmakers, are also absent.

Even with all this careful packaging, European and Anglophone philosophers have developed another mode of protection against thinking of Diotima as important to the history of philosophy—treating her as a fiction. Luis Navia, in his work on the problem of establishing an accurate account of who Diotima was, offers this symptomatic view: "The friends and acquaintances of Socrates appear distinctly drawn throughout the dialogues, and there are no compelling reasons to believe that any of them are fictitious or imaginary characters, expect perhaps for Diotima, the Mantinean seer who plays an important role in the *Symposium* (201d–212b), and about whom there are no other references outside of this dialogue."[18]

Perhaps, in the crowds that fill Plato's dialogues, there is one fiction, Diotima. Navia further notes two of the most important pieces of evidence that feed opposing sides of the controversy of Diotima's (non)being. First, he notes that Plato is not known to have constructed from whole cloth any other character in the dialogues, and second, he claims that no other record of Diotima exists except that given to us here by Plato.

On the first point, A. E. Taylor provides one defense of Diotima's historical existence, emphasizing Plato's otherwise perfect record in fictionalizing real persons:

> I cannot agree with many modern scholars in regarding Diotima of Mantinea as a fictitious personage; still less in looking for fanciful reasons for giving the particular names Plato does to the prophetess and her place of origin. The introduction of purely fictitious named personages into a discourse seems to be a literary device unknown to Plato . . . and I do not believe that if he had invented Diotima he would have gone on to put into the mouth of Socrates the definite statement that she had delayed the pestilence of the early years of the Archidamian war for ten years by "offering sacrifice" at Athens. . . . The purpose of the reference to the presence of Diotima at Athens about 440 is manifestly not merely to account for Socrates' acquaintance with her, but to make the point that the mystical doctrine of the contemplative "ascent" of the soul, now to be set forth, was one on which the philosopher's mind had been brooding ever since his thirtieth year. This, if true, is very important for our understanding of the man's personality, and I, for one, cannot believe that Plato was guilty of wanton mystifications about such things.[19]

Taylor's strong defense of Diotima's historicity, however, is undercut when he writes: "To all intents and purposes, we shall not go wrong by treating the 'speech of Diotima' as a speech of Socrates."[20] In other words, even if we believe that Diotima was a real person we need not concede to her any philosophical authority.

Other scholars—even those with feminist commitments—dismiss Diotima's historicity altogether. Martha Nussbaum, for instance, writes in *The Fragility of Goodness*: "Socrates' teacher is a priestess named Diotima. Since she is a fiction, we are moved to ask about her name, and why Plato should have chosen it."[21] Nussbaum then engages in exactly what Taylor dismissed as fanciful, that is, a reading of Diotima's name and its importance to the meaning of the dialogue.

Richard Hunter gives a slightly different, perhaps more cunning, view when he writes:

> There has been much discussion of the historicity of Diotima, though her role in the *Symposium* is obviously a fictitious one (she has even had an advance inkling of Aristophanes' speech, 205d10–e7),[22] and we should no more wonder when she and Socrates used to meet than we should inquire when Er of Pamphylia told Socrates the story which concludes the *Republic.* It was common enough at symposia for the male guests to impersonate characters, including women, through the recitation of poetry, whether one's own or another's . . . and Socrates' gambit must be seen, in part, as appropriate to the setting in which he finds himself.[23]

Hunter does not claim so much that Diotima is a fiction as that Socrates has taken liberties that make her *role* fictitious. Even if she did exist, she certainly was not at the symposium described by Plato; rather, she may have been impersonated by Socrates, a common enough practice, according to Hunter. Here Diotima is allowed existence but only as a vehicle for male ventriloquism. Nussbaum and Hunter's treatments of Diotima both appear in works published well after feminist interest in Diotima had been established. Thus, both treatments indicate a resilient tradition of thinking about Diotima as either fictional or a vehicle for Socrates's view that has continued with little or no trouble despite feminist debates and sometimes within feminist work.[24]

Motivated by Mary Ellen Waithe's reclamation of Diotima and appreciating the significance of Diotima's relegation to fiction, Margaret Urban Walker uses the case of Diotima to present her concerns about the future of European and Anglophone feminist philosophy. She writes: "Waithe's restoration of just a small sampling of women philosophers throughout history, and her concern with Diotima's reality serve as a cautionary tale."[25] Inasmuch as, Walker reasons, women have already produced philosophy and been forgotten, there is reason to worry that this could happen again, regardless of how open the field seems at the moment. Walker's essay title reflects both the main point of the essay and the importance of Diotima as a figure in it: "Diotima's Ghost: The Uncertain Place of Feminist Philosophy in Professional Philosophy." The cautionary tale that Walker finds in Waithe's work revolves around not so much the importance of women philosopher's historical existence, but their philosophical authority, and the ways the disciplinary practices of European and Anglophone philosophy threaten them with rhetorical "nonbeing." Diotima's ghost is not a remnant of her historical existence, in Walker's rendering, but a specter of her lost authority.

But are feminists right to spend so much time on such a troubled case? After all, there are plenty of other candidates for reclamation.[26] I take up this question in different forms in the first four chapters. I argue that Diotima *is* worth a fight, but there are better and worse strategies to employ. Of particular importance, I show, is resisting the attempt to prove Diotima's historical existence as the foundation for her philosophical authority.

We are unlikely to find sufficient empirical evidence to substantiate Diotima's historicity. But that problem of the archive is not simply unfortunate or frustrating, that problem is a result of women's exclusion. The gaps, silences, and muted voices of the archive have been produced through myriad practices of prohibition and elimination. We must have theories of exclusion that grapple with these productive effects and pursue reclamation anyway. Not just Diotima's philosophical authority is at stake, but also our contemporary practices of conferring philosophical authority.

To make the point slightly differently, the history of European and Anglophone philosophy is more than incomplete; it has been constructed through practices of exclusion that we can critique. We need practices of reclamation that comprehend the myriad modes of prohibition and erasure employed to deny philosophical authority. Without such grounding in theories of exclusion, reclamation risks permitting some women into the history of European and Anglophone philosophy in ways that strengthen philosophy's exclusionary practices, because the practices of producing philosophical authority have not been changed. As difficult as Diotima's reclamation is, hers is not the most troubling. Indeed, Diotima's name appears in philosophical history, even if she is invoked only to be disregarded. But there are other exclusions at work, all the more powerful for the faintness of their traces, which have given the philosophical canon its form. In some disagreement with Le Doeuff, then, this book appreciates the cunning of permissive prohibition *and* prohibition to create a tradition that insults some while failing even to mention others. Given that systematic practices of exclusion have so shaped our understanding, I argue that feminist reclamation's goal should not be the supplementation of philosophy, but rather its transformation.

To that end, I reclaim two texts afforded little credence in European and Anglophone philosophy. Both have legendary status in feminist, and to some extent popular, history. *The Declaration of Sentiments* and Truth's speech in Akron, Ohio, in 1851 are not in need of reclamation because they have been forgotten. Rather, they are remembered in ways that make philosophical engagement with them seem unnecessary. They are legendary texts and, even if they were not, they are not likely texts for philosophical canonization. What is this document of the early women's movement and this speech by a former slave, for which there is not even an authoritative version, to philosophy? This book shows that while they are currently pretty much nothing, they could be quite something.

CHAPTER OVERVIEWS

In the first chapter—"Reclamation Strategies"—I explore the different ways scholars, primarily feminist philosophers, have tried to reclaim women's writing in the history of European and Anglophone philosophy. I identify and outline four strategies that are the most common approaches employed for treating women as part of philosophical history. The different strategies offer, implicitly or explicitly, different ways to conceive of the problem of European and Anglophone philosophy's erasure and prohibition of women and, following from those conceptions, different remedies. Beyond identifying these four strategies, I also argue that the only strategy that can succeed at establishing women's philosophical authority is the fourth approach, which seeks to transform European and Anglophone philosophical practices.[27] In the first chapter, I take the time to survey the other strategies and investigate examples of each in order to show how they can reinforce women's exclusion.

The first approach seeks to enfranchise women into European and Anglophone philosophical history. Arguments in this line advocate for understanding women philosophers as being just like men philosophers and important to philosophical history for the same reasons as recognized, canonical philosophers in that tradition. The second approach offers women's work as an alternative to traditional or mainstream European and Anglophone philosophical history. This move seeks to substantiate an independent tradition of women thinkers, either from within or from without the European and Anglophone philosophical traditions; it offers us new answers to questions and problems the mainstream tradition cannot resolve. A third approach seeks to correct philosophical history with the inclusion of women. In this approach, traditional ideals of European and Anglophone philosophy are used to critique practices of excluding women and justify the inclusion of women. Important work on historical women's philosophical writing has been done using these approaches, but each also risks operating as a method of permissive prohibition. They have this unintended consequence because, in different ways that I examine, they do not displace the practices of conferring philosophical authority that exclude women. I argue that we need reclamation approaches that not only engage with historical women's texts as philosophical, but do so in ways that contend with how the contemporary field of European and Anglophone philosophy has been and is constituted through women's exclusion.

Such approaches have been developed and are what I call transformative reclamations. I include under this approach any reclamation that identifies women's exclusions as a means by which European and Anglophone philosophy has substantiated itself as a discipline, and recognizes that redressing women's exclusion entails transforming the practices of philosophy. I explore different examples of how philosophically engaging with historical women's texts can reshape contemporary practices of European and Anglophone philosophy. My overview in the first chapter, and foregrounding of transformative reclamation, makes clear how consequential our theories of women's exclusion are for how we engage historical women's work and how those engagements can impact our practices now.

Because how we theorize exclusion is so consequential for how reclamation proceeds, the subsequent three chapters of this book outline three very different approaches to theorizing women's exclusion. Chapters 2, 3, and 4 consider the influential theories of Genevieve Lloyd, Luce Irigaray, and Michèle Le Doeuff, as well as investigate the reclamation practices they could or do support. While Lloyd and Irigaray offer important insights about exclusion for the field of reclamation, I conclude that Le Doeuff's method leads to the most promising reclamation practice.

In chapter 2—"Conceptual Exclusion"—I reconsider Lloyd's *The Man of Reason: "Male" and "Female" in Western Philosophy*, a critique of how reason has been conceptualized as masculine throughout European and Anglophone philosophical history. Lloyd's approach to the masculinization of reason has great potential as a basis of transformative reclamation. The particular strength of her method consists in its demand to treat thinkers as part of the history of conceptualization and to show the role metaphor plays within that history. Her project comes into productive crisis when she engages the work of Simone de Beauvoir. Lloyd does not give an explicit account of how Beauvoir managed to make a philosophical contribution, but Lloyd's account hints at the possibility that Beauvoir was able to do so by sacrificing her femininity.

This thesis is productive because it makes clear that the concepts of "femininity" and "women" need not always align. While these two categories are closely allied—in their denigration and exclusion from European and Anglophone philosophy and within feminist work to challenge that denigration and exclusion—Lloyd's inclusion of Beauvoir as a woman philosopher who participated in the marginalization of femininity allows us to glimpse a crucial distinction. Tina Chanter more fully articulates this distinction in tracking how Beauvoir participated in the exclusion of women from European philosophy in order to do her own philosophical work. Chanter's account brings with it an important methodological insight. We must read for the way women who philosophize navigate the exclusion of femininity and women from philosophy. In other words, the epistemic norms that have worked to exclude women's philosophical authority can, and often will, operate in the philosophical work of women.

In chapter 3—"Reclamation from Absence"—I argue that Irigaray provides the example of a method for reclaiming women's work in her essay "Sorcerer Love: A Reading of Plato, *Symposium*, 'Diotima's Speech.'" In that work, Irigaray offers a model of reclamation as love. She develops that method in conversation with the absent Diotima. By using Diotima's absence from the *Symposium* as the basis for engaging the words Plato attributes to the priestess, Irigaray shows that reclamation must transform philosophical practice through introducing the question of sexual difference that this tradition has all but excluded. I examine how Irigaray, through conceiving of philosophy as a practice of loving engagement with traces of feminine subjectivity, imagines and performs new forms of philosophical authority. While conceding the power of this approach, this chapter also surveys problems with Irigaray's account that limit its transformational potential.

In the fourth chapter—"Insults and Their Possibilities"—I highlight the importance of Le Doeuff's attention to insult and innuendo in European and Anglophone philosophical history and the practice of uchronic history she develops in response to that history. To understand "uchronic," think first of "utopia." If a utopia is a placeless place in which we can imagine a world ordered by our ideals and their consequences, then uchronic history is a timeless time in which we can similarly imagine a world ordered by our ideals and their consequences. Uchronic history is a species of counterfactual narrative: one imagines a history in which women's writings were not excluded and projects the possible contemporary consequences of this. While I find Le Doeuff's theory of exclusion deeply promising, I argue (following Penelope Deutscher) that her method is also problematic insofar as it often fails to critique the duplicitous involvements with patriarchal power, to use Spillers's words, of those historical ideals. In other words, these historical texts need to be examined not just for their promise in helping us to understand and critique our contemporary situation, but also for how they reproduce hierarchies and marginalizations. I suggest that a critical uchronic practice can make both moves possible, and I employ such a method in the final chapter.

Chapter 5—"From Exclusion to Reclamation"—compares the contributions of Lloyd, Irigaray, and Le Doeuff, so as to clarify the advantages and pitfalls of how they theorize women's exclusion. First, I consider how Lloyd, Irigaray, and Le Doeuff can respond to charges that how they reconstruct history is fatally inaccurate. Although reclamation depends upon careful historical work, it cannot stop there. The historical archives to which reclamation can turn for texts have been shaped by massive exclusions. Reclamation must highlight the limitations of our archives—limitations that are not the result of unfortunate historical accidents (missing files, disintegrating documents, and the like), but rather the consequence of enduring practices of interdiction.

Further, as Irigaray and Le Doeuff demonstrate, we can read the texts we do have in imaginative ways in order to open new avenues of thought. (Lloyd, by contrast, does not read archival limitations as a form of exclusion, nor does she offer imaginative ways to deal with the limitations of the archive.) In comparing forms of reclamation developed by Irigaray and Le Doeuff, I suggest that the latter's method encourages more freedom in speculating from historical texts to new contemporary possibilities. Decisive for my assessment, however, is that Le Doeuff is the only one of the three who recognizes and regularly engages with women in the history of European and Anglophone philosophy. Lloyd and Irigaray tend to tell the history of European and American philosophy as the history of men or masculine subjectivity, respectively. While their stories serve feminist critiques, they also reinforce the fallacy that the history of European and Anglophone philosophy has proceeded without women. The chapter concludes with a response to charges that Le Doeuff's feminism is suspect because of her loyalty to philosophy.

In the final chapter—"Injuries and Usurpations"—I reclaim two texts. The first text is a document important in Le Doeuff's reclamation of Harriet Taylor Mill, the *Declaration of Sentiments*. The *Declaration of Sentiments* was signed at the Seneca Falls Convention in 1848, which launched the women's rights movement in the United States. Using Le Doeuff's uchronic method to think through some of the demands of the *Declaration*, I also attend to the problematic hierarchies the document employs. To deepen concerns about the problems of the *Declaration*, I pivot to Sojourner Truth's speech at the Akron, Ohio, meeting on women's rights in 1851. Truth's speech not only critiques the understanding of women's rights reflected in the *Declaration*, but also offers a significantly different vision of freedom. I again use the uchronic method, but the uncertainties around what

Truth said at the meeting (we have many reports, but no text from Truth's hand) require reading multiple versions of the speech to speculate on what Truth may have been saying. I argue for the importance of reading uchronically *with* the uncertainties of the text to engage Truth as a philosophical thinker. And I draw out the consequences of this engagement for contemporary practices of European and Anglophone philosophy.

The aim of this project is to reflect on what is at stake in the work of reclaiming women philosophers in and for the history of European and Anglophone philosophy. Feminist reclamation has its origin in an impulse to redress the silencing of women, but the mechanisms of that silencing have remained un- or undertheorized. In the absence of sufficient theorization, views about the nature of women's exclusion and the nature of what they have been excluded from have operated nonetheless. Through explicit theorization of exclusion, we can appreciate how some modes of reclamation have reinforced powerful forms of exclusion. Conversely, through assessing theories of exclusion through the methods of reclamation they suggest, we can also appreciate how some theories of women's exclusion have reinforced powerful forms of marginalization and erasure already operating in philosophy. Ultimately, this book does not identify one sure strategy for reclamation arising from the right theory of exclusion. Philosophy is a living practice, and my aim is to make us aware of how our practices of history telling are central to what it is possible for us to think.

WHERE ARE THE WOMEN?

1

RECLAMATION STRATEGIES

When feminists first turned their attention to the history of European and Anglophone philosophy during the revival of feminism in the latter half of the twentieth century, energy was primarily directed toward critiquing the tradition and its canon for widespread misogyny and its exclusion of women. Few asked about women's historical involvement in European and Anglophone philosophy. Interest in women philosophers intensified in the mid-1980s, a trend both exemplified and fueled by the publication in 1987 of the first of the four-volume *History of Women Philosophers*, edited by Mary Ellen Waithe.[1] There are now many resources making available and engaging with women's writing in the history of European and Anglophone philosophy in what has come to be known as feminist reclamation.[2]

Within the field of reclamation, there have been four dominant strategies for engaging with women's work as philosophically authoritative. (1) Enfranchisement. The first strategy reclaims women as philosophers who belong in traditional philosophical histories. (2) Alternative history. The second type claims that women's philosophical writing offers us something other than the masculine philosophical tradition. (3) Corrective history. The third strategy treats reclamation as an endeavor that will make philosophy more philosophical. (4) Transformation. The fourth and final type reclaims women's writing as a force that will change philosophical history and, thereby, contemporary philosophical practice.

These classifications are heuristic, showing that reclamation projects tend toward certain argumentative strategies. These strategies can be deployed to varying ends. Perhaps surprisingly, some reclamation projects have little concern about the exclusion of women from the history of European and Anglophone philosophy or, more surprisingly still, even endorse it. Others, by contrast, treat the exclusion of women from European and Anglophone philosophy as a failure whose correction will change the nature of philosophy. In other words, within the field of reclamation, there is a great deal of disagreement about what the problem of women in the history of European and Anglophone philosophy has been and how it ought to be remedied. By classifying and analyzing these different strategies, I illuminate how each strategy entails a theory of women's exclusion.

We need such an overview because women's exclusion is, by and large, insufficiently theorized within the field. By attending to the theories of exclusion already at work in the field of reclamation—and thematizing them—it becomes clear that what is needed is not a bridge between reclamation and exclusion, but more conscious attention to how the relationship is conceived. In other words, the mechanisms of exclusion have, understandably, been secondary to making available and engaging women's work. But reclamation must turn its attention to exclusion, or it stands to redouble the exclusion of women's philosophical authority. We need to take stock of how the philosophical norms of exclusion can and sometimes have migrated to European and Anglophone feminist philosophy. While no strategy can prepare for all contingencies, this chapter argues that transformational approaches to reclamation, because they are enacted through attention to how exclusion has happened, offer the most promising path for reclaiming women's philosophical authority.

THE ENFRANCHISEMENT MODEL

Enfranchising reclamations argue that women should be included in the history of European and Anglophone philosophy because they already meet established criteria for inclusion. Women, the argument goes, wrote and write philosophy *just like* recognized canonical European and Anglophone philosophers. Mary Ellen Waithe advocates for women's inclusion in philosophical history, for instance, by arguing: "women were engaged in precisely the same kind of philosophical enterprises that have historically characterized male philosophers."[3] That sentiment sounds like the more general version of Mary Warnock's claim that the women she treats "are (or were) mostly philosophers in the same sort of sense as, all would agree, Hume was a philosopher."[4] I focus on Waithe and Warnock in this section, in part, because they use this hallmark enfranchisement strategy of claiming a lack of difference. Women's work has been just like men's, so it also should be included.

Their projects are also exemplary of enfranchisement methods in their acceptance of existing conceptions of European and Anglophone philosophy. Waithe's claim about philosophical enterprises in the paragraph above, for instance, signals her acceptance of prevailing conceptions of those enterprises. Yet, Waithe also asks: "Might we come to a different understanding of the nature of philosophy itself as a result of an acquaintance with women's thought?"[5] In this question, she reconsiders whether women really have been involved in precisely the same kind of philosophical enterprise that has historically characterized male philosophers. In other words, Waithe troubles what counts as philosophy. Warnock never puts "the nature of philosophy itself" under such scrutiny. Instead, Warnock finds grounds for dismissing the enterprise of feminist philosophy within her conception of philosophy: feminist work fails the criterion of gender-neutrality. In other words, Waithe troubles the strategy of enfranchisement with transformative questions, while Warnock models just how effectively the enfranchisement strategy maintains a certain philosophical border against women's work.

Finally, neither author puts into question the category of "women." Both treat this category as self-evident, although they do come close to interrogating it. Waithe does so by questioning whether the topic of women's place in society can be summarily dismissed from the purview of European and Anglophone philosophy, even if it traditionally has been. Warnock comes close to interrogating this category through a discussion of "the Woman Question." Warnock uses this Victorian term to introduce "broadly 'feminist' literature."[6] Ultimately, however, neither questions how the category of "women" has been constructed over time or the role of philosophical exclusion in that construction. And this acceptance of the category of "women," despite its historical vicissitudes and contestations, is also a hallmark of enfranchisement. Focused on inclusion in the practice of philosophy, enfranchising strategies accept that in some instances members of the category have been unfairly or erroneously excluded. Through appeal to existing standards of inclusion within philosophical history, acceptance of prevailing conceptions of what counts as philosophy, and acceptance of the category of "women" as self-evident, these two thinkers offer illuminating, and quite different, examples of enfranchisement.

Waithe: Enfranchisement with Transformative Tendencies

Waithe's *A History of Women Philosophers* is such an early work within reclamation that when she became interested in women in the history of European and Anglophone philosophy, she thought she would find only enough material for a journal article. The resulting four-volume collection was the surprising result of her tenacious leadership and the recently developed networks of feminist scholars willing to help (the newsletter for the Society for Women in Philosophy played a crucial role, for instance).[7] Perhaps more surprising was that finding women in the history of European and Anglophone philosophy was not that difficult. Women, Waithe discovered, had not so much been prohibited from practicing philosophy, nor had there been a concerted effort to hide their work. Rather, Waithe speculates that women were not included in dominant conceptions of European and Anglophone philosophy because philosophers have been beyond careless and lacked curiosity. She writes: "The very existence of what in retrospect appears to have been not terribly well hidden (after all, all the writings of the Pythagorean women excepting the letters were preserved by Stobeaus) suggests that philosophers have been more than careless about knowing the history of their discipline, and certainly not very inquisitive about it."[8] Undaunted, Waithe "decided to attempt to restore women's contributions to the history of philosophy."[9]

Waithe's foray into philosophical history to find those it had neither remembered nor forgotten quickly led her to a set of philosophical issues. How was European and Anglophone philosophy's inertia about women in its history related to the nature of the discipline? She writes:

> I could not presume to undertake the task of re-defining the discipline of philosophy, so I chose a purely *ad hoc* device for identifying philosophical works: use a definition of "philosophy" that has been an accepted definition of philosophy for some identifiable historical period. Unfortunately, this *ad hoc* device, uncontroversial though it may at first seem, begs an important feminist question. If traditional philosophy has always been an essentially male enterprise, by selecting works of women that fit those traditional definitions, am I not merely selecting works by women who "thought like men" or who "did what men did?" Perhaps. Examining the question whether philosophy as we have come to know the discipline defines essentially masculinist enterprises that necessarily exclude women is a worthwhile undertaking. But it is far beyond the expertise of this philosopher, and beyond the immediate task of the Project. The women were engaged in precisely the same kind of philosophical enterprises that have historically characterized male philosophers.[10]

Waithe signals that redressing the exclusion she has ascribed to (more than) carelessness and incuriosity may have transformational potential for the discipline, requiring its redefinition. She attempts to hold at bay such implications to begin the work of reclamation, but, as I discuss below, she was tellingly unsuccessful.

By way of introduction to the problem of determining whether or not something was philosophy Waithe noted that the reclaimed Pythagorean women in the first volume discussed issues of running a family, a topic not traditionally considered philosophical. Waithe reports that the Pythagorean women did so by applying ethical theory, using the concept of *harmonia* to compare the state and the family, and, therefore, approached the topic philosophically.[11] In other words, she introduces the problem of determining who counts as a philosopher by performing a feminist recasting of what is "properly" philosophical; discussions of child rearing cannot be dismissed a priori from the purview of philosophy, even if it has traditionally been dismissed. We must analyze the approach to a topic, Waithe implies, before deciding if philosophy has been done. And our analysis may lead us into new conceptions of philosophy, along with a changed understanding of "the standard philosophic reference works and histories of philosophy."[12]

Waithe then sidesteps the transformative potential of what she is up to by claiming that she is unqualified to determine the extent to which European and Anglophone philosophy is a masculine enterprise and that it is outside the scope of the current project. We can well understand how Waithe, faced with the enormous project of reading and presenting this material by and on women philosophers, was eager to present it, not to determine the extent to which European and Anglophone philosophy could or should be changed by it. Waithe attempts to settle the concerns, perhaps because she is aware of the risk that her readers will resist engagement with women's work if it is too challenging to their conceptions of European and Anglophone philosophy. Her conclusion that women were involved in the same kind of enterprises as men offers a clear example of reclamation as enfranchisement. Women belong in the history of European and Anglophone philosophy because they have done work just like men who are remembered.

In the midst of claiming women's importance for philosophical history on the model of men's work that has been previously legitimized, Waithe then suggests that women bring a particular perspective to philosophical work. She claims: "While both males and females have inquired into the basic principles of science, mathematics, and human behavior, when women philosophers examined the principles underlying human behavior, they frequently did so from the perspective of a woman."[13] To substantiate this characterization, she notes that they raised issues of law and justice in the home, marital infidelity, normative standards of women's behavior, women's rationality (arguing for it), and women's social, economic, and political rights.[14] Notably, this list does not make clear what Waithe means by a woman's perspective. She seems to be suggesting that women have been positioned to care enough about these issues to philosophize about them, rather than making a stronger claim to some sort of eternal or essential women's perspective. Regardless, on either a weak or a strong reading of the "woman's perspective," Waithe's enfranchisement strategy is in trouble. Because enfranchisement relies on women belonging in philosophical history in the same way that men do, women's attention to and contestation of their status present something of a problem. After all, men have not spent much time on these issues. Thus, if the grounds of women's legitimacy are that they have practiced philosophy just like men, then evidence that women have introduced topics and questions not typical of men philosophers undermines the case for enfranchisement. In this strategy, canonical concerns are necessary for legitimate philosophical authority.

After surveying the tradition of women who discussed the role of women, Waithe reestablishes her enfranchising tack when she writes: "Yet, the majority of women philosophers' writing do not reflect concern with the nature, status, and rights of women."[15] Then, she talks about Diotima adopting "a masculine perspective" and the gender-neutral way Hypatia discusses astronomy, and concludes her survey of topics about which women wrote with the observation that "Indeed, the philosophical topics and theories of the women philosophers are every bit as diverse and interesting as are those which characterize 'traditional' male philosophers."[16] Women did not spend all their time talking about women, Waithe assures us, and not only did they talk about diverse and interesting things, but often the same diverse and interesting things with which men like Leibniz were concerned. This assurance shows the continued importance of traditional standards of what counts as philosophy to Waithe's project of establishing women's philosophical authority and is consistent with the enfranchisement strategy.

Yet, at the end of her introduction, Waithe considers three questions that indicate that the relationship between reclamation and European and Anglophone philosophy was far from being settled by *A History of Women Philosophers*, but was rather being given initial form. She introduces the questions by writing: "What has struck me as fundamentally serious is the ramification that the contents of these four volumes will have for philosophy itself."[17] The three questions she asks are "What *is* the history of philosophy?"; "Have philosophers failed at the most basic task of philosophy—to question one's basic assumptions thereby to discover the truth?"; and "Might we come to a different understanding of the nature of philosophy itself as a result of an acquaintance with women's thought?"[18] With her questions, Waithe reopens transformative queries into the field of reclamation that her enfranchisement strategy had largely sidelined. What work will excluded perspectives do to and within European and Anglophone philosophy? Thus, while Waithe's project often relies on strategies of enfranchisement, at moments she also questions philosophy and philosophical practice. Waithe's introduction is an instructive record of the challenges of incorporating women's philosophical authority. She is clearly excited and motivated to take women's work seriously, to the point of questioning her home field and seeking help from outside of it.[19] Yet, she continually reasserts standards of her discipline to legitimize her engagement with women's work.

Diotima

While the above analysis has emphasized the way Waithe's enfranchisement strategy gives way or is troubled by transformative questions, if we turn to her reclamation of Diotima, an enfranchisement strategy dominates. Further, this strategy is not up to the challenge Diotima presents. Waithe grounds her reclamation of Diotima with what is perhaps the most modest claim of enfranchisement—Waithe argues for Diotima's existence. Acknowledging the then recent trend in scholarship to think of Diotima as a fictional character, Waithe reports: "Other disciplines, especially classics and archeology, have considered this issue, and in following sources outside philosophy I came across two different types of evidence bearing upon it. First, it appears that in the fifteenth century a scholar suggested that it was 'silly' to think that a woman would have been a philosopher. Second, there is ancient archeological evidence which classicists and archeologists have interpreted as support for the claim that Diotima was indeed a historical person."[20] Waithe suggests that the fifteenth-century scholar set the tone for European and Anglophone philosophy's reception of Diotima as a fictional character. Until that time, Diotima's historical existence was not debated, nor was it considered pertinent to the issue of Diotima's philosophical authority. Further, Waithe contends that archeological evidence may substantiate Diotima's existence.

In addition to that evidence, Waithe also maintains that Diotima's arguments differ from that of either Plato or Socrates. Thus, she seeks to show that analysis of the content of Diotima's speech urges us to consider her a real person with views independent from the author or the character reporting them. While Waithe does not think the evidence she considers or the arguments she presents can fully decide the issue of whether or not this was the person whose arguments Socrates recounts in the *Symposium*, the material on Diotima is included as a spur to further research.

Waithe's intent is to raise the possibility that we need to reassess how we have accorded—or rather not accorded—Diotima philosophical authority. By putting into question the convention of treating Diotima as fictional, Waithe is attempting to put into question the reduction of Diotima's philosophical contribution to that of Socrates or Plato. Waithe, through the issue of Diotima's historical existence, tries to open up the possibility that women have been active participants in the work of philosophy since its beginning—well before women are commonly believed to have been involved. In other words, Waithe's advocates for a reassessment of Diotima's historicity as a first step in enfranchisement. Diotima must be recognized as a historical figure, the argument goes, if she is to become a figure of historical philosophical authority.

This implicit argument can be seen at work in one of the first reviews of *A History of Women Philosophers*. There, the feminist philosopher Mary Anne Warren gives special emphasis to Waithe's reclamation of Diotima. She writes: "This careful scholarship lends weight to what is probably the most important finding of the volume—i.e., that Diotima of Manitea was almost certainly an historical figure, rather than a fictional character created by Socrates or Plato."[21] Warren does not explain the importance of establishing Diotima as a historical figure. The volume reclaims writing by other ancient women, yet Warren singles out Diotima's historicity as its most important finding.

Perhaps the importance Warren gives Diotima in her analysis relates to the broader importance she sees in Waithe's project. Warren writes: "The gaps and distortions in the history of western philosophy resulting from millennia of suppression of female thought cannot be overcome in a single volume or series of volumes. But Waithe and her fellow researchers are making a significant contribution to that goal. Further research and analysis will be necessary to determine the accuracy of their specific conclusions and occasional speculations. If this volume leads to such further work, then it will have proved its value."[22]

Warren is satisfied with a volume that she criticizes for "lack[ing] a clear unifying theme" because she sees the enormity of the project of establishing women as part of philosophical history.[23] Waithe, as mentioned, does not claim to decide the issue of Diotima's historical existence, but Warren seems swayed by the presentation of the evidence. To establish a woman's presence so early in European and Anglophone philosophy's history and in conjunction with figures no less important to its development than Plato and Socrates would, Warren implies, make it all the more difficult to maintain that women have had no impact on the history of European and Anglophone philosophy. In other words, Diotima's reclamation is powerful because it troubles philosophical history telling (almost) all the way back to its beginning. Importantly, Warren does not address the problem that even if Diotima was a historical person, we do not have a record of her writing.

Warren's review contrasts sharply with another review that appeared in the same issue of *Hypatia*. R. M. Dancy concludes his assessment with this: "In sum, the chapters by Zedler and Wolfskeel are good, and the translations and all too infrequent comments by Harper are first rate. But the rest of the books is so frought [sic] with half-truths, wishful thinking and downright misinformation based on poor or incomplete scholarship that it utterly fails to attain the goals it set out to achieve."[24] Dancy describes the chapter on Diotima as "the centerpiece of this book,"[25] by which he means it is the focal point of a work with little value in his estimation. He writes: "Perhaps Diotima was a historical person. If so, she may have held the theory of forms we associate with Plato, if what Plato makes Socrates makes her say in the *Symposium* is true to her, she certainly did. But we have been given no reason whatever for supposing that she must have been a historical person, or that, if she was, she held the views put into her mouth in the *Symposium*."[26]

Whether she was fictional or fictionalized, Dancy highlights the seemingly intractable problem of attributing any view to Diotima. In attacking the claim to historicity, Dancy attacks the first step taken by Waithe in the case for enfranchising Diotima into philosophical history. He also anticipates the further steps when he argues that even if Diotima's historicity was admitted, her views as reported by Plato do not stand on their own and we do not have a record of what she might have thought if Plato's report is inaccurate.

Dancy's resistance to Waithe's project is not based on a simple allegiance to the way history has already been rendered. He writes: "No doubt the prospect of having to rewrite the history of Greek philosophy does not disturb Waithe. Nor does it disturb me. But it cannot be done this way. Too much work has been done to separate out the genuine from the spurious in

Pythagoreanism, and some account must be taken of this no matter how we do our rewriting. Waithe does not mention this work."[27] Dancy advocates for the importance of the progress already made on the history of Greek philosophy. He is not against putting that history into question in some ways, but he condemns what he sees as Waithe's apparent disregard for the work already done to determine genuine sources. In other words, Dancy questions Waithe's method for establishing Diotima's philosophical authority with charges of historical inaccuracy.

Enfranchisement, with its acceptance of dominant terms of conferring philosophical authority, cannot answer this problem. We will need some other strategy to answer Dancy's concerns. But if Dancy's concerns are not to become another cover for dismissing women's philosophical authority, we do need to answer them. And the answer cannot be that we need Diotima, or that cannot be the sum and substance of our answer. Waithe and Warren are right that Diotima is a potentially powerful site of reclamation, but enfranchisement does not give us a way to utilize this potential.

Warnock: A More Thoroughgoing Enfranchisement

Now to a very different use of the enfranchisement strategy. Mary Warnock's anthology *Women Philosophers* seeks to dissuade its readers from considering the impact feminism might have on European and Anglophone philosophy. I include it as a project of feminist reclamation advisedly. Warnock rejects feminism as properly philosophical, but her volume is often cited as a resource for further reading on women in the history of European and Anglophone philosophy, both as a collection of primary source material and for her perspective on issues of reclamation.[28] Warnock employs enfranchisement strategies, and in so doing offers perhaps the clearest example of their limitations.

Warnock begins with the question of who should be considered a philosopher. In answer, she writes: "First, I think, a writer must be concerned with matters of a high degree of generality, and must be at home among abstract ideas. . . . He or she would claim not only to seek the truth, but to seek a truth, or theory, that will explain the particular and detailed and the everyday."[29] Warnock uses Hume as her model—someone who never held an academic post, who argued for his views, wrote essays and dialogues, and was in conversation with other thinkers, responding to and refuting their ideas. The women in *Women Philosophers* "are (or were) mostly philosophers in the same sort of sense as, all would agree, Hume was a philosopher."[30] Warnock's use of Hume indicates her reliance on an enfranchisement strategy.

With Hume as her model, Warnock notes that she had "considerable difficulties" with "what used to be called 'the Woman Question.' There is, understandably, an enormous quantity of broadly 'feminist' literature written by women. How much of this should count as philosophy?"[31] She notes that much of it meets the generality criteria. The paragraph turns bibliographical, reporting on feminist works from the 1980s and 1990s "all plausibly purporting to be philosophical."[32] Yet, Warnock's judges: "there tends to be too much unexamined dogma in these writings, too much ill-concealed proselytizing, too little objective analysis, to allow them to qualify for inclusion among philosophical writing proper."[33] This writing *deserves* to be excluded, in other words. Warnock deems feminist writing to be insufficiently critical and too biased to be considered properly philosophical.

But Warnock also reverses her initial judgment that the work meets the criteria of generality. She continues:

> Moreover, as we look at these titles and others like them it becomes clear that they fail, after all, the test of generality. For the great subjects of philosophy, the nature of human knowledge, the limits of science, the foundations of morality or aesthetics, the relation between our language and the world, must be concerned with "us" in the sense in which "we" are all human. The truths which philosophers seek must aim to be not merely generally, but objectively, even universally, true. Essentially, they must be gender-indifferent.[34]

With a line drawn between feminism and philosophy, the only feminist Warnock includes is Mary Wollstonecraft.

In this passage, Warnock reveals the overshot optimism of Linda Lopez McAlister's claim in 1989 that "feminism has expanded the bounds of what we have considered to be philosophy both in terms of subject matter and the forms that it may take. There is no longer any denying that women who theorize, e.g., about the rights or liberation of women, whether in the eighteenth century or today, are engaged in a philosophical pursuit."[35] Warnock denies exactly what McAlister says can no longer be denied; women writing on women is anthropology, according to Warnock, not philosophy.

Warnock gives another reason, in addition to lack of objectivity, poor quality, and insufficient universality, for Wollstonecraft as the only writer she included on the "Woman Question." She writes: "My other reason for omitting most writing that would be called specifically feminist is that I wanted to show the variety of philosophical topics on which women have written, and written well. It may still be asked whether or not women have a particular 'voice' as philosophers, but it would prejudge the answer to that question if too great a proportion of the extracts I selected were concerned with 'women's' subjects."[36]

Warnock wants to show a variety of writings by women. She seems also to want to complicate the issue of whether men and women do philosophy differently—have different "voices." So, she excludes feminist works or works that are concerned with "women's" subjects. She makes that move because the question of "voice" would be prejudiced by attention to "women's" subjects.[37] While Warnock notes that we could ask questions about the category of "women"—for instance, does it entail a different voice?—her commitment to enfranchising a few women into the philosophical canon takes precedence. Perhaps not surprising, given that she has excluded work that might (prejudicially) substantiate such a conclusion, Warnock concludes: "In the end, I have not found any clear 'voice' shared by women philosophers."[38]

Without wishing to change what counts as philosophy, Warnock seeks to correct, at least in a few cases, the neglect of women's writing, but that corrective does not call European and Anglophone philosophy to be more philosophical or change its practice. When Warnock writes, "Anne Conway seems to me to be one of the few women philosophers who may be said to have been unjustly neglected," the implication is that other women's work has been justly neglected.[39] She may put in doubt what counts as women's subjects, but what counts as philosophy has been established on the model of Hume, and her anthology should be read as evidence that women worth reading have been philosophers like him. Anne Conway belongs in philosophical history because she has done work just like men who are already there.

Although Warnock and Waithe both claim the status of philosopher for historical women on the model of traditional conceptions of who a philosopher is, the overall tenor of their projects is quite different. Warnock's rejection of feminism as properly philosophical lends consistency to her definition of philosophy and minimizes the impact reclamation might have on it. Indeed, her view of feminism has led some of her critics to wonder why she wrote a book about women philosophers.[40] Waithe, on the other hand, while tending to make claims for women's inclusion in European and Anglophone philosophy based on their similarity to men, also shows her thinking about European and Anglophone philosophy altering through her encounter with historical women's work, and so she encourages more thinking about how feminist reclamation might change European and Anglophone philosophy. Both Waithe and Warnock are cited by feminists undertaking diverse projects of reclamation. While Warnock's intent may have been to more firmly draw the boundary between philosophy and feminism, in presenting the writing of women she has aided feminist efforts in redressing the exclusion of women in the history of European and Anglophone philosophy. One thing to appreciate about this appropriation of Warnock's work for feminist ends is that simply making women's work more widely available, regardless of how that work is framed, can increase engagement with women's writing. The use of Warnock's work for feminist ends is a testament to feminist philosophers' resourcefulness in the fight against sexist oppression. With better methods of reclamation, however, women's writing not only stands a better chance of philosophical engagement, but can profoundly affect philosophical practice, history, and the construction of the category of "women." Enfranchising women into a canon that all but denies women's philosophical writing and doing so by using the criteria through which that writing has been excluded risk failing to promote robust engagement with women's work. With these implications of enfranchisement clarified, we can appreciate that the moments in which Waithe destabilizes and troubles the enfranchisement strategy hold more promise for transformative engagements with women's work.

THE ALTERNATIVE HISTORY MODEL

Another strategy of reclamation is the alternative history approach. In this approach, reclamationists argue that women have established a tradition of thinking independently of men's and that there are now compelling reasons for us to turn to this other tradition. I focus on the work of Andrea Nye and Karen Green in this section because they offer two apparently different versions of this strategy that reveal its basic structure. Nye argues that there is an independent tradition of women thinkers *outside* of European and Anglophone philosophy that can help us with issues that have failed to produce nourishing results within the discourse of European and Anglophone philosophy. Green, by contrast, identifies an alternative tradition *within* European and Anglophone philosophy that can help us with some of the most intractable philosophical problems, especially within political theory. As in the enfranchisement model, the alternative history approach cedes the nature of philosophy and how its history has been constructed to dominant or prevailing conceptions. In the alternative tradition strategy, however, women's writing contains resources for us because it has been immune to the main tradition of European and Anglophone philosophy. Thus, rather than advocating that women ought to take their rightful place within the philosophical pantheon (or largely be excluded from it), Nye and Green argue that women's writing has resources for us as a result of its independence from traditional European and Anglophone philosophy.

Women's work is now valued for how it has *not* been like men's, but the risk remains that we continue to conceive of philosophy as men's domain. It may be stale or in need of help from feminism according to these models, but European and Anglophone philosophy is treated as an independent entity with which feminism interacts. Even Green, who identifies a feminist humanism that has been submerged in the tradition of European and Anglophone philosophy, sees this reclaimed tradition as a competitor with a masculinist humanist tradition. Alternative strategies lead away from considerations of how men and women share contexts of thinking, which leads away from several problems, two of which are crucial in this study. First, some women were considered philosophers in their own time. Some women, and their contemporaries, did not understand their work to be part of an alternative tradition. If the alternative tradition framing gave us more insight into the women's work, then we might dismiss this concern, especially since women's exclusion can occur through permissive prohibition that denies their work philosophical authority. But this framing can obscure that, second, women's work can inherit processes that contribute to the exclusion of women (among other problems). That is to say, women's work can share many of the problems of men's work, since it developed in conversation and context with it.

Alternative tradition strategies conceive of women as outside philosophical practice, and credit this exclusion with their power to offer solutions where European and Anglophone philosophy has failed. Nye is wary of essentialism, but implies that women are the excluded other to philosophy. European and Anglophone philosophy has failed to answer some of our most pressing questions, and so Nye suggests that we look to those who were excluded from European and Anglophone philosophy for answers. Women's work offers hope to a moribund philosophy because women's exclusion from European and Anglophone philosophy has been so successful that they developed an alternative tradition. Green conceives of a transhistorical category of "women" as necessary to the project of feminism and the guarantor of a tradition within European and Anglophone philosophy that can offer us a gynocentric humanism. She argues, for instance, that "The human self which emerges from the writings of feminist humanists is not the same self that emerges from the writings of male humanists, nor is she a completely different being. She is rational but also thoroughly aware of herself as an embodied and emotional being."[41] Green relies on a framework of women's fundamental and universal difference. While Nye's conception appears more historically contingent than Green's, they both rely on an opposition between women and philosophy in order to argue for the necessity and importance of an alternative tradition.

Nye: An Alternative History Outside of Philosophy

In *Philosophia: The Thought of Rosa Luxemburg, Simone Weil, and Hannah Arendt*, Nye uses the notion of leavening as a central metaphor, which she first introduces in her epigraph: "The Kingdom of Heaven is like unto the leaven which a woman took and hid in three measures of meal until the whole was leavened. *Matthew 13:33*."[42] In her conclusion, she writes: "the redemption of thought is that even in failure, even in lost causes, something is left alive, to be saved, to be used again, in another recipe, with a bit more or less kneading, more care in handling."[43] What appears as a rather straightforward use of Christian terms, "redemption" and "saving," takes a provocative turn when the saving is for a new recipe. Redemption and saving are on the model of a sourdough starter and not that of salvation through Christ.[44]

What needs to be leavened, according to Nye, is contemporary existence, and European and Anglophone philosophy is no longer a powerful agent. As she puts the point in her conclusion: "What I have tried to show is that if European and Anglophone philosophy is just a bit old and stale, and not as nourishing as we might wish, there may be other recipes, other ways of thinking, remembered and conserved, able to enliven the heavy stuff of postmodern existence."[45] Nye advocates for remembering and conserving another tradition of thinking, something fresh, one she finds in the work of Luxemburg, Weil, and Arendt.

Nye does not try to present these women as somehow involved in a common project, but rather sees their commonality in that they differ from the "mainstream philosophical tradition."[46] They return to experience, insist on materiality, are open to many disciplines, and reject "knowledge as a privileged representation of reality"[47] and the traditional oppositions of Western philosophy. As Nye writes: "the very thickness and confusion of reality provides new material for this other thought that, like leaven, has its source in material reality and its aim the preservation and enhancement of human life."[48]

But in reconstructing this tradition of women thinkers, Nye is clear that she is not offering a *feminist* alternative tradition. Notice how Nye describes these women and their authority:

> Sexism was a dimension of oppression virtually untouched in their theoretical work. They used suspect generic language. They

> drew on no body of feminist scholarship; they relied on no supportive network of women scholars. Although they had close women friends and allies, they did not identify themselves primarily as women. If this was a weakness in their thought—and it was—it was also a strength. Bypassing the very real fact of women's oppression, they took upon themselves the authority to rethink the human condition.[49]

That language of authority returns in her conclusion. She writes:

> These are women who take upon themselves the authority to speak for both women and men. They are also women whose thinking differs from the style of most philosophy written by men. I have not meant to argue that their grasp of the human condition is privileged because they are women, any more than I have meant to argue that their neglect of gender issues is unimportant. But there is a sense in which that neglect made it possible for them to address the deepest of human concerns offstage from the drama of Western philosophy.[50]

Nye suggests that neglecting or bypassing a facet of oppression made this alternative tradition possible. Although Nye is an avowed feminist philosopher whose other works contribute to the field, in this project she is offering an alternative tradition of women and not feminists. She describes European and Anglophone philosophy as that which excludes women and women as that which has been excluded. Alternative strategies rely on exclusion: that is, exclusion creates a unified alternative.

Nye even offers us a name for this alternative tradition. Though the term is not thematized, or even indexed, in the book, "philosophia" is in both the title and the conclusion. Nye asks: "What kind of knowledge or truth could such a philosophia, without the closure of masculine ending, produce?"[51] Philosophia is a different tradition, one that relates to European and Anglophone philosophy, and treats some of its main figures (Descartes, Kant, Marx, to name a few), but that does not continue a tradition of abstraction that Nye understands to be *the* continuity of European and Anglophone philosophy.

Indeed, on closer reading, Nye's conception of "alternative" appears so strong that it is misleading to call her project a reclamation *in* the history of philosophy. She writes: "To ask whether women could have played—would have played if they had been allowed—major roles in this drama is futile. The history of Western ideas has been written by men for male characters; in its narratives women have been occasionally an object of concern but never the agents of change."[52] Nye's view is that reclamation of women for European and Anglophone philosophy is futile. Nye does not speculate on why European and Anglophone philosophy has been a male tradition or what relationship its maleness might have with its failure. Although Nye does not explain why they were neglected, the neglect of these women is directly related to their ability to offer us an alternative to a failed tradition. Further, these women somehow bypass women's oppression to address the deepest of human concerns, as though oppression were not one of these and as though it were the kind of thing an individual could choose to bypass.

Nye continues to use women's exclusion as the unifying principle of the alternative tradition in how she situates her project. Nye claims that she does not take a side in the dispute between feminists of difference and feminists of equality.[53] Yet, Nye contrasts her approach to what she describes as the "retreat to an expressive, nonrational 'woman's language,' embraced by some 'French feminists,' which is an exhausted and despairing project that denies women access to logic and politics."[54] Nye may not take sides, but she takes pains to distance her work from any association with familiar, if contestable, characterizations of feminisms of difference.

In focusing on establishing the bounds of an alternative women's tradition, Nye recognizes that the category of "women" must be clarified. She distances her own conception of that category from essentializing conceptions that can be found in European and Anglophone philosophy and feminist work.[55] Nye does not give a positive account of what constitutes the category of "women" or, more narrowly, philosophia, but her account relies on an exclusion of women from European and Anglophone philosophy so successful that an infusion of what women have been doing while not doing philosophy may save European and Anglophone philosophy. What remains unclear in Nye's account is why European and Anglophone philosophy has been a male tradition, what role gender plays in its failures, and the way the neglect of women's voices relates to its failure. Nye need not give a causal story—such as that European and Anglophone philosophy has excluded women and failed to gain traction on central questions (riveting as such a story might be)—but her suggestion that these women offer a more promising tradition because they were neglected and somehow bypassed the oppression that has something to do with that neglect simplifies these three women's complex relationships both to European and Anglophone philosophy and to their status as women. More generally, Nye offers a strategy of reclamation that looks away from such complex negotiations in favor of finding a separate tradition among women that will solve intractable problems.

Green: An Alternative History Within Philosophy

Karen Green, in *The Woman of Reason: Feminism, Humanism, and Political Thought*, seeks to reinvigorate the connection between feminism and humanism by arguing that "a careful adherence to the methods of humanism, and a scholarly reappraisal of past feminist humanists, while it shows the inadequacy of masculinist humanisms, offers an alternative viable form of gynocentrism, a feminist humanism."[56] Like Nye, Green advances her project as an alternative to the dominant tradition. In Green's case, feminism is right in rejecting masculinist humanism, but she urges us to reassess humanism in light of the alternative tradition she traces in the works of Christine de Pisan and Wollstonecraft, among others. Green, unlike Nye, seeks an alternative within philosophical tradition.

Green excavates that tradition to provide current feminist political theory with a history of gynocentrism in the service of strengthening contemporary feminist work, or as she puts the point, "one way of understanding this book would be as part of the project of 'creating' woman's past in order to shape our future."[57] Green's understanding of history as a practice we engage in, and one we engage for certain ends, is a crucial point—and a transformative one. Indeed, although Green characterizes her project as creating an alternative, and I follow her self-characterization in my analysis, there are important transformative tendencies in Green's project. This tendency is clearest in Green's understanding of history as a practice of the present that can affect our understanding of philosophy.

Also with potential for transformative results, she acknowledges the importance of the category of exclusion within her project. While she is seeking to uncover a gynocentric tradition, she attempts to give that tradition an open and flexible definition; her failure to do so is instructive. She writes:

> This gynocentrism is nonessentialist in so far as it rejects the idea that there is a biologically given feminine nature, or a universal feminine essence, which *determines* social possibilities. . . . There are commonalities in women's experience which have a biological origin, and biology places *constraints* on possible social forms and their acceptability. Women, I will argue, should be interpreted as having constructed their own identity through their interpretations of the more or less similar situations in which they find themselves. The position I develop is gynocentric, in that it takes women's points of view seriously, but it rejects those strands of gynocentrism which too hastily associate women with the rejection of rationality and representationalism. Indeed, it will be argued that out of the philosophical tradition, a distinctive feminine conception of rationality and objectivity that can provide the basis for feminist political theory can be seen to emerge.[58]

Note the development of this quotation. Green distances herself from essentialist understandings of feminine nature or subjectivity, but recapitulates powerful ideas of commonalities with biological origins and the idea that women across time have shared similar situations. These are seductive ideas that seem to make a nod to a sensible understanding of what we mean when we say "woman" or "women" without the baggage of strict definitions of who compose that group.

And Green is attentive to the construction of women's status—she illustrates how ideas shape the status of women. Reclaimed history can help us to think of contemporary life differently, Green argues, specifically in nonpatriarchal ways.[59] But in the last line of the quotation the idea of "a feminine conception" creeps into the account. A unity develops in this approach: people with similar situations share a conception we can call feminine. Green builds on her insistence in the first chapter that "Feminism requires the possibility of speaking of women as an identifiable group with identifiable interests."[60] Green's approach, in its pursuit of an alternative humanist tradition, seems to displace the production of an identifiable group as outside the work of European and Anglophone philosophy. There is an identifiable group that has been affected by exclusion, but Green does not interrogate how that (and other) exclusion(s) may be constitutive or productive of that identifiable group. Even when she acknowledges that women may have had a hand in constructing their own identity, it is in relation to their (more or less similar) situations. Green can speak of a woman of reason, rather than women of reason, because women are more or less the same as a result of biology and the constraints of biology on social life.

Green has grossly underestimated just how different women's lives can be, or just how powerful normative conceptions of women can be in producing subjects to whom anything can and will be done.[61] Denise Riley captures the loss for feminism when this category is so flattened:

> To put it schematically: "women" is historically, discursively constructed, and always relatively to other categories which themselves change; "women" is a volatile collectivity in which female persons can be very differently positioned, so that the apparent continuity of the subject of "women" isn't to be relied on; "women" is both synchronically and diachronically erratic as a collectivity, while for the individual, "being a woman" is

> also inconstant, and can't provide an ontological foundation. Yet it must be emphasised that these instabilities of the category are the *sine qua non* of feminism, which would otherwise be lost for an object, despoiled of a fight, and, in short, without much life.[62]

In other words, considering how the category of "women" has been constructed is different than asking how women's status has changed throughout time. We need to question how the category has been constructed, rather than relying on it to launch our feminist critiques.

Relatedly, Green's rejection of Luce Irigaray's work seems to follow from a transhistorical reading of the category of "woman." Green writes:

> At times it appears as though Irigaray herself is caught up by the image of woman, excluded from the rational order, which is the legacy of patriarchal thought. But accepting that woman is the beyond of reason is accepting that woman is what she is for this patriarchal philosophy: its repressed Other. The very possibility of woman speaking then becomes paradoxical for it can seem that the only position available from which to conceptualize oneself as a subject is the masculine one.[63]

In the third chapter, I consider and argue against such readings of Irigaray. For now, it is important that Green recognizes that accepting certain versions of "woman" presents challenges to reclamation, hence the feminist bent of her project. Green's investment in the category of "women," however, obscures the contestation of the meaning of that category in European and Anglophone philosophy's history. And Green's analysis obscures the critical approach of Irigaray's work.

Green's reading of Beauvoir is similarly structured. The former's commitment to a transhistorically identifiable category obscures the critical purchase of the latter's analysis of woman as Other. She writes: "De Beauvoir's claim that woman has been Other, even for herself, is examined and ultimately rejected, because it undermines the possibility of taking earlier feminists seriously, and leads to the bizarre and rather arrogant view that it is only in the late twentieth century that women have acquired the capacity to judge their own interests."[64] Green rightly notes that how the relationship of women to thinking is theorized has implications for how we can engage the history of women's thinking. Also rightly, as I'll argue in chapter 2, Green argues that Beauvoir's understanding of exclusion presents difficulties for reclamation that we must attend to. But problematically, Green contends: "The most fruitful way forward from de Beauvoir's thought is not to attempt to speak from the impossible position of the Other of discourse, but to discover our own feminist subjectivity and reason in the cultural legacy left us in the writings of women."[65] Women's historical work can bequeath us feminist subjectivity and reason, rather than offer us a record of contestation and argumentation through which we can consider the construction of the category of "women."

Despite their points of agreement, Nye's and Green's conclusions about philosophy are very different. Nye seeks an alternative from the philosophical tradition in the writing of some women, while Green seeks an alternative deposited within European and Anglophone philosophy. Although they both model reclamation in the pursuit of alternative traditions, the meaning of "alternative" takes very different shape in Nye's and Green's projects. In proposing women's writing as an alternative to European and Anglophone philosophy, however, they both encourage a view of men's and women's writing as constituting different traditions. They raise the possibility that the women's tradition will save us from the failures of the men's, but that is a limited view of interaction in which women save the day. With the pursuit of reclamation through an alternative tradition, we lose the shared contexts of thinking, the history of men and women responding to and shaping each other's thinking and writing. Perhaps most importantly for reclamation is the loss of focus on women's exclusion as a problem that has shaped our conceptions of European and Anglophone philosophy, as well as our conceptions of women. Exclusion has perhaps contributed to the staling process of European and Anglophone philosophy, and it has certainly produced versions of feminism that purport to speak universally while using the voice of a few. We need, however, reclamation efforts that acknowledge exclusion as a dynamic process that has never fully produced a truly alternative tradition.

THE CORRECTIVE MODEL

In corrective projects, reclamationists argue that including women in the history of European and Anglophone philosophy will help philosophy to fulfill its critical aspirations. The corrective model takes to task traditional histories of European and Anglophone philosophy for excluding women because in so doing philosophy has failed to be properly philosophical. For instance, Janet Kourany uses the image of the gadfly to illuminate the problem of European and Anglophone philosophy's misogyny. Insofar as philosophers have failed to question biases against women, it has failed to live up to its role in rousing us out of our complacency. European and Anglophone feminist philosophy is a project of correcting this problem, including through its scrutiny of philosophical history and engagement with historical women's writing. Therese Boos Dykeman takes a different tack by arguing that the philosophical tradition has been incomplete because it has ignored women in its history. Like Kourany, Dykeman thinks philosophy has erred in ignoring women and sees historical women's writing as a particularly important resource to redress this problem. However, Dykeman does not use a traditional European and Anglophone philosophical ideal, like the gadfly, to launch her critique. Instead, Dykeman points to the incompleteness of a tradition that purports to think about human experience that has not considered women's experiences. These two theorists of corrective reclamation offer particularly compelling versions of philosophical practice to set the stage for reclamation and thus give the corrective strategy two of its most compelling renderings.

The promise this model makes is that women's work will make European and Anglophone philosophy better. There are two problems with this strategy. First, if philosophers have had sufficient ideals to prevent or correct their own misogyny, why has feminism been necessary to correct it? Could there be something in how the ideals of European and Anglophone philosophy operate that has prevented that critical turn? By relying on European and Anglophone philosophy's ideals, corrective models do an excellent job of showing that this tradition has fallen short of its own ideals, but they do not address how the ideals of European and Anglophone philosophy may have contributed to the historical exclusion of women.

In not addressing European and Anglophone philosophy's shortcoming, this model also does not sufficiently problematize the category of exclusion. So, second: Why is women's work corrective? What gives it that power? Is inclusion of women's work sufficient to correct European and Anglophone philosophy or must the work meet certain standards? Are those standards generated from within European and Anglophone philosophy? Are they feminist standards? The corrective model rightly points out that European and Anglophone philosophy has been insufficiently critical about its exclusionary practices, but, like the alternative model, it accepts the category of exclusion as a well-defined and well-justified category. Thus, we need to correct philosophical practice to reverse this exclusion, but it is not clear how this category has been formed through this exclusion and how it may be formed differently through new practices.

Kourany: The Feminist Gadfly

In her introduction to *Philosophy in a Feminist Voice: Critiques and Reconstructions*, Kourany writes: "Far from functioning as the proverbial gadfly that rouses everyone from complacency on every question, this philosophy tends to ignore women even while it reflects and reinforces or in other ways perpetuates some of the most deeply entrenched and abusive biases against women in our society."[66] Evoking one of European and Anglophone philosophy's most famous metaphors for philosophical activity, Kourany suggests that this tradition of philosophy has failed in its social responsibility. Feminism, therefore, far from contaminating it with social or political matters, calls it to remember the importance of its role in questioning everyone about everything. Kourany provides a powerful counternarrative to Warnock's conception of philosophy as too universal to consider gender.

Kourany frames her essay with a question for its title: "Philosophy in a Feminist Voice?" Kourany affirms the importance of a feminist voice, but in a way that does not limit that voice to women. She writes:

> In contrast to the overwhelmingly male-dominated philosophical enterprise that most Western philosophers engage in and teach and study, all of this new work—these new directions in philosophy, as well as the critiques that have motivated them—aim in one way or another to make visible and improve women's situation. And, again in contrast to the male-dominated philosophical enterprise, almost all of this new work is being done by women. It is thus appropriate to speak of this book and the work it deals with as philosophy in a different voice—indeed, philosophy in a *feminist* voice. But the new work this book deals with is relevant and helpful to men as well as women, and in fact promises to more adequately fulfill the aims that philosophers espouse for themselves than the philosophical enterprise that most Western philosophers now engage in.[67]

Kourany suggests that a feminist voice is a critical one—the voice that raises questions as philosophy is supposed to do. Through the metaphor of voice, Kourany provides an image of philosophy and feminism together.

Kourany contends that European and Anglophone philosophy's history must undergo scrutiny as part of feminism's improvement of European and Anglophone philosophy. Included in the volume is an essay by Eileen O'Neill, which Kourany claims "makes clear [that] philosophers in the past, especially women philosophers, were at least sometimes engaged in [philosophy in a feminist voice], though most of us are now completely ignorant of their contributions. To profit from their contributions, it is necessary to redo the history of philosophy so as to make them visible."[68] Here again, the image that Kourany gives us is of philosophy and feminism together, a redoing of European and Anglophone philosophy's history with feminist voices. Our ignorance of women's historical writing is a failure of European and Anglophone philosophy to question everything and is one of the ignorances that must be corrected for this tradition of philosophy to live up to the image Socrates has given us.

Yet, by the end of her introduction, a set of vital questions remains unaddressed. Why has European and Anglophone philosophy needed a spur on the question of women? What's the relationship between being a woman and being a feminist or launching a feminist critique? Does reclaiming women, even if we wouldn't retroactively call her work feminist, constitute feminist work? Or does a woman's work need to seek to improve women's situations? Should women who offered (sometimes partially) nonprogressive views or did not offer views on women's situation be excluded? To develop answers to these questions, European and Anglophone philosophy does not need simply to be practiced better; it must undergo a more fundamental transformation to overcome its self-constitution through the exclusion of women. To use a concept that Kristie Dotson has adapted from organizational change theory, a third-order change is required. Such change requires "recognition of the limits of one's overall epistemological framework."[69] It is not just that European and Anglophone philosophy has inefficient epistemic resources for engaging with women in the history of philosophy, which would require first-order changes to make better use of our epistemic resources, or insufficient epistemic resources, which would require second-order changes within the discipline to develop new resources; "a third-order exclusion is a compromise to epistemic agency caused by *inadequate* dominant, shared epistemic resources."[70] Because women's work challenges the epistemic resources of European and Anglophone philosophy, it is rejected and we witness, again and again, what Dotson calls "the epistemological resilience of a maladjusted system."[71] Epistemic norms, built on the exclusion of women, continue to operate, sometimes quite cleverly, as in the relegation of Diotima to fiction, to exclude women. The norms, the ideals, the images European and Anglophone philosophy produces of itself are all part of exclusionary practice and so must all undergo transformation.

Dykeman: The Incomplete Tradition

In *The Neglected Canon: Nine Women Philosophers First to the Twentieth Century*, Dykeman presents a multicultural history of women in philosophy. Dykeman challenges geographical exclusions upon which European and Anglophone philosophy has constituted itself as a tradition through engagement with excluded women. She writes: "From fragments and completed writings we have learned that thinking women from antiquity forward have chafed under mental restrictions placed upon them, and that among these women thinkers, there have always been philosophers. This text provides philosophy of nine women from China to modern Europe and America who formulated feminist philosophy as they advance their individual arguments—metaphysics to political theory."[72] The women she presents are bound together by their reactions and responses to the limitations they have faced as women. Dykeman claims for these women a unified tradition without claiming that they understood themselves to be part of such a tradition, or even knew of one another. Rather, they are bound together by their arguments for women's full humanity.[73] Thus, Dykeman offers a provocative use of attention to contestations of the category of "women" to expand the scope of European and Anglophone philosophy.

Dykeman, like Kourany, sees the voices of these women as a corrective to philosophy: "Voices of women philosophers demand participation in the male-stream of philosophy; for they celebrate women's contributions already made, and they richly construct a more complete tradition of philosophy. The aim of this anthology is to let these nine 'powers of the mind' be taken into account."[74] The tradition will be more complete when these women's writings have been taken into account, for their works are "testaments . . . to philosophy's fuller 'truth.'"[75] Dykeman does not gloss the scare quotes around truth, but whatever doubt they are meant to engender is undermined by the idea that the works by these women offer testament to it. That is, Dykeman argues that these works deserve our consideration because they evidence a fuller version of philosophy. The idea of philosophy's truth may be suspended in some doubt, but its augmentation is offered as a motive for reading women as philosophers.

Dykeman's principle of selection is particularly interesting in contrast to Warnock's. Dykeman writes: "I have chosen in historical sequence works by women philosophers that demonstrate century after century a consciousness of women being barred from full participation in those human endeavors which elevate the species."[76] Not just their advocacy for women earns them a place in Dykeman's anthology, but also their advocacy for admission to the fullness of human activity. Thus, Dykeman, contra Warnock, sees emphasis on and attention to particularity as a means of helping to make human endeavors more fully human. Reductively: because humans are different, attention to difference is necessary to theorize the human.

Compelling as Dykeman's corrective is (and her expansion of the geography of philosophy for European and Anglophone philosophical sources is quite compelling), her reliance on the categories that preexist her critique signals trouble. She seeks to add women to "the male-stream of philosophy," to celebrate their contributions, and to illustrate women's consciousness of their having been barred from "human endeavors which elevate the species." The enfranchisement of women into the male-stream of philosophy and human endeavors serves the corrective aim of expanding philosophy's truth. But the notion of expansion implies that what needs to change is women's access to the categories, male-stream philosophy and the species, for instance. Left unquestioned is how our ideals of philosophy and the species were constructed through the exclusion of women. As Hortense Spillers has written: "That the feminist writer challenges certain symbolic formations of the past in correcting and revising them does not destroy the previous authority, but extends its possibilities."[77] In other words, the corrective move, while critical, strengthens the symbolic formations that were predicated on women's exclusion. Those symbolic formations, the categories of philosophy and the species, for instance, might now have room for some women—or a category of them—but that should not be read as a feminist transformation of those symbolic formations. As Spillers writes: "My point is that the analytical discourse that feminists engage in different ways and for different reasons must not only keep vigil over its procedures, but must also know its hidden and impermissible origins."[78] Corrective models leave the hidden and impermissible origins of philosophy too well alone.

Kourany and Dykeman both contend that feminism can challenge philosophy to do its job, which will have broader positive effects, either for society or for the species. Although the corrective model is closely related to the transformative model, the difference consists in the distinction between making philosophy more what it is and changing what philosophy is. In the corrective version, philosophy is not meeting its own standards or it is incomplete. By contrast, in transformative reclamation projects, there is a problem with our conceptions of philosophy that can be redressed through attention to women's work. The corrective model does not make the same sort of concession to preexisting notions of European and Anglophone philosophy that are central to the enfranchisement model. Indeed, the corrective model allows us to contemplate available conceptions of European and Anglophone philosophy and appreciate how incompatible misogyny is with those conceptions. Yet, there is still little contestation over the adequacy of existing notions of European and Anglophone philosophy or how they have been developed and deployed. The corrective model insufficiently questions why European and Anglophone philosophy is in need of correction.

Put differently, corrective strategies do not interrogate how the practice and history of European and Anglophone philosophy have been constructed through the exclusion of women and how the category of "women" has been constructed through its exclusion from European and Anglophone philosophy. If European and Anglophone philosophy will more successfully be what it is imagined to be through the inclusion of women, then we have reason to pause and consider what women are being used to strengthen.

THE TRANSFORMATIVE MODEL

The transformative model investigates norms of philosophical engagement and offers new norms that not only countenance work by women, but also highlight its importance. More precisely, this model shows how women's exclusion has shaped prevalent notions of what is considered philosophy and shows how European and Anglophone philosophy must be reshaped to redress this exclusion. Here I examine two very different approaches to transformative reclamation, one that argues for transformative reclamation through close attention to generic choices women have employed and the other through metaphilosophical reflection on who can be countenanced as a philosopher. In the first approach, Catherine Gardner proposes a transformation of the field of ethics through her engagements with the work of women writers who employed genres that have been previously deemed nonphilosophical. In the second, Charlotte Witt claims that establishing a lineage of historical women philosophers transforms the nature of the philosophical "us." By changing the available concepts of who can be a philosopher, that is, making it possible to think of women as philosophers, Witt maintains European and Anglophone philosophy will be transformed.

Gardner interrogates the interrelation of practices of policing of the boundaries of the discipline and the exclusion of women. She looks beyond the bounds of European and Anglophone philosophy as she has been trained to understand them and discovers that those boundaries have produced limitations on her own ability to engage the thinking of women. Gardner is clear that there is no necessary relationship between sex and genre. Rather, women's access to certain forms and the exclusion of those forms from philosophy have been expedient and historically contingent means of excluding women's work. Witt analyzes how "philosopher" has been coded male. Witt identifies reclamation's power in its ability to trouble that image. She leaves open the form that trouble will take, claiming neither that a woman's voice will emerge, nor that a feminist one will. She instead argues that engaging women's work will instigate greater reflection on how exclusion has shaped European and Anglophone philosophy. Witt retains the language of "canon" and "philosopher," which I will argue in the fifth chapter are likely, in different ways, to aid exclusionary processes, but this is a disagreement about transformative strategies. For now, I am just making the case that feminist reclamation needs to pursue transformational reclamation.

Gardner: Transformation Through Attention to Genre

In her introduction to *Rediscovering Women Philosophers*, Gardner writes: "Inspired by Mary Ellen Waithe's four-volume work *A History of Women Philosophers*, I wanted to learn more about our philosophical foremothers; and I wondered what, if anything, their work may have to offer modern theorizing in feminist ethics."[79] When she embarked on this work, Gardner reports that genre quickly became an issue. Some of the forms employed by figures she wanted to analyze were letters, novels, poetry, and allegory. Gardner reflects: "As a philosopher from what is typically called the Anglo-American tradition, I did not have the analytic and conceptual tools immediately at hand to read philosophy in these other forms of writing. I had been trained to read purely for argumentative content and to discuss style and form only if and when they obscured comprehension."[80] The limits of Gardner's training, which are widely shared in the discipline of philosophy, made some forms of writing inaccessible to her for philosophical consideration.

Gardner's account substantiates the claim Jane Duran makes in her preface to *Eight Women Philosophers: Theory, Politics, and*

Feminism that "Work on women philosophers asks us to retain an open-mindedness about what is constitutive of philosophical thought that is often sadly lacking in professional philosophical circles, while at the same time asking us to be prepared for some surprises insofar as theory is concerned."[81] Gardner does not, however, choose to remain in her philosophical circle. Rather, Gardner shows an exemplary open-mindedness. Instead of discounting the authors and works that she was not immediately able to engage, Gardner took stock of her own inability. She writes: "I realized that if we are to work towards including the work of these philosophers properly, then one thing we must do is to look further into the reasons for the assignment of non-philosophical status to certain forms."[82] In other words, Gardner's inability to encounter certain forms led her to investigate the creation of that inability.

As for why it is women's work that presented this opportunity, Gardner concedes that limited access to education and publishing opportunities may have contributed to the form in which women wrote, but she is clear "that there is no essential connection here between form and sex."[83] While Gardner supports work on the history of women's exclusion from European and Anglophone philosophy, her motivation was to discover "what an interpretation of the work of some of these philosophers can offer modern ethical, specifically feminist, theorizing."[84] Gardner argues that putting women's thinking to use contributes to revaluing this past work more forcefully than arguing for its merit.[85] More important, however, than revaluing the work was finding out how it could enrich contemporary theory. Thus, Gardner turns to women's work to find out if there is any help to be had. Up against problems that require new approaches, she sought work she had not been taught to accord philosophical authority. Exclusion plays a role in why these women can potentially offer help to Gardner, because through processes of exclusion, these women have not been included in her training. Yet Gardner treats that exclusion as a problem for European and Anglophone philosophy that must be addressed through changes to philosophical practice, rather than ascribing the exclusion to women's different nature or rendering that exclusion so successful that historical women developed an alternative tradition. Form was, however, a formidable obstacle for Gardner to make such reclamations of the work she was encountering. As she writes: "Despite bringing all my objectivity and critical thinking skills to bear on some of these works, this approach did not allow me to deal with the type of case where the form is part of the argument of the work. . . . I began to understand that this classification of some forms as part of the philosophical genre, and the exclusion of others, is not a 'given' or somehow independent of modern conceptions of what moral philosophy is."[86] Thus, Gardner first reconstructs "how and why certain forms become excluded—and will remain so—on this model of moral philosophy."[87] Gardner sets up her engagements with Catherine Macauley, Christine de Pisan, Mary Wollstonecraft, George Eliot, and Mechthild of Magdeburg by educating her readers about the dominant models of European and Anglophone moral philosophy. The chapters on the women thinkers are then guides to how to read their writing, given their choice of form.

Gardner is not just interested in giving us access to women's texts. She also uses her engagement with nonstandard forms to question the dominant model of European and Anglophone moral philosophy.[88] The subtitle of *Rediscovering Women Philosophers, Philosophical Genre and the Boundaries of Philosophy*, could be rewritten to read: *Transforming the Boundaries of Philosophy with Attention to Genre.* Gardner's project is as much a critique of philosophical practice as it is a reclamation of women's work. Indeed, it is a critique of philosophical practice *through* engagement with women's work. In Gardner's hands, then, reclamation makes it possible for us to question the standards by which writing is judged as philosophical and to become readers capable of judging differently. Gardner does not massify the women excluded throughout European and Anglophone philosophy's history. For a variety of contingent reasons (related to women's exclusion from European and Anglophone philosophy in complex ways), women used forms that provide productive friction for contemporary philosophical practices.

Witt: Philosophy's Self-Image

Witt provides a different, metaphilosophical view of reclamation in her overview of feminist approaches to the history of European and Anglophone philosophy, "Feminist History of Philosophy." Witt writes:

> Feminist historians of philosophy have argued that the historical record is incomplete because it omits women philosophers, and it is biased because it devalues any women philosophers it forgot to omit. In addition, feminist philosophers have argued that the philosophical tradition is conceptually flawed because of the way that its fundamental norms like reason and objectivity are gendered male. By means of these criticisms, feminist philosophers are enlarging the philosophical canon and re-evaluating its norms, in order to include women in the philosophical "us."[89]

The philosophical "us" is the organizing idea of Witt's essay. Feminism's work, the importance of its historical work, in particular, is to transform who is included in the "us."

Note the metaphor Witt uses to emphasize the nature of this transformation: "The philosophical canon can allow the luster of some of its members to be tarnished by feminist criticism, just as it has weathered criticisms from analytic or continental perspectives. The most radical feminist critics, however, have urged that the canon's central philosophical norms and values, like reason and objectivity, are gendered notions."[90] Feminism is not like other critiques—at stake is not just the luster of a few reputations. Not a tarnishing critique, but a critique that may require complete rebuilding after the storm. Witt categorizes this storm into three approaches: feminist criticisms of the canon as misogynist, feminist revisions of the history of European and Anglophone philosophy, and feminist appropriation of canonical philosophers. She grapples with women's reclamation in the first two categories, so let's look at those successively.

In her review of critiques of the misogyny of the philosophical canon, Witt identifies Genevieve Lloyd as an exemplary feminist synoptic interpreter: that is, as an interpreter who argues that the history of European and Anglophone philosophy is implicated in gendering reason and objectivity male. Witt notes that Lloyd's critique focuses on the symbolic, as opposed to the psychological or social, maleness of reason.[91] Witt aligns Irigaray's work with Lloyd's insofar as they focus on "symbolic associations of images and concepts."[92] Witt then argues that Irigaray's critique is more radical in suggesting that "patriarchal thinking attempts to achieve universality by repressing sexual difference."[93] Yet, in a common move that I argue against in the third chapter, Witt once again aligns Lloyd's and Irigaray's projects, arguing that "each of these panoramic visions of the history of philosophy delivers the same moral, which is that the central norms that inform our philosophical culture today are gendered male."[94]

For feminist philosophy, Witt argues: "these synoptic narratives of the philosophical tradition provide historical justifications for feminist philosophers who are critical of our central philosophical norms of reason and objectivity. Does the feminist synoptic critical reading of the history of philosophy justify either the conclusion that traditional conceptions of reason ought to be flat-out rejected by feminists or the conclusion that traditional conceptions of reason ought to be subjected to critical scrutiny?"[95] Two groups have now formed in Witt's analysis: philosophers who have shared norms of reason and objectivity, and feminists who share the same critique. With differences effaced on both the side of European and Anglophone philosophy and that of feminists, Witt sets up a dilemma: Should feminists reject philosophical concepts or submit them to critical scrutiny?

Witt answers by arguing that feminist claims that the traditional concepts of reason and objectivity are male-biased ought to lead to the conclusion that we need better concepts, not that we ought to reject the concepts altogether. Rejection, Witt argues, would only be called for if the concepts *ought* to be male-biased. What needs to be redressed is the fact that the concepts have been biased when they should not have been. We need critical engagement and not rejection. Here, Witt rejects enfranchisement and alternative history approaches to philosophical history. There is a problem with how conceptualization has tended to operate; hence whether or not women have so conceptualized (i.e., practiced philosophy just like men) means we must take stock of and work to change practices of conceptualization. And Witt is arguing that this engagement ought to be done not as an alternative to European and Anglophone philosophy, but as a project within it. Perhaps, however, Witt is arguing for a corrective understanding of reclamation? Let's turn now to Witt's second category, feminist revisions of the history of European and Anglophone philosophy, for her more radical understanding of reclamation.

Witt writes:

> Feminist canon revision is most distinctive, and most radical, in its retrieval of women philosophers for the historical record, and in its placement of women in the canon of great philosophers. It is a distinctive project because there is no comparable activity undertaken by other contemporary philosophical movements, for whom canon creation has been largely a process of selection from an already established list of male philosophers. It is a radical project because by uncovering a history of women philosophers, it has destroyed the alienating myth that philosophy was, and by implication is or ought to be, a male preserve.[96]

Witt attributes to this branch of feminist critique the power to destroy the alienating myth of European and Anglophone philosophy's absolute maleness. By placing women in the canon, reclamations remakes European and Anglophone philosophy, depriving it of its sustaining myth as a male preserve.

Witt claims neither that all women in European and Anglophone philosophy's history speak in the same "feminine" or "woman's" voice, nor that they are all protofeminists. Thus, she notes: "The diversity of women philosophers raises the question why their recovery or re-valuation is an important project for contemporary feminist theory."[97] While this work is important to correct mistaken beliefs and counter the effects of discrimination, Witt argues that reclamation's importance extends beyond either of these issues, and this is where Witt's work makes transformational purchase. Witt writes: "*What is really at issue is not philosophy's past, but its present; its self-image as male.*

That self-image is created and maintained in part by a tacit historical justification. It is a damaging self-image for women philosophers today, and for women who aspire to be philosophers. The real significance of uncovering the presence of women in our history and in placing women in our canon is the effect that has on the way we think about the 'us' of philosophy."[98] Witt argues that reclamation makes it possible for *us* to think of women as philosophers. She leaves open what the results will be for the future of European and Anglophone philosophy, but by broadening the concept of "philosopher," reclamation promises to transform European and Anglophone philosophy, and who is seen as capable of it.

Interestingly, Witt seems to be making a rather straightforward enfranchisement argument: engagement with women philosophers and inclusion of them in the canon will improve women's self-image and help overcome the male-bias of philosophical history. Yet, Witt locates the power of engagement with historical women in its ability to destabilize the image of a men's only canon. The canon in which Witt envisions women being placed is not one that preexists the work of engagement with historical women, but rather one that is transformed through that engagement. She is, therefore, interested not in bringing women into the canon, but rather in what happens to the history and practices of European and Anglophone philosophy when we begin to engage women as philosophers. In distinction from Green, Witt does not argue that an identifiable group with identifiable interests has sustained an alternative tradition in the shadow of a male philosophical tradition. For Witt, there is a group that has been excluded, but engaging with its members will not necessarily reveal a voice, a feminine subjectivity, or even resources for feminist work. Rather, such engagements will broaden our understanding of who practices European and Anglophone philosophy, overcoming the work that has secured a male philosophical self-image. Attending to exclusion is the feminist task, and it is one that will change not just our understanding of European and Anglophone philosophy's history, but who can be a philosophical authority. Witt does not tell us who the us of philosophy will become, but she insists that it must become through attending to exclusion.

Gardner and Witt agree that attention to women philosophers will transform philosophy. For Gardner, the transformative potential of women's writing lies not just in what they said but also in how they said it; how historical women approached philosophy can benefit current work. For Witt, the radical work of reclamation consists in overcoming the perception of European and Anglophone philosophy's maleness. Witt focuses on the question of who wrote and writes philosophy, while Gardner focuses on what has been written and how we can best approach it. Thus, while agreeing on the transformative potential of reclamation for contemporary European and Anglophone philosophy, they have different notions of how this tradition of philosophy can be transformed by women's philosophical authority. Their reasons differ, in part, because they attend to the diversity of those who are collected under the category of "women." The category does not operate as a natural kind, but it does indicate a mechanism of exclusion.

Transformational models answer Waithe's question—"Might we come to a different understanding of the nature of philosophy itself as a result of an acquaintance with women's thought?"—with a resounding "yes." Further, they explore *how* our understanding can be changed. These models can be identified by the way they attend to exclusion. Transformative models make clear that European and Anglophone philosophy has sought to constitute its proper domain as a discipline (what genres are permitted, for instance) through exclusions that require our critical interrogation.

FROM RECLAMATION TO EXCLUSION

There is something counterintuitive about arguing that reclamation should be guided by exclusion. After all, exclusion is what reclamation seeks to address. Yet, as my overview of the recurring strategies of reclamation has meant to show, the role of women's exclusion in producing European and Anglophone philosophy as a field has powerful effects that can be seen at work even within projects seeking to reclaim women's philosophical authority. The writings of historical women can be put to many uses, including making the point, as in the very different cases of Warnock and Nye, that we can largely be complacent about women's exclusion from European and Anglophone philosophy. In Warnock's case, exclusion has mostly been appropriate, whereas Nye's exclusion has been so complete that women's writing constitutes an alternative tradition. Historical texts cannot dictate their own effects. Rather, as readers and reclaimers of these texts, we engage them for our own ends, ends that are always shaped by the discursive practices and norms with which we have been trained, have succeeded, and have failed in our own practices of philosophy. If one of our ends is to overcome the exclusion of women from philosophical history and/as practice, then we must investigate how exclusion has operated and imagine how it might operate differently.

The next three chapters consider three theorists of exclusion whose work has been influential within European and Anglophone feminist philosophy: Genevieve Lloyd, Luce Irigaray, and Michèle Le Doeuff. Ultimately, I argue that Le Doeuff offers the most promising approach to exclusion and imagining its redress through reclamation. Yet, in thinking through the practice of fictionalizing Diotima, I have found the work of Lloyd and Irigaray crucial to gaining perspective on European and Anglophone philosophy as an exclusionary practice. Further, in my engagements with the *Declaration of Sentiments* and Sojourner Truth's speech in Akron in 1851, I have found myself relying on key insights they develop in their work on exclusion. The next two chapters, therefore, highlight those insights, even as I argue that Lloyd and Irigaray offer theories of exclusion with important limitations. And, indeed, although Le Doeuff's method has been most effective in helping me gain insight into the ways European and Anglophone philosophy operates through exclusion, it too has limitations with which we must contend. Perhaps those limitations in Le Doeuff's method are part of why I have not been able to leave behind Lloyd's and Irigaray's approaches. More importantly, the work of exclusion has always been the work of many hands. Not surprisingly, then, its redress is also the work of many hands.

2

CONCEPTUAL EXCLUSION

In *The Man of Reason: "Male" and "Female" in Western Philosophy*, Genevieve Lloyd argues that while the Western philosophical tradition has idealized gender-neutral conceptions of reason, it has actually been masculinizing reason. To explain how European and Anglophone philosophy has been so self-deceiving, Lloyd analyzes the arguments about reason by philosophers from the pre-Socratics through Simone de Beauvoir. Lloyd shows that philosophers have employed gendering metaphors to conceptualize reason throughout European and Anglophone philosophy's history. The result is not just the masculinization of reason, but also the conceptualization of femininity as that which is excluded from reason. Lloyd's focus is on the symbolic work of masculinization, but as her title implies, the effects of this symbolization hinder women's access to philosophical authority.

While Lloyd's project is important for understanding and redressing women's exclusion, it may appear that she has little to offer reclamation. Lloyd recounts a fairly traditional history of European and Anglophone philosophy; she analyzes Pythagoreans, Plato, Aristotle, Augustine, Aquinas, Bacon, Descartes, Hume, Kant, Hegel, Sartre, and Beauvoir. And Lloyd maintains that reason has always been gendered masculine, supporting the development of a tradition of male thinkers. How could we hope to find women in such a tradition? Lloyd may be able to help us recognize femininity's exclusion from reason so that we may redress it going forward, but she does not seem to offer a method of reclamation.

This chapter argues that Lloyd *almost* gives us a method of reclamation. In so doing, she offers us crucial insights into what reclamation requires and why it must transform philosophical practice. First, Lloyd shows how concepts can be gendered through nonobvious processes. A philosopher need not say that only (white) men have the capacity for reason, which is asserted often enough in the history of European and Anglophone philosophy, but there can be other ways in which reason is coded masculine. Lloyd focuses on the role of metaphors in this masculinization of reason. Further, Lloyd argues that while metaphors are necessary for philosophical work, they can be critiqued. Thus, there is nothing essential about the particular metaphors that have aided in the masculinization of reason, even if metaphors cannot be eliminated from philosophical work. Lloyd exposes the contingency of masculinizing reason and how much work, even if unintentional, is required to continually reassert its masculinity.

Second, Lloyd does include a woman, Simone de Beauvoir, in her history of philosophy. Lloyd shows how Beauvoir contributes to the masculinization of reason. That analysis illuminates that just because we are reading a text by a woman does not mean it is somehow immune from the effects of masculinization or incapable of contributing to it. We can analyze women's work for its contribution to the masculinization of reason, even as that woman's work violates the exclusion of women from practices of reason. Tina Chanter's reading of Beauvoir as a negotiator of women's exclusion from practices of reason helps to develop this point beyond Lloyd's analysis. Chanter details how Beauvoir negotiates the relationship of philosophy and gender. That account is a crucial supplement to Lloyd's history because, given the exclusion of women, symbolically and literally, from European and Anglophone philosophy, it is not clear how Beauvoir managed to produce philosophy. Chanter foregrounds how the exclusion of women from European and Anglophone philosophy shapes Beauvoir's contributions, and thereby provides a model for critically reading other historical women.

Finally, while Lloyd shows us a robust diachronic project of exclusion, she also shows us cracks in that project. Lloyd tends not to pry at those cracks, but we can. Lloyd shows again and again that the history of reason's masculinization has never been totally successful. We can look for openings and opportunities to create new orientations to that history. We can read philosophical history differently. While Lloyd calls for reading differently in her reflections on philosophical history, she does not develop a model of reclamation based on reading differently. In other words, Lloyd tends to note breakdowns in reason's masculinization, but then to conclude that masculinization was ultimately successful. We, however, can resist that move. And, as I explore in the next chapter, Luce Irigaray offers a model of utilizing those breakdowns to transform philosophical practice.

To illustrate the importance of Lloyd's insights for methods of reclamation, I read Lloyd's analysis of Diotima with and against Lloyd's own reading. Lloyd gives us the means to reclaim Diotima's speech as part of the conceptual history of reason, though she does not take up this possibility in her treatment of the priestess. By using Lloyd's approach to concepts for Diotima's speech, we can engage Diotima's words as both a product of and a force in producing our concepts of reason. With such analysis, we can think about how to render that history in light of how we have been formed by it. But Lloyd offers no reason or method for us to treat Diotima as a woman in the history of philosophy. This shortcoming is significant, given European and Anglophone philosophy's defenses against women's philosophical authority. Without more explicit attention to women's philosophical authority, Lloyd's work risks reinforcing the exclusion of women, even though it aims to diagnose a major force of exclusion.

Lloyd shows us the power of constructing history through critical engagement with how concepts are shaped by symbolic practices. With that power, Lloyd does not promise us full mastery over concepts, but she does illuminate critical practices for reclamation. Yet, Lloyd often depicts the masculinization of reason as too totalizing. Further, Lloyd's account too quickly moves from analyzing the symbolic operations of gender to concluding that, as her title implies, there have only been men of reason. These problems in her work are revealing for reclamation, and can guide our practices to change how we engage with the history of European and Anglophone philosophy.

MASCULINIZING REASON

To understand Lloyd's account of the masculinization of reason, we must note that it was in looking back at her work that she recognized the importance of metaphor, especially the symbolic operations of male and female, in her work. In the preface to the second edition, Lloyd explains: "If I were now to articulate the central claims of the book, I would give much more prominence to metaphorical aspects of the male-female distinction as it occurs in philosophical texts."[1] That retrospective articulation explains why one must look elsewhere than *The Man of Reason* to gain greater clarity about how the terms "male," "female," "masculine," and "feminine" operate in the text. Lloyd did not fully recognize the register of her critique of these terms as she wrote *The Man of Reason*. In retrospect, she adopts Sandra Harding's concept of "symbolic gender" to describe the target of her analysis.[2] Thus, in reading the text it is crucial to keep in mind that key concepts of her methodology were undertheorized but operative (and perhaps this undertheorization helps explain why Lloyd tends to totalize women's exclusion and does not register the need to account for Beauvoir's appearance in philosophical history). So, what does Lloyd mean by symbolic gender?

Lloyd clarifies the nature of symbolic gender in a later article, "Maleness, Metaphor, and the 'Crisis' of Reason."[3] She writes, "But even though people can identify with symbolic maleness or femaleness, their proper subjects are not men and women but concepts."[4] In other words, analyzing the symbolic operations of gendered terms requires recognizing that individuals are not always the referents of those terms. *Concepts can be gendered.* That point is crucial to understanding Lloyd's critique of reason. The concept of reason has been gendered masculine in the history of European and Anglophone philosophy through the metaphors that thinkers use to elaborate their meanings. Indeed, Lloyd seems to largely limit the meaning of symbolic operations to the use of metaphors.

Lloyd clarifies her project in response to criticisms: "My own concern is not with the processes by which social gender and symbolic gender interact but rather with getting a better understanding of symbolic maleness and symbolic femaleness independently of that interaction."[5] *The Man of Reason* is interested in how male and female are deployed and shaped as discursive symbols. That clarification is an important one for reading Lloyd's analysis. Lloyd is not arguing that symbolic gender is in fact unrelated to social gender. Rather, methodologically she isolates symbolic gender in order to gain a critical perspective on the history of European and Anglophone philosophy. Lloyd notes that "The symbolism of the male-female distinction has had all too real repercussions for the self-images of men and women."[6] But to understand those repercussions properly, Lloyd argues, we must first understand the symbolic functioning of the male-female distinction.[7]

Lloyd argues that "Those who talk of mere metaphor here imply that we can keep our received ideals of reason while cleaning up the offensive metaphors through which they have been articulated. But the problem goes deeper than this—not just because metaphors have their nonmetaphorical effects on our understanding, but also for reasons that pertain to the relations between reason and metaphors that express it. Metaphors have their philosophical import as well as their cultural effects."[8] In other words, Lloyd is concerned with metaphors insofar as metaphors do philosophical work. Lloyd argues that conceptual continuity throughout philosophical history has been made possible by the circulation of gendered symbols. She writes, for instance, "From the beginnings of philosophical thought, femaleness was symbolically associated with what Reason supposedly left behind—the dark powers of the earth goddesses, immersion in unknown forces associated with mysterious female powers."[9] Though the concept of reason changes, as well as the deployment of gendered metaphors, the masculinity of the concept persists, as does the use of gendered symbols to articulate ideals of reason.

Metaphors are not, however, above critique. Lloyd also argues, and this point is crucial to the hope for reclamation, that acknowledging the need for metaphor in thinking does not entail the endorsement of any particular metaphor. Lloyd is clear both in "Maleness, Metaphor, and the 'Crisis' of Reason" and in *The Man of Reason* that the content of philosophical metaphor is contingent. She writes, "To grasp the contingency of philosophical metaphor is often to gain insight into philosophical content even when this does not bring with it any clear idea of how we might think differently."[10] Gendered metaphors have been important in European and Anglophone philosophical conceptualizations of reason. We can recount the history of how those metaphors have shaped and been shaped by philosophical discourse. The use of gendered metaphors are not, therefore, a necessary feature of philosophical thinking. Though philosophy cannot jettison metaphors, gendered metaphors are not essential. While this means that we will always need to reflect on the metaphors we encounter and use, there is reason to believe that we can make progress on ending the exclusionary functions of gendered metaphors in European and Anglophone philosophical thinking.

Linda Martín Alcoff succinctly articulates the upshot of Lloyd's theory of conceptualization for women in European and Anglophone philosophy: "we cannot simply remove women from the sphere of the 'body' and claim for ourselves the sphere of the 'mind' and 'reason' when these later concepts have been constructed on the basis of our exclusion. Such a strategy would only participate in the violent erasure of women, continuing the valorization of the masculine as the only gender that can achieve full humanity."[11] We must expose and explore the way the masculinization of reason has occurred through metaphors.

Lloyd's discussion of Descartes's method exemplifies the sort of analysis she performs on the history of European and Anglophone philosophy: "Descartes's emphasis on the equality of

Reason had less influence than his formative contribution to the ideal of a distinctive kind of Reason—a highly abstract mode of thought, separable, in principle, from the emotional complexities and practical demands of ordinary life."[12] Lloyd explains that the abstract mode of thought became associated with already extant ideals of masculinity, *even though* Descartes's separation of mental and physical substances is inimical to the idea of gendered reason. Descartes's view has resources, utilized by some historical actors, for arguing that there can be no difference between men and women as far as reason is concerned.[13] Yet, the association of masculinity with that which transcends the corporeal, the emotional, the everyday labor of reproducing life—all coded feminine—in order to arrive at truth won out in the history of ideas. As Lloyd writes, "Women have been assigned responsibility for that realm of the sensuous which the Cartesian Man of Reason must transcend, if he is to have true knowledge of things."[14] The good news, for reclamation and European and Anglophone philosophy more generally, is that these associations, these metaphors can be critiqued.

BEAUVOIR'S NEGOTIATIONS

While Lloyd might make us look for masculinizing metaphors, she does not necessarily lead us to a project of reclamation. Indeed, in a quotation that appears almost unaltered in both *The Man of Reason* and an article from the same year, "History of Philosophy and the Critique of Reason," Lloyd paints a traditional history of European and Anglophone philosophy as the history of philosophy. She writes:

> Philosophers have been at different periods churchmen, scientists, men of letters, university professors. They have expressed

> their understanding of Reason and of what matters about in terms of their own self-perceptions; and this has left marks on successive paradigms of rationality. But one thing philosophers have had in common throughout the history of the activity: they have been *predominantly male*. The *absence of women* from the philosophical tradition has meant that *the conceptualisation of Reason has been done exclusively by men*. It is not surprising that it should reflect their sense of philosophy as a male activity.[15]

The predominance of maleness in one line has transformed into the exclusivity of it in the next. Lloyd has made a masculinizing move. I say this not to catch Lloyd at what she critiques, but rather to underscore how easy it is to move from acknowledging women's exclusion from European and Anglophone philosophy to speaking as though that exclusion has always been totally effective.

Indeed, in an early review of *The Man of Reason*, Carole Pateman wrote:

> [Lloyd's] focus on Woman and "the feminine" obscures the fact that the Man of Reason and his female companion are only part of the story of the construction of femininity. Femininity as it appears in the classic texts has both drawn on and helped shape the lives of women, but they have also criticized this construction and attempted to develop their own, autonomous womanhood. Moreover, there is a long history of feminist criticism of philosophy going back to the seventeenth century, when modern individualism (the emergence of the modern "individual" as the *man* of reason) became the basis of general social theories.[16]

It is certainly true that Lloyd does not give an account of women's contestations of the gendering of reason. One could read Lloyd's history as confirmation of the belief that women have been successfully excluded from philosophical practice by the masculinization of reason. Yet, Lloyd's inclusion of Simone de Beauvoir seems to trouble this reading.

But that troubling may only confirm Pateman's critique. For Beauvoir is the only woman whose work receives sustained attention in *The Man of Reason*.[17] And according to Lloyd, Beauvoir holds that it is only through women becoming like men that their oppression can be overcome. Lloyd's reading is based on the fact that Beauvoir does not address the crucial problem that the two thinkers most influential for her analysis, Hegel and Sartre, both understand men's transcendence as a transcending of the feminine. By modeling the possibility of women's transcendence on the transcendence that Hegel and Sartre describe, Beauvoir cannot escape the denigration of the feminine that their models require. Beauvoir would have needed to alter or undermine their accounts of transcendence as transcendence of the feminine.

While Lloyd's interpretation of transcendence is compelling, there is an issue of more fundamental significance for reclamation. Lloyd does not account for how Beauvoir came to make a philosophical contribution. After explaining how women, through the symbolic shaping of the meanings of rationality, male-female, and masculine-feminine, have been excluded from practices of rationality for centuries, and despite Beauvoir's own denial that she was a philosopher, Lloyd does not pause to consider how this woman managed to enter philosophical discourse. Nor does Lloyd address the troubled status of *The Second Sex*, a text that even its first English translator failed to identify as a work of philosophy.[18] The analysis of Beauvoir's text appears in a chapter with Hegel and Sartre as part of a lineage of thinking about transcendence. Given Lloyd's account of exclusion, it seems remarkable that Beauvoir made a philosophical contribution. What are we to make of this woman who is an heir to masculine reason and male philosophy? Do we have the material for a reclamation or do we rather need to stage an intervention?

In the opening to the chapter, Lloyd offers the following that could serve as an explanation of how Beauvoir, or any woman, could contribute to philosophy. Lloyd writes: "Women's general disinclination to reach for the sky of transcendence is connected not only with practical obstacles, but also with conceptual ones. The 'status of manhood' has been seen as itself an attainment, in ways in which femininity has not. Women have shared in these ideals only at the expense of their femininity, as culturally defined."[19] What this suggests is that the price to enter philosophical discourse was her femininity. In other words, in traditional philosophical history, there is no need for an account of how a woman broke through the exclusion to write a work of philosophy; neither Beauvoir nor any woman could enter philosophical discourse as feminine.

That conclusion creates an interesting problem for reclamation. If Beauvoir did not enter philosophical discourse as a woman, if any woman who entered philosophical discourse did not do so as a woman, then we might be able to reclaim women philosophers, but only those who paid the price of their femininity to produce philosophy. That consequence seems very close to Irigaray's claim, explored in the next chapter, that feminine subjectivity has not yet spoken. Yet, Lloyd's focus on the relationship between concepts and metaphor use does not necessarily lead to the conclusion that women have not spoken, only that the ways European and Anglophone philosophy has been practiced lead to a history in which women can only speak as masculine—defining transcendence as transcendence of femininity, as in Beauvoir's case, for instance. Lloyd's analysis suggests that people will only be able to share in the history of reason without sacrificing their femininity once we expose the masculinization of reason and change our conceptual practices. We must change the processes by which we conceive of reason in order to construct narratives in which women do not have to pay the price of admission with their femininity. Importantly, according to this argument, without redressing the masculinization of reason, men also have to sacrifice their femininity as the price of admission to philosophy.

But, of course, that cannot change what Beauvoir wrote. Changing our understanding of the history of reason and paying attention to the operation of gender in conceptualization do not alleviate the troubling associations of masculinity and reason in Beauvoir's work. We are back to the possibility that Lloyd has little to offer reclamation. Even when someone is socially gendered a woman, she must, in some way, give that up to be a philosopher.[20] Tina Chanter helps open up this problem in a way that is potentially beneficial for reclamation. Chanter asks how Beauvoir succeeded in producing philosophy even within such an exclusionary tradition. Chanter helps us to appreciate that careful reassessment of the category of "woman," and thereby "philosophy," must be done *because* of the exclusions that Lloyd illuminates. That is, because of this history of construction through exclusion, we can fruitfully interrogate the work of someone who, at least apparently, flouts the exclusion of women from European and Anglophone philosophy.

Chanter does so through care in analyzing how Beauvoir made a philosophical intervention. Chanter situates Lloyd's interpretation of Beauvoir within a larger tendency in feminist discourse to conflate the influence of Hegel and Sartre on Beauvoir's work. In the course of doing so, Chanter writes in a footnote:

> Lloyd sets out "to trace de Beauvoir's diagnosis of the condition of women back to its Hegelian origins," and she has a helpful discussion of Hegel's master-slave dialectic. However, because she assumes that "de Beauvoir's application of Hegel's philosophy is taken not from the original version, but from Sartre's adaptation of it in *Being and Nothingness*," Lloyd concentrates most of her attention on Sartre's (rather than Hegel's) discussion of the subject's relation with others.[21]

Chanter does not speculate on why Lloyd or others tend to conflate the Hegelian and Sartrean influences in Beauvoir's work. Or, more precisely, why commentators tend to reduce Hegelian influences *to* Sartrean influences. Yet, Chanter's analysis is evidence that there is a great deal to be gained in attempting to resist that conflation and understand Beauvoir as a reader of both Hegel and Sartre. By grappling with how Beauvoir engaged in philosophical practice, Chanter illuminates a history, even in feminist work, of seeing Beauvoir's ideas as the result of influences. By approaching Beauvoir as a reader of Hegel and Sartre, Chanter attributes Beauvoir's alignments with and differences from Hegel and Sartre to philosophical work. For reclamation, one important effect is that we must read Beauvoir's alignments with and differences from these two thinkers as the result of philosophical work, rather than mere parroting or mistakes.[22]

Her analysis leads Chanter to explicitly ask: "What do we make of Beauvoir's equation between the writer and the male when she says that she was treated 'both as a writer [read man] . . . and as a woman?' "[23] Chanter suggests that Beauvoir's ability to make a contribution to philosophical thought required a negotiation of the history of women's exclusion from the role of writer. Chanter proposes that "Beauvoir sets up the problem of finding the appropriate standpoint of women in a way that builds her privileged position into her theoretical approach."[24]

There is, of course, a long history of feminist concern that what Beauvoir considers her privilege in fact amounts to a repudiation of femininity that threatens to make *The Second Sex* a repetition of European and Anglophone philosophy's exclusion of women. Chanter moves through those concerns by tracking Beauvoir's negotiations of women's exclusion from philosophical work and, in doing so, relates the contradictions within Beauvoir's texts to those negotiations. The benefits of such an approach are many. The one most relevant to the project here is that if, with Lloyd, we are concerned with exclusion in the conceptual history of reason, Chanter's approach locates women as writers within the history of that exclusion and assumes neither that they will be immune from its effects nor that they will be simply determined by them. Rather, part of the importance of reading women's texts is to understand how the history of women's exclusion has never been merely exclusionary or totally successful, but has also had productive effects. Indeed, Chanter convincingly argues that "In order to think about women's otherness, feminism also needs to take history seriously. Not only do we need to think through the history of women's otherness, but also the history of feminism itself. To do so is not to acquiesce to that history, but to appreciate both the limitations and the radicality of feminist theories by situating them in their theoretical, historical, and political context."[25] If we think of women's exclusion producing complicity and resistance, then Beauvoir (and many others) can be read for both tendencies. We can appreciate the work of historical women as both limited and radical, in need of critique and available to us as critical resources.

Lloyd argues that the exclusion of femininity from rationality has shaped femininity, and Chanter here reminds us that such shaping may lead women, unconsciously or with intent, to treat femininity as inimical or opposed to their work as thinkers. By investigating how Beauvoir engaged both Hegel and Sartre, Chanter resists the narrative that would have Beauvoir receive philosophy from Sartre. But in highlighting Beauvoir's problematic negotiation of her role as woman and writer—as Chanter puts it, "her eagerness to identify herself as having overcome her status as other"—Chanter ushers into view the importance of woman's status as other.[26] By giving greater insight into how a woman's philosophical writing was shaped by the tradition of her exclusion from European and Anglophone philosophy, Chanter extends Lloyd's project in a fruitful way for reclamation. Chanter shows us that women can participate in philosophy in ways that reinforce the exclusion of femininity from rationality. Thus, the mere presence of women in European and Anglophone philosophy or the fact that a work is written by a woman is not protection against the symbolic operations of exclusion that Lloyd targets.

Thus, we can use Lloyd's conceptual analysis on the work of women writers, even though Lloyd largely does not. While we will find critical responses, as Pateman assures us, we will also find writing that shares in the conceptual history of reason. Reclamation cannot alleviate women's work of the shaping it has received by a tradition that has conceptualized reason in opposition to femininity. We can, however, engage women's writing by looking for the way it resists the exclusion of femininity *and* the way exclusion operates in it. We can look not only for how women's work has contributed to the masculinization of reason, but for how it can help maintain many other boundaries and exclusions that are not isomorphic, analogous, or unrelated to the exclusion of women, such as those of race and geography.

HOW TOTAL?

Lloyd's work is critical for reclamation in another way. As Penelope Deutscher has argued, Lloyd's analysis always concludes that femininity has been excluded from reason. Deutscher calls this move Lloyd's "stabilising tendency."[27] That is, Lloyd's account reflects no historically impactful contestation or conflict about the symbolic masculinization of reason, whether generated by men or women. Gendered metaphors operate in a predictable manner. The net result has always been deceptive concepts of reason that exclude femininity and, by extension, actual women, without appearing to be the source of the exclusion. While Lloyd sometimes notes inconsistencies in this story, she discounts their importance for the history of European and Anglophone philosophy and for our practices of constructing histories of European and Anglophone philosophy. Thus, her account is not only stabilizing, but also totalizing: reason is fully masculinized.

For instance, Lloyd writes, "We owe to Descartes an influential and pervasive theory of mind, which provides support for a powerful version of the sexual division of mental labour."[28] But we also owe to Descartes a theory of mind that does not tolerate distinctions based on gender.[29] Lloyd's explanation for the consistency of the masculinization of reason, not just in Descartes's case but in the case of all the philosophers she treats, is the momentum of masculinization already at work in the concept of reason by the time of Descartes's writing. While there are moments in which Descartes's texts open to nonexclusionary possibilities, the history of reason's conceptualization in ancient and medieval thought bolstered readings of Descartes's account that emphasized the connection between reason and masculinity. In particular, the metaphors by which Descartes's arguments could be developed and understood were masculinizing metaphors.

To capitalize on the possibilities that Lloyd touches on, but does not linger with, we need to appreciate that when femininity is excluded from the realm of reason, not only is it possible that women could still practice philosophy, but it is also possible that the exclusion has cracks and fissures in it. The man of reason may contribute to the exclusion of femininity and be shaped by that exclusion, but that does not mean such exclusion is ever fully successful. François Poullain de la Barre's use of Cartesian resources to argue for women's equality in the late seventeenth century offers an important counterexample.[30] Thus, if we follow Lloyd in making the analytic distinction between symbolic gender and social gender, we can look not only for how women philosophers might masculinize reason, but also for how philosophers throughout history have failed to.

DIOTIMA

Lloyd's analysis of Diotima offers a rich starting place for reclamation, though she does not present it as such. Indeed, her analysis leaves untouched all of the major feminist concerns that have developed about Diotima in the past three decades. Lloyd does not discuss Diotima's historicity or her absence from the dialogue. Nor does Lloyd interpret the relationship between the views of Diotima, Socrates, and Plato. Indeed, Lloyd presents Diotima's speech as a development in Plato's thinking about the tripartite soul while also attributing a view about love to Diotima and explicating it. Yet, Lloyd's treatment of Diotima could still form the beginning of a reclamation. Lloyd's analysis of Diotima shows us how words attributed to a woman can contribute to the exclusion of femininity while *at the same time* showing how the work of a man can suggest nonexclusionary possibilities. I take each point in turn. By way of introduction to the chapter "The Divided Soul: Manliness and Effeminacy," Lloyd gives an account of Plato's views on reason. Lloyd presents Diotima's views on love as part of the later Plato's attempt to incorporate passion and desire into the pursuit of wisdom. Lloyd explains: "The pursuit of wisdom is a spiritual procreation, which shares with physical procreation the desire for immortality through generation—the desire to leave behind a new and different existence in place of the 'old worn-out mortality.' The pursuit of wisdom thus shares a common structure with physical procreation; but its aim is a superior form of immortality."[31] Lloyd does not offer a critical reflection on this hierarchization of rational procreation over physical. Lloyd also speaks of those who achieve this immortality as men—though she does not attribute to Diotima the view that it can only be men.[32]

Lloyd concludes the discussion of Diotima with the observation: "The old conflicts between Reason and the transcended fertility mysteries are here subsumed in a treatment of Reason as itself generative."[33] Yet, it is not clear how we are to read subsumption here. Lloyd moves from that observation to a critique of the way Plato's idea of the divided soul became incorporated into later philosophers' conceptions of reason. We are left without a clear sense of how to understand Diotima's role or the role of her view in the masculinization of reason. Lloyd seems to indicate a new end to an old conflict: reason and the passion of the fertility mysteries are brought together under the rule of productivity. We might read this as the incorporation of rationality and physicality into a transcendent concept of procreation.

Lloyd does not question the valorization of rational procreation above physical generation that she attributes to Diotima. As explored in the next chapter, Irigaray labels this form of subsumption—the prioritization of production, whether rational or physical, over exchanges between persons—Diotima's miscarriage. While Lloyd calls the productivity of pursuing wisdom a superior form of immortality to physical generation without critically reflecting on that hierarchy of production over relation or generative reason over physical generation, Lloyd certainly has resources for a critique. By this point in *The Man of Reason*, Lloyd has already discussed the Pythagorean table of opposites that forms the context of not only the Platonic dialogues but, as much feminist ink has been spilt to show, the history of Western thinking. While Lloyd lists the ten oppositions, I will present them here in columns to more clearly show the associations:

Limit	Unlimited
Odd	Even
One	Many
Right	Left
Male	Female
Rest	Motion
Straight	Curved
Light	Dark
Good	Bad
Square	Oblong

Lloyd observes: "Thus 'male' and 'female,' like the other contrasted terms, did not here function as straightforwardly descriptive classifications. 'Male,' like the other terms on its side of the table, was construed as superior to its opposite."[34] Indeed, there is only one clearly normative pair in the list—Good/Bad—but even without the centuries of metaphorical work done by Light/Dark the appearance of those norms within each list underscores the hierarchy at work. Lloyd quickly links this list to the opposition of Reason/Matter. We could argue that Lloyd's reading of Diotima contributes to the history of masculinizing reason.

Clearly, however, Lloyd offers critical resources for addressing such hierarchization. As we saw, an implication of Lloyd's analysis is that conceptual masculinization will happen in women's, as well as men's, writing. Thus, we need not be surprised—thanks to a point available, but not explicitly made, in Lloyd's work—to find that Diotima does not offer us a concept of reason free of masculinizing tendencies. Rather, we are ready to look for possible sources and to trace the effects of the hierarchizing in the history of European and Anglophone philosophy. Lloyd's focus on the history of concepts, and the way that history operates whether or not we are aware of it, directs reclamation's attention to the concept of reason. Diotima's speech incorporates the importance of physical passion into the pursuit of wisdom, but it also maintains reason as superior to the physical body. The second move is part of the history of associations that pair masculinity with reason and femininity with the body. Thus, while the first move appears to bring together reason and body, the second move shows that such subsumption reestablishes a hierarchical binary. The progress that may be made by bringing together reason and the passions gets reinvested in the masculinization of reason.

Further, Plato attributes the words, even in a highly attenuated way, to a woman. A woman can masculinize reason, and thus the introduction of a woman as a source of wisdom does not, prima facie, guarantee feminist possibilities. But we can also consider Diotima as a site of the negotiation of the masculinization of reason in another interesting way. Is Diotima a woman in the history of philosophy? As I explored in the introduction to the book, such a claim is highly contentious. Lloyd's model does not offer a way to settle Diotima's historicity or philosophical authority. With supplementation from Chanter, however, we can look at Plato's use of Diotima as a negotiation of women's exclusion. Why does Plato use the figure of a female priestess at this point on these questions?[35] Why does Plato so rarely include women in his dialogues and what role has that played in subsequent philosophical practices of masculinizing reason?[36] These questions, and others that follow from seeing women's exclusion as an ongoing project that thinkers must negotiate, are an invitation to reflect on women's philosophical authority. Rather than quickly consigning Diotima to fiction, we can consider what role her nonappearance plays in the conceptual work of the dialogue.

CONCLUSION

With Lloyd's guidance neither Diotima nor Beauvoir becomes a hero for feminist philosophy. Rather, Lloyd's analysis allows us to give up the false hope for thinkers who can radically reorient history to free us from it. Lloyd's model instead urges reclamation to engage women's writing as part of reason's conceptual history. We can engage the complexities of that history. Lloyd gives us one history of reason's successful masculinization by staying close to traditional renderings of philosophical history. With the help of Chanter, Lloyd can point to the importance of tracing the effects of metaphors on conceptualization and the way the history of concepts builds across texts, thinkers, time periods, and traditions, even in the writing of women thinkers. We can appreciate, then, possibilities for new histories.

As Lloyd's treatment of Beauvoir shows, including women in the history of reason's masculinization is not the same as overcoming the masculinization of reason. Indeed, like Warnock, Lloyd offers us a strong case against enfranchisement methods of reclamation. By simply trying to include some women in traditional philosophical histories, we risk enfranchising women into masculine reason, rather than engaging with the complexity of women's work, as well as interpretative possibilities in any philosopher's work. Lloyd's approach also warns against reclamation as the construction of an alternative history because her analysis shows the continuity of conceptual development across thinkers. By advocating for women's writing as an alternative tradition within the tradition or as an alternative outside the tradition, we risk presenting women's thinking as free from reason's conceptual history. Again, as Lloyd's treatment of Beauvoir shows and as Chanter helps to develop, women's writing must be understood as part of conceptual history, even if it also offers resistance to some of the dominant trends of that history. Finally, Lloyd does not point to a corrective approach to traditional philosophical history, because in her view philosophical thinking cannot be cleansed of its reliance on metaphor. We cannot erase the history of concepts to correct philosophical history. Instead, Lloyd emphasizes that aspirations for neutral concepts help to hide the work of a concept's history. We must engage in ongoing critique of the metaphors by which we conceptualize.

Lloyd urges us to a project of self-reflection about our concept use. Moreover, Lloyd urges us to think of our history as an ongoing and always contemporary project of construction that is informed by and informs the concepts we use. Philosophical history is thus a communal project and one to which we not only can, but must, bring contemporary concerns. That "must" is descriptive. In other words, Lloyd does not show us that we should bring our contemporary concerns, demands, views, and understandings to the work of past thinkers; rather Lloyd shows that we inevitably do so. Lloyd's acknowledgment of the inevitability of involving our contemporary investments in our renderings of philosophical history does not lead her to argue for greater objectivity or more faith in texts of the past. Instead, Lloyd writes:

> To highlight the male-female distinction in relation to philosophical texts is not to distort the History of Philosophy. It does, however, involve taking seriously the distance that separates us from past thinkers. Taking temporal distance seriously demands also of course that we keep firmly in view what the thinkers themselves saw as central to their projects. This exercise involves a constant tension between the need to confront past ideals with perspective drawn from the present and, on the other hand, an equally strong demand to present fairly what the authors took themselves to be doing. A constructive resolution of the tensions between contemporary feminism and past Philosophy requires that we do justice to both demands.[37]

Lloyd's proposal for how work on the history of European and Anglophone philosophy ought to proceed in light of feminist criticism highlights the fact that we, from our perspectives, construct that history. By speaking of doing justice to opposing demands, Lloyd signals that feminist work on the history of European and Anglophone philosophy will have an impact on how we understand that history. Lloyd recognizes that attention to the masculinization of reason in European and Anglophone philosophy's history, a feminist demand, disturbs accepted practices for how we recount the projects of past philosophers. That disturbance is necessary if we are to interrupt the operations of metaphors that shut down our ability to read the history in ways not anticipated by philosophers of the past.

Note that Lloyd does not render the feminist disturbance of philosophical history as necessarily antagonistic to the practice of philosophy. She connects feminist critiques of reason to "a very old strand in the western philosophical tradition."[38] In other words, she proposes using the tools of European and Anglophone philosophy against its history of conceptualizing reason as masculine. Lloyd makes this proposal while recognizing that it is only with feminist pressure that those tools have been put to such use. Thus, it is aspirational when Lloyd writes: "Philosophy has defined ideals of Reason through exclusions of the feminine. But it also contains within it the resources for critical reflection on those ideals and on its own aspirations."[39] We can bring the tools of European and Anglophone philosophy to bear when we register the gendering of reason. While there is not a necessary antagonism between European and Anglophone philosophy and feminism, Lloyd sees that feminist work on the concept of reason *is* antagonistic to the masculinization of reason both found in and supported by traditional philosophical histories.

Lloyd urges us to become more conversant with what we bring to philosophical history, in particular through understanding the history of our concepts. Further, understanding the history of our concepts changes what we bring to our work of constructing the history of European and Anglophone philosophy. Lloyd thus gives us a model of philosophical practice in which conceptualization is a communal process that occurs over time and that cannot be made totally or finally transparent. That open and historically oriented conception of philosophical history makes it possible for questions about women's writing to become part of the work of constructing philosophical history—and that, as Lloyd's history shows, is a transformation indeed.

Rather than seeing women as supplemental to, external from, or in some way immune to philosophical history, we can read them as part of that history. We can do so with attention to how their thinking responds to and is shaped by the concerns, assumptions, facts, prejudices, and insights of their time, as well as by the mechanisms of oppression specific to their time and their position within it. Lloyd tends to present the history of European and Anglophone philosophy as something from which women are absent. We can, however, use Lloyd's work as a call and a guide to giving greater attention to the women Lloyd moves so quickly past: Diotima, Elizabeth of Bohemia, and Mary Wollstonecraft, perhaps even Virginia Woolf. Lloyd gives us many of the elements of a transformative reclamation, and certainly her philosophy of history calls for such practices.

3

RECLAMATION FROM ABSENCE

Because of her radical diagnosis of women's exclusion, Luce Irigaray's work does not present an obvious resource for projects seeking to reclaim women in the history of European and Anglophone philosophy. Indeed, many authors introduce their reclamation project with an argument against conceptions, attributed to Irigaray or "French Feminists" more generally, that the feminine is the excluded other of discourse.[1] These authors argue that if the feminine is the excluded other of discourse, then women are relegated to a nonrational language outside of logic. This chapter shows not only that a method of reclamation can follow from Irigaray's critique, but that she has modeled such a method in her reclamation of Diotima. Irigaray does not abandon philosophy, discourse, or reason. Instead, she proposes that the logic of discourse must be changed to make possible a culture of sexual difference. Further she models how this might be done through engagement with texts from the history of European philosophy, including with a reclamation in "Sorcerer Love: A Reading of Plato, *Symposium*, 'Diotima's Speech.'"[2] There, Irigaray shows that reclamation entails thinking and doing discourse—and thereby philosophy—differently. Irigaray challenges us to rethink and practice differently our relationship to history. In "Sorcerer Love," Irigaray challenges us to engage with history as an act of love.[3]

"Sorcerer Love" is the only text in Irigaray's corpus to offer a model for reclamation of women philosophers. The model Irigaray offers is consistent with, and develops themes from, her other work, but this essay is the only one in which Irigaray models substantive engagement with the philosophical work of a woman in the history of philosophy. "Sorcerer Love" is not, however, Irigaray's only text on love. In *I Love to You*, for example, Irigaray engages with questions of history, discourse, negative critique, and "the labor that love represents in sexual difference."[4] Although my focus is on one essay, it is likely that the method of reclamation Irigaray models in "Sorcerer Love" could be further developed, and complicated, based on this later work on love.

Yet, before we can appreciate Irigaray's approach, we need to distinguish her approach from Genevieve Lloyd's. While Lloyd's analysis has important points of connection to Irigaray's, ultimately Irigaray breaks much more radically from traditional philosophical practices of reading and constructing history (to the point that she is not uncommonly charged with negligence toward philosophical history). To appreciate the importance for reclamation of this radical turn, we must understand how Irigaray takes her critique of women's exclusion further than Lloyd. To do that, I review how Irigaray's and Lloyd's contributions have been elided in feminist work.

Then, I recapitulate Irigaray's diagnosis of the fundamental and ongoing work of exclusion in philosophical discourse, what she calls its sexual indifference. Irigaray shows how philosophy has been made possible by denying the possibility of feminine subjectivity. Irigaray's diagnosis of the sexual indifference of discourse does not lead her to despair, irrationality, or silence, as some commentators have claimed. Rather, she urges new modes of discourse, built in light of the critique of the history of sexual indifference. Of particular importance for reclamation is Irigaray's reading of Diotima's speech. In that reading, Irigaray models reclamation as a practice of love. This loving practice allows Irigaray to engage Diotima as a source of philosophical authority, even though the priestess did not leave us a text (and may not have been capable of doing so). Irigaray *uses* Diotima's absence from the dialogue as an example of sexual indifference, but then reads the words attributed to Plato for the traces of new possibilities for sexual difference.

By using Diotima's absence, Irigaray models reclamation with one of the toughest cases for reclamation. The case of Diotima has an unparalleled intractability within the field. As shown in the first chapter, especially through Dancy's critique of Waithe, but also in the persistent acceptance of Diotima's fictionality, questions about Diotima's historicity have delegitimized attempts to read her as an authoritative philosophical thinker. Irigaray's approach situates Diotima's marginalization within a bigger project of repression and silencing, and she offers a means of relocating philosophical authority to thwart those practices of marginalization. Irigaray uses Diotima's absence as an invitation to authorship, moving the site of philosophical authority from texts to our practices of engaging (reading, but also reading out loud and writing in response to) texts.

To highlight the creative reenvisioning of authority in Irigaray's reading of Diotima, I look closely at Andrea Nye's critique of Irigaray's reading. Nye's critique is meant to set the stage for a different reclamation.[5] Nye's approach, however, cannot overcome Diotima's absence from the dialogue. Nye's failure to establish Diotima as a philosophical authority is not only helpful for showing how Irigaray's reclamation works, however. Nye also offers important historical detail about the priestess and her context that offers compelling reason to think Diotima could have been a person of some authority in her own day. The loss of her thoughts, or the lack of an attempt to record them in the first place, becomes even more clearly worthy of lament.

Finally, I conclude with several concerns about Irigaray's approach. First, Irigaray's strategy of using Diotima's absence to critique the sexual indifference of European philosophy *and* to model relational philosophical authority is undeniably powerful. Problematically, however, Irigaray tends to treat the history of European philosophy as devoid of women. She thus implicitly, and thereby powerfully, reinforces women's exclusion. Second, Irigaray's theory of exclusion, to use Judith Butler's language, engages in an "epistemological imperialism."[6] That is, Irigaray often writes as though all discourse represses, censors, and fails to recognize feminine subjectivity through the same processes. Third, Penelope Deutscher identifies appropriative moves in Irigaray's work that she inherits from the tradition of Western philosophy. Without a more thoroughgoing self-critique of the appropriations in her own work, Irigaray's critique of the sexual indifference of discourse consolidates other forms of exclusion. Finally, when Irigaray speaks of sexual difference, she tends to speak of a duality, male and female. For reclamation, this move forecloses conceiving of philosophical authority as multiplicitous and potentially surprising in its forms and circulation.

DISENTANGLING CRITIQUES

This section continues work begun in the last chapter and finished in the fifth chapter that shows that Lloyd and Irigaray have quite different views of the exclusion of women from the history of European and Anglophone philosophy. Such differentiation is necessary because of a tendency in feminist scholarship to elide their critical views. Take, for instance, Elizabeth Grosz's overview of the development of feminist theory from the 1960s through the 1980s, in which she argues that Lloyd and Irigaray are part of a recent radical turn in feminist theory. Grosz writes: "Within philosophy, for example, the presumed eternal, timeless values of the discipline—Truth, Reason, Logic, Meaning, Being—have been shown by feminists . . . to be based on their implicit but disavowed relations to their 'other'—poetry, madness, passions, body, non-sense, non-existence. These 'others' are thus defined as feminine in opposition to the privileged concepts, and become the silent but necessary supports of masculine speculation."[7] Lloyd and Irigaray appear in this description to be offering similar critiques of European and Anglophone philosophy: this tradition has gained apparently stable concepts through the exclusion of the feminine, and the feminine has come to be defined as the other to the valorized concepts.

In her groundbreaking study of Irigaray's work, *Luce Irigaray: Philosophy in the Feminine*, to offer another example, Margaret Whitford also associates Lloyd and Irigaray insofar as they critique European and Anglophone philosophy for excluding the feminine. Whitford writes: "Male/female symbolism has been used 'to express subordination relations between elements of a divided human nature' [according to Lloyd] and reason, conceptualized as transcendence, in practice came to mean transcendence of the feminine, because of the symbolism used, despite the fact that 'it can of course be pointed out that mere bodily difference surely makes the female no more appropriate than the male to the symbolic of "lesser" intellectual functions' [according to Lloyd]."[8] Whitford further observes that Irigaray's critique also uses symbolism, through the symbolism of psychoanalysis, to expose the exclusions of European philosophy.[9] Thus, while marking the important difference in regard to the role of psychoanalysis, Whitford aligns Irigaray's and Lloyd's use of symbolism in understanding the subordination of femininity.

These first two examples of authors aligning Lloyd and Irigaray are brief and in the service of projects that have little connection to issues of reclamation. Thus, though they contribute to an elision of Irigaray and Lloyd, their influence is perhaps more in shaping general perceptions of their work than in directly forming reclamationist practices. To understand the importance of differentiating these thinkers, which allows us to see that their critiques operate at quite different levels, let's return to Charlotte Witt's "Feminist History of Philosophy," which I discussed in the first chapter. To reiterate, Witt is concerned with feminist approaches to philosophical history and reclamation in particular. In that essay, Witt aligns Lloyd and Irigaray to set up a dilemma for feminists: rejection or critical scrutiny of reason and objectivity. Witt resolves the dilemma by arguing that if the traditional concepts of reason and objectivity are male-biased, then we need better concepts, not the rejection of the concepts altogether. Rejection, Witt argues, would only be called for if the concepts *ought* to be male-biased. What we need to redress, Witt maintains, is the fact that they have been when they should not have been, which requires critical engagement and not rejection.

Although Irigaray does not reject discourse, reason, or philosophy, in line with Witt's suggestion, Irigaray's critique requires doing them very differently. The changes to discourse and thinking that Irigaray argues for and models happen at a different level than Witt's resolution to the dilemma. Based on Irigaray's diagnosis, we need to do far more than revise our concepts of rationality and objectivity. Revising concepts leaves the logic of concept use—discourse—intact and, thus, Witt's solution is insufficient to meet Irigaray's critique. Irigaray's theory of exclusion is much more radical than the elision with Lloyd's theory would suggest.

By contrast, Witt's solution is apt for Lloyd. Lloyd points to the need for critical revisions of the concept of reason. Lloyd does not attend to the way that women's practices of philosophy will be shaped by the exclusion of femininity from European and Anglophone philosophy, because she moves quickly from diagnosing the masculinization to concluding that only men have practiced philosophy before the twentieth century. In conversation with Lloyd's work, Chanter charts a more complex interpretive path that attends to the negotiations women's philosophical work conducts with entrenched practices of exclusion. But Lloyd does not offer the sort of upheaving critique that Irigaray does.

Put another way, Witt indicates the difference that make a difference: Lloyd focuses on the historically contingent way that Western conceptions of reason have been framed, whereas Irigaray seeks to expose the way thinking has been made possible by the exclusion of femininity within the historical practice of European philosophy. In the last chapter, we saw that Lloyd's account needs supplementation in order for her method to offer transformative engagement with the history of European and Anglophone philosophy. Lloyd's account does not tackle the way femininity has been constructed as that which lacks reason and European and Anglophone philosophy has been constructed as that which lacks femininity. This chapter considers Irigaray's more radical diagnosis that European and Anglophone philosophy and femininity have been constructed through their mutual exclusion.

SPEAKING OF OR ABOUT WOMAN

Irigaray critiques the sexual indifference of philosophy to show how arguing about women may always be a means of excluding meaningful change about who can speak and be heard—who can act and develop as subjects. Irigaray warns: "to speak *of* or *about* woman may always boil down to, or be understood as, a recuperation of the feminine within a logic that maintains it in repression, censorship, nonrecognition."[10] That is, under the current logic of discourse, to speak of woman, whatever one says, may aid in the repression, censorship, and nonrecognition of feminine subjectivity. On Irigaray's theory, feminine subjectivity has been not just lost or accidentally forgotten in the writing of European philosophy; rather, the exclusion of feminine subjectivity has been a mode of discourse production. Thus, for Irigaray, the logics of discourse must be changed for sexual indifference to be overcome.

Irigaray famously counsels: "the issue is not one of elaborating a new theory of which woman would be the *subject* or the *object*, but of jamming the theoretical machinery itself, of suspending its pretension to the production of a truth and of a meaning that are excessively univocal. Which presupposes that women do not aspire simply to be men's equals in knowledge."[11] In proposing that we need to jam the machinery, Irigaray commits both to discourse and to the possibility of changing it. When we are changed as readers of discourse, when we jam the machinery with our reading and writing, for Irigaray, we disrupt the sexual indifference of discourse. For reclamation specifically, Irigaray's theory means that we cannot merely advocate for the texts of women philosophers or seek their representation in the canon as the solution to the history of exclusion: that would be the aspiration to be the same as men. Further, amassing evidence of women's contributions to philosophical history alone is unlikely to change discourse, for it does not disrupt practices of reading and writing. Neither can women's writing be reclaimed as an alternative to traditional philosophical history. Again, a reader's practices of engagement would be left intact, unmoved. Nor can European and Anglophone philosophy be corrected according to its own ideals, for those ideals have been formed through making sexual difference impossible. Irigaray's work shows us, rather, that we must become the sort of readers who can disrupt discursive practices.

Irigaray critiques the sexual indifference of European and Anglophone philosophy with the tools of psychoanalysis. Psychoanalysis has uncovered, Irigaray argues, "*the sexual indifference that underlies the truth of any science, the logic of every discourse.*"[12] But fatefully for the discourse of psychoanalysis, Freud failed to consider the "*sexualization of discourse* itself."[13] In other words, Freud has not interrogated how discourse assumes a single model of desire, coded masculine. That failure, Irigaray maintains, is actually the fault of European philosophy. Psychoanalysis relies on the metaphysical presuppositions the "discourse on discourse" supplies to it and all other discourses.[14] Psychoanalysis relies on European philosophy's ability to "*reduce all others to the economy of the Same.*"[15] In other words, all apparent psychoanalytic acknowledgment of sexual difference is actually a variation of a single theme. One of Freud's most famous theories, penis envy, is illustrative. While many interpretations of the theory are possible, the deployment of the term "penis" to explain human sexuality anchors sexual difference in a shared signifier. Radical sexual difference is thus foreclosed.

Overcoming that failure of psychoanalysis requires, Irigaray argues, engaging with the master discourse at fault for the failure. We must expose the sexual indifference of discourse itself.

So, how can we hope to disrupt the sexual indifference of discourse with such powerful dynamics already at work? How does Irigaray jam the machinery? In *Speculum of the Other Woman*, Irigaray engages the master discourse "by 'beginning' with Freud and 'ending' with Plato," which is "already going at history 'backwards.'"[16] Yet, she has already noted that *Speculum* has no beginning or end; it "confounds the linearity of an outline, the teleology of discourse, within which there is no possible place for the 'feminine,' except the traditional place of the repressed, the censured."[17] For even reversal, Irigaray notes, does not make a place for the feminine. And it is not enough that her readings expose moments of the repression of the feminine in a text for, according to Irigaray, woman has provided the place for European and Anglophone philosophy to unfold. Thus, in *Speculum*, Irigaray writes: "And if one day her sexuality was recognized, if it did enter into 'History,' then his-story would no longer simply take place or have a place to take."[18] From the point of view of the history that has taken place in and through the repression of the feminine, it remains unclear *how* discourse could unfold differently. Yet, it is clear that continuing to engage in discourse as it has been done will not overcome the sexual indifference that European and Anglophone philosophy has used so productively.

Note how Irigaray concedes and performs the difficulty of conceptualizing discourse differently: "What a feminine syntax might be is not simple nor easy to state, because in that 'syntax' there would no longer be either subject or object, 'oneness' would no longer be privileged, there would no longer be proper meanings, proper names, 'proper' attributes. . . . Instead, that 'syntax' would involve nearness, proximity, but in such an extreme form that it would preclude any distinction of identities, any establishment of ownership, thus any form of appropriation."[19] In other words, Irigaray's positive project is *all but* unimaginable.

Even the notion of "syntax" must be suspended in its meaning when projecting what might be.[20]

But Irigaray is not without suggestions for how a place might be made for the feminine. Foremost among them: mimicry. Which means, Irigaray writes, for a woman "to resubmit herself—inasmuch as she is on the side of the 'perceptible,' of 'matter'—to 'ideas,' in particular to ideas about herself, that are elaborated in/by a masculine logic, but so as to make 'visible,' by an effect of playful repetition, what was supposed to remain invisible: the cover-up of a possible operation of the feminine in language."[21] Irigaray makes this recommendation because the feminine has already been ascribed the role of the mimic.[22] Thus, by suggesting that women take up the role of mimic, Irigaray is suggesting that women exploit a position already assigned to woman. We cannot skip to representing the feminine in language, but must use the role already assigned to women, that of mimic, to jam those operations of discourse. The moments of textual repression can become opportunities for imagining new possibilities.

SO WHAT ABOUT RECLAMATION?

While this sort of mimicry seems to offer a way forward that engages the work of repression, does it give us a way forward to engage women's historical philosophical authority? The possibility remains that historical exclusion was so successful that no women wrote philosophy. If the repression, censorship, and nonrecognition of the feminine are the condition of possibility for philosophical work as we know it, then even if we read women's work, we are not reading feminine subjectivity. So, while it may be important for feminist projects to examine philosophical history, the goal would have to be, it seems, overcoming European and Anglophone philosophy, or at least its history. That is, we need to overcome this practice of repression, censorship, and nonrecognition, rather than look for women in philosophy's history.

Irigaray, as I have explicated her project, offers a structural explanation of European and Anglophone philosophy's relationship to the feminine and, thereby, seems to thwart the possibility of reclamation. Woman has not spoken. Thus, historical women (or men) who have spoken have not brought feminine subjectivity into discourse. A close reading of the following passage illustrates this point. The passage is from "Any Theory of the 'Subject' Has Always Been Appropriated by the 'Masculine,'" an essay title that expresses the structural view. Irigaray writes:

> But if, by exploits of her hand, woman were to reopen paths into (once again) a/one logos that connotes her as castrated, especially as castrated by words, excluded from the work of force except as prostitute to the interests of the dominant ideology—that is of hom(m)osexuality and its struggles with the maternal—then a certain sense, which still constitutes the sense of history also, will undergo unparalleled interrogation, revolution. But how is this to be done? Given that, once again, the "reasonable" words—to which in any case she has access only through mimicry—are powerless to translate all that pulses, clamors, and hangs hazily in the cryptic passages of hysterical suffering-latency. Then. . . . Turn everything upside down, inside out, back to front. *Rack it with radical convulsions*, carry back, reimport, those crises that her "body" suffers in her impotence to say what disturbs her. Insist also and deliberately upon those *blanks* in discourse which recall the places of her exclusion and which, by their *silent*

> *plasticity*, ensure the cohesion, the articulation, the coherent expansion of established forms.[23]

At first, Irigaray seems to suggest that there are paths to be reopened into discourse that will overturn its sexualization. She reiterates the sense of reopening by saying that woman would *once again* do so with the exploits of her hand. Thus, perhaps, one might hopefully propose, the exclusion of women has been historical and not structural. But, she continues, woman has only had access to reasonable words through mimicry. And those words are put into question as truly reasonable by Irigaray's use of quotation marks. Woman's exclusion can only be recalled by attention to *blanks* in discourse that lend themselves *silently* to many forms that ensure discourse.

Such a description does not sound promising for reclaiming women's writing; woman appears only as blanks and silences and not as an articulator of philosophical discourse. But before we concede the impossibility of reclamation, it is important to note that Irigaray speaks of "woman," not "women." As Elizabeth Weed notes: "Irigaray may write about women and their political, economic, psychic, and bodily betterment, but it is through woman that she speaks."[24] Thus, we misplace hope for the reclamation of women's writing if we invest it in the idea that woman reopens paths with the exploits of her hand. Rather, by using woman, Irigaray repeats a trope of discourse, one we can recognize in formulations like "The Woman Question," but she also, as Weed highlights, speaks through it. Speaking through woman has the sense both of speaking by way of woman and of woman being a concept through which Irigaray strains to be heard: the difference between speaking through a receiver and speaking through a wall. Irigaray's use of "woman" both sustains the possibility of speaking and troubles it. The way Irigaray is playing with the idea of "woman" does not yet easily lead to a practice of reclamation, but we are getting a clearer picture of what Irigaray thinks any such attempt to establish women's philosophical authority is up against.

Irigaray signals with her use of "woman" that the unparalleled interrogation and revolution of a certain sense, which still also constitutes the sense of history, will not be achieved by enfranchising certain voices into discourse. Woman does not speak. Woman is a trope of discourse. Words, like woman, are powerless to translate all and will always be so, but we do not have to leave uninterrogated the sense, which is also the sense of history, with which we engage discourse. Body thus appears in quotation marks in the above passage. When we write "body" we no more bring that which exceeds discourse into discourse than when we write "woman." Marking off "body" in quotation marks encourages an encounter with it as a concept that has a history in discourse of marking some sort of limit, excess, or disturbance. Irigaray invites us to apprehend every appeal to "body" as a citation with which we engage and through which we are constituted in discourse. Words, as Irigaray writes, are powerless to translate all that pulses, clamors, and hangs hazily in the cryptic passages of hysterical suffering latency, but that does not lead her to abandon discourse. Instead, she tells us to turn everything upside down, inside out, back to front. She tells us to insist, insist on the blanks of discourse and not on the coherence they enable.

For reclamation, this means our relationship to discourse can be changed. We can become readers who pay attention to the blanks and silences of discourse, who read with a sense of the history of discourse, who write with an ear for silences and the history upon which our meaning relies. Exclusion has been both historical and structural. The structure is changed by reading and writing differently, thereby giving us a new historical relation to discourse. As Weed writes:

> Consciousness has a history—perhaps, Irigaray observes, the logic of consciousness and the logic of history "add up to the same thing in the end, in a way"—and that history can change and be changed. And, of course, to change the logic of consciousness is to change the relationship of conscious/unconscious: "Since the recognition of a 'specific' female sexuality would change the monopoly of value held by the masculine sex alone, in the final analysis by the father, what meaning could the Oedipus complex have in a symbolic system other than patriarchy?"[25]

It is the history of consciousness—the logic of consciousness—that can be changed. That history and logic are what must be changed for women to have philosophical authority.

The power of discourse will always be its power to subordinate—to fix everything along vertical and horizontal axes to determine what is above and what is below. But must readers remain powerless in the face of this power? Must we accept the feminine as that which provides the place of this ordering? In the "The Power of Discourse and the Subordination of the Feminine," Irigaray indicates a different possibility in the conjunction of the title. The power of discourse has been the subordination of the feminine, but we can read, write, and rewrite differently. And in practicing differently, we can create the possibility of reclaiming women's work through our reading, writing, and rewriting. We can make a history in which women's writing is part of history, not as the other to discourse and not as its alternative, but as part of a discourse we are powerful enough to practice differently.

In "Power of Discourse," after describing European philosophy's power to "*reduce all others to the economy of the Same*," Irigaray writes: "Whence the necessity of 'reopening' the figures of philosophical discourse—idea, substance, subject, transcendental subjectivity, absolute knowledge—in order to pry out of them what they have borrowed that is feminine, from the feminine, to make them 'render up' and give back what they owe the feminine. This may be done in various ways, along various 'paths'; moreover, at minimum several of these must be pursued."[26] Irigaray does not dictate what sort of readers we must be; at minimum, we must pursue several paths. Irigaray's work records many different attempts at prying out of discourse what it has borrowed and writing discourse differently. Now that we have a sense of what Irigaray thinks reclamation is up against we can ask: What does Irigarayan reclamation look like? The approach is wily.

SORCERER LOVE

Irigaray's concept of the "sensible transcendental" provides one path for reclamation. One way to understand the sensible transcendental is as a highly condensed act of mimesis. Irigaray uses the form of a concept, a basic unit of discourse, but in an anomalous repetition. Our eyes cannot glide over the concept, but we must repeat the terms to ourselves and try to pull together "sensible" and "transcendental." It plays the game of discourse, but it uses the rules to disrupt discourse. Sensible and transcendental do not belong together, but in opposition, comfortably across the chasm within discourse.

Irigaray develops the idea of the sensible transcendental in "Sorcerer Love: A Reading of Plato, *Symposium*, 'Diotima's

Speech,'" as something attainable; it is "the material texture of beauty."[27] In a sense, the idea is the accomplishment of the text, one prefigured by Irigaray's use of the "accessible transcendental" and the "inaccessible transcendent" in "Sorcerer Love." In order to resist the easy deployment of the sensible transcendental as a definable concept—to read it as disruptive—we must appreciate "Sorcerer Love" as Irigaray's reclamation of Diotima's philosophical contribution, but not by putting the words back in Diotima's mouth; Irigaray speaks "Diotima's Speech." Further, in her lecture, Irigaray does not decide the issue of who should take the blame for problems of argumentation. Indeed, Plato is only mentioned in the title to the piece and once obliquely in the text; thus, the author is all but absent from the text. Irigaray will suggest that missteps in arguments are perhaps Socrates's fault, but she also speaks of these missteps as errors in Diotima's method. Irigaray's voice, as reader of the speech, tells us what is true to Diotima's argument and what is a departure from it.

The love to which Diotima and therefore Irigaray refer is Eros, the not quite human, not quite divine child of Plenty and Poverty.[28] This daimon—this spirit—is never one thing or the other, but the middle that makes relationships between the unalike possible. By lending her voice to Diotima to elaborate that argument, Irigaray takes on a potentially daimonic role. She asks us to engage with her as listeners and readers. As Irigaray writes, "If we did not, at each moment, have something to learn from the encounter with reality, between reality and already established knowledge, we would not perfect ourselves in wisdom."[29] Thus, "Sorcerer Love" does not ask us to trust this instance of discourse because it is a woman reading a woman, reclaiming her from her embedding in a man's text. Rather, she asks us to perfect ourselves in wisdom by being the readers of her reading. She asks us to consider this activity as philosophy:

"Philosophy is not a formal learning, fixed and rigid, abstracted from all feeling. It is a quest for love, love of beauty, love of wisdom, which is one of the most beautiful things."[30]

That is to say, we do not just read for the theme of love, but our reading can be an enactment of love. The exchange can be immortalizing if there is a constant movement between text and reader. "Love is fecund prior to any procreation," Irigaray writes, "And its fecundity is *mediumlike, daimonic*, the guarantee for all, male and female, of the immortal becoming of the living."[31] Indeed, Irigaray writes that Diotima "miscarries" when she suggests that procreation is the cause of love. Irigaray writes: "Something becomes frozen in space-time, with the loss of a vital intermediary and of an accessible transcendental that remains alive. A sort of teleological triangle is put into place instead of a perpetual journey, a perpetual transvaluation, a permanent becoming."[32] The perpetual journey, the perpetual transvaluation, the becoming of dialogue that flows between people are what Irigaray calls the accessible transcendental. And it is that accessible transcendental that is lost in a procreative or teleological concept of love. As Somer Brodribb observes, "This methodological error of Diotima has fixed [love] on the space-time plane, and lost a vital conduit from living beings to the transcendental."[33] The image of the child as telos is a sad image compared to the child who, empowered to love and be loved, achieves immortality through loving. Irigaray does not negate the importance of children or texts, but is rather trying to help us reevaluate familiar images and ways of thinking about love that would funnel our thinking immediately to procreation and productivity—to a fixed goal as the means of immortality.

Irigaray argues that the *inaccessible* transcendent becomes "the ideal when daimonic love is suppressed."[34] That is, when children, texts, the truth become the means to immortality, the transcendent becomes inaccessible to us. When the circulation of dialogue becomes subordinate to the product of its work, the transcendent becomes inaccessible—we are merely mortal with dreams of achieving an immortality totally alien from us. Which is not to say that we should not have children, write texts, or pursue the truth. Indeed, if Irigaray attempts in "Sorcerer Love" a daimonic reading of Diotima's speech, it results in a text. She is dependent on our reading of it, whether we hear the lecture or read it. If we read the text as the goal of Irigaray's engagement with Diotima, Socrates, and Plato, then we have certainly taken up one possibility of that text. But in having done so, we stop the circulation of dialogue and the text becomes inaccessibly transcendent—we have turned away from a possibility of philosophical authority. On this model, we might agree or disagree with a text, but it is not ours to change through engagement with it. Rather, the text somehow subsists through our interpretations of it. The text becomes, to use Irigaray's words, *beloved*, rather than a *lover.*

Irigaray gains these categories—lover, beloved—from Diotima, but, as mentioned, she also argues that Diotima is inconsistent in her treatment of love. Diotima, she suggests, also maintains that procreation becomes the goal of love. In such a view, "[love] risks losing its internal motivation, its 'inner' fecundity, its slow and constant generation, regeneration. This error in method, in the originality of Diotima's method, is corrected soon afterward only to be confirmed later. Of course, once again, *she is not there. Socrates relates her words.* Perhaps he distorts them unwittingly or unknowingly."[35] Irigaray exposes a contradiction in Diotima's argument. Love is first daimonic, but then Diotima miscarries and links love to procreation. But we cannot be sure who is speaking, whose error and whose method we encounter in the dialogue. Perhaps Socrates is to blame, Irigaray suggests.

We do not know who to blame, because as Irigaray reminds us, no one can read the words of Diotima. We can read Plato's rendering of Socrates's speech that he attributes to Diotima. As Irigaray repeats throughout "Sorcerer Love": *she is not there.* The challenge before Irigaray, as it is before reclamation, is reading and voicing (for "Sorcerer Love" *is* a lecture) Diotima's speech without appeal to it as a historical text on which our authority about matters of love and beauty can be grounded. *She is not there*, and yet we can be lovers in the style Diotima suggests. We can seek immortality through our exchange. Diotima fails to be present at all *and* yet she has something for us. Irigaray becomes the author of Diotima's speech in dialogue with Plato's authorship. We can recognize the philosophical authority developed in reading and engaging, and we can take part in it. We have a sense, as Carolyn Burke observes, that we are reading a reading and this invites us to read also.[36]

To approach the importance of intermediacy for philosophical authority in Irigaray's work from another angle, consider the closing passage of "An Ethics of Sexual Difference":

> Beyond the circularity of discourse, of the nothing that is in and of being. When the copula no longer veils the abyssal burial of the other in a gift of language which is neuter only in that it forgets the difference from which it draws its strength and energy. With a neuter, abstract *there is* giving way to or making space for a "we are" or "we become," "we live here" together.
>
> This creation would be our opportunity, from the humblest detail of everyday life to the "grandest," by means of the opening of a *sensible transcendental* that comes into being through us, of which *we would be* the mediators and bridges. Not only the mourning for the dead God of Nietzsche, not waiting passively for the god to come, but by conjuring him up among us, within

> us, as resurrection and transfiguration of blood, of flesh, through a language and an ethics that is ours.[37]

What Irigaray called immortality in "Sorcerer Love" appears divine in this description. Not the God of divine authority that all but died with the advent of modernity, nor God the son who will rise again to end our human suffering, but a divine among and within us. And that divinity is "a new birth, a new era in history" only when we have moved beyond the sexual indifference of discourse that pretends to neutrality through forgetting the placenta that sustains it.[38] The becoming is both divine and mucosal. Transcendental and sensible. It does not close itself off through the forgetting of the maternal body, the elements, especially air, that sustain it. We can be readers who remember: "Language, however formal it may be, feeds on blood, on flesh, on material elements."[39] We can be readers who resist turning away from this materiality of discourse, jamming the machine with love.

How can love jam the machinery? That question introduces a positive trajectory into the project of jamming the machinery without simply replicating the imperative to produce more discourse. For love, as Irigaray reads Diotima, is an intermediary that does not end in the production of discourse, but rather flows through dialogue with each other, texts, and readings. The machinery of discourse production is jammed by lovers who do not value the product of discourse as a means to immortality, but rather the becoming that is possible with each other, even in and through discourse. The possibility of discourse circulating differently opens the door for reclamation. For the circulation of philosophy does not have to be guaranteed by the disavowed place of its happening—other norms can shape the circulation of discourse. We can, for one, conceive authority together, reading Diotima's words as hers, not hers, Irigaray's, not Irigaray's, ours, and not ours.

Reclamation as a practice of love does not have a telos outside itself; it opens up room to experience ourselves as readers of texts and the way the text responds to our reading. Irigaray writes: "Like love, the philosopher would be someone poor, dirty, rather down-and-out, always unhoused, sleeping beneath the stars, but very curious, skilled in ruses and tricks of all kinds, constantly reflecting, a sorcerer, a sophist, sometimes exuberant, sometimes close to death."[40] Reclamation that is divine and mucosal will have to be skilled in ruses and tricks of all kind. But it is also dependent upon readers who are sometimes exuberant, sometimes close to death. Readers who wonder at what they encounter, capable of "attraction to that which is not yet (en) coded" and "curiosity (but perhaps in all senses: sight, smell, hearing? Etc.) vis-à-vis that which we have not yet encountered or made ours."[41] Curious, rather than appropriative, we work with the uncertainty of whose text we read. We can appreciate and engage the uncertainty as a wellspring of fecund possibilities for love.

How can we be readers who appreciate and engage the uncertainties of texts? That is the challenge Irigaray puts to reclamation. The heterogeneity with which she reads, rewrites, mimics the texts of European philosophy does not just jam the machinery once, setting up a situation in which we wait for new parts to be ordered or a new machine to be built. Irigaray's readings offer a model of reclamation in which discourse is jammed with dialogue and style interrupts meaning. Her writing models an invitation to the reader to become author also, as the partner in an exchange that may result in texts, but that does not end in texts. Reclaiming women as philosophers and reclaiming European and Anglophone philosophy for women does not require that new idols be erected for our reverence and obedience. But if they are not to become such figures, we must be readers powerful enough to wonder at what we have not yet appropriated.

To come at Irigarayan reclamation from another angle, we can look at Penelope Deutscher's description of Irigaray's political project: "Irigaray's politics is based on a notion of impossible difference. What concepts of identity and difference have most repeatedly been excluded—rendered most impossible—in a given culture, context, or history? Against what possible alternative identities have hegemonic forces most concentrated? Proposing a methodology for the interpretation of overdetermined, repeatedly consolidated exclusion of certain kinds of alternative possible identities, Irigaray reinterprets this pattern of exclusion as a kind of anticipation."[42] Irigaray imagines a philosophical history in which Diotima is a philosophical authority. European and Anglophone philosophy may have concentrated and consolidated its practices through the exclusion of the feminine, and Diotima, in particular, but there is no reason we must interpret these practices by hegemonic or traditional means. We can practice disruptive means of interpretation, as a kind of anticipation, rather than appropriation.

DIOTIMA

Another way to appreciate the radical nature of the transformation in philosophical practice that Irigaray urges is through Nye's critique of it. In "The Hidden Host: Irigaray and Diotima at Plato's Symposium," an essay that appeared in *Hypatia* with the first English translation of "Sorcerer Love," Nye presents a different Diotima, one whose argument is consistent throughout the speech in the *Symposium*. The successful student of

Diotima, Nye argues, "glimpses no universal, abstracted from imperfect particulars, but an indwelling immortal divine beauty, an attracting center that foments fruitful creation in all areas of existence,"[43] and Diotima never wavers from developing this line of thought. Nye agrees with Irigaray's daimonic reading of Diotima's speech, but disagrees that Diotima's speech ever miscarries. "Irigaray judges Diotima as a lapsed French feminist," Nye writes, "struggling to maintain the 'correct method' against philosophical orthodoxy."[44] In other words, Nye's criticism is not only that Irigaray relies on an overliteral translation of the *Symposium*, which she also argues, but that Irigaray's method of reading causes her to misread Diotima and to misread her as failing in the French feminist method of reading. The source of Irigaray's misreading, Nye contends, is in the "conceptual infrastructure of Irigaray's feminist strategy in deconstructive method and textual practice, in '*écriture féminine*,' and in the concept of feminine '*jouissance*.'"[45] Nye explains Irigaray's inability to read well through using the concepts of deconstruction, *écriture feminine*, and *jouissance*.

One could respond to this criticism by showing the complicated manner in which Irigaray adopts deconstructive methods, thereby countering the image of her as an acolyte of Derrida, or by mentioning that Irigaray does not use the term *écriture féminine*,[46] or by analyzing the way that Irigaray deploys *jouissance* with and against Lacan. Indeed, one could show that Nye fails to be the historically informed, subtle reader of Irigaray that she claims Irigaray fails to be of Diotima. But here, we can more fruitfully remember that while Nye can read Irigaray, no one can read the words of Diotima. We can read Plato's rendering of Socrates's speech that he attributes to Diotima. As Irigaray repeats throughout "Sorcerer Love": *she is not there.* Thus, Irigaray's problem is not that she "judges Diotima within the context that gives meaning to her own deconstructive practice as if Diotima were a twentieth-century Parisian '*intellectuelle*' struggling against the authority of a male academic establishment to produce an '*écriture feminine*.'"[47] Irigaray is not diagnosing Diotima as a failed French feminist. Irigaray is grappling with the fact that Diotima fails to be present at all *and* yet she has something for us.

More interesting for reclamation than Nye's accusation about how Irigaray fails is that Nye and Irigaray disagree about authority. For Irigaray, Diotima's absence and the importance of her lesson allow us to conceive of authority differently. Irigaray becomes the author of Diotima's speech, not as Plato did, but in dialogue with Plato's authorship. Further, Diotima's absence from the scene of philosophy is imperfect, for a view is still attributed to her, even if quite tenuously. Yet, Irigaray takes the role given to a woman and exploits it to raise the question of sexual difference. She does so by engaging with the assigned role as though it did generate a woman's speech. Irigaray's approach to establishing Diotima's authority is consistent with her view of the imperfect yet powerful exclusion of sexual difference from philosophical discourse.

Nye, of course, is not unaware of the means by which Diotima's speech has been transmitted. She negotiates worries about the authenticity or veracity of Socrates's via Plato's rendering of it in two ways. First, Nye provides historical detail about "a sophisticated Minoan culture" that persisted through Greek culture that granted some authority to women, especially in religious contexts.[48] She concludes, "In historical context, then, it is neither surprising nor anomalous that Diotima would appear in an authoritative role as the teacher of Socrates. As prophetess/priestess she was part of a religious order that has maintained its authority from Minoan/Mycenean times."[49]

This contextualization helps to account for Socrates's appeal to the authority of a woman, according to Nye, and his reverence for her as his teacher. Nye contends that even though Diotima was absent *she could have been an authority*. That, Nye's argument suggests, is grounds for considering her an authority now. Nye's second strategy is more complicatedly related to Irigaray's work. Nye claims that Diotima is the host of the *Symposium*. In her introduction to the essay, she writes: "The root meaning of 'host' is a physical body on whose flesh parasites feed. The host is the nourishment they steal and convert to prolong their own dependent existences. The host is a sacrificed animal body offered up to placate heaven. The host is the physical bread the faithful eat at communion to become one with the insubstantial god. If we take 'host' in these root sense, then, as I hope to show, it is Diotima and not Agathon, Socrates, or Plato who is the real host of the *Symposium*."[50] It is not, from that etymological lesson, clear why Nye wants to show that Diotima is the host. It appears as if she would then be (a) the physical body feeding parasites so that they may, in dependence, prolong their existence, (b) the animal body placating heaven, or (c) the physical bread through which the faithful make contact with an insubstantial god. None of these is an obvious base for establishing Diotima's authority. Nye does not return to the image of the host to provide alternative meanings or to help us reevaluate the meanings she made available in her introduction. But Nye does return to the idea of Diotima as the host. In her conclusion, Nye writes: "If, with Diotima, [Irigaray's] usual sure touch falters, it is because Diotima does not play the feminine role as deconstruction or Lacanian psychoanalytic theory has conceived it. She is not the uninvited gatecrasher, but the host of the *Symposium*. She is the spokesperson for the ways of life and thought that Greek philosophy feeds on, ways of thought whose authority

Plato neutralized and converted to his own purposes."[51] Diotima is the host upon which Greek philosophy feeds and the basis for the authority that Plato neutralizes and converts. Interestingly, the image that Nye gives of her here resonates with Irigaray's rendering of the feminine as the disavowed material of discourse; for Nye, Diotima is the absent body on which the *Symposium* feeds. Diotima, who by the history Nye gives us should have some authority to speak her own ideas, does not speak in the *Symposium*. She is not the gatecrasher at the party because *she is not there*. Nor can she be, in her absence, the spokesperson for a way of life and thought. Plato or Socrates, perhaps, but not Diotima; *she is not there*.

We can read Nye's strategy to illuminate Irigaray's. Nye urges that through contextualization and proper translation we can gain access to what Diotima really meant, despite even the difficulty that the text we have of her speech does not even pretend to be an accurate record of her speaking. Nye's work raises questions about the style we ought to use to write about, represent, give voice to women's thinking. Nye's contextualization does more to raise questions about reclamation than it does to answer them, however. At the heart of Nye's condemnation is the observation that Irigaray's approach does not take up questions of historical accuracy or the project of contextualization. Irigaray, Nye suggests, cannot be trusted as Diotima's reader because she is not sufficiently knowledgeable, she has not taken the care the text requires, and there is too much of her in the material. Yet, as I have argued, Nye's approach cannot bring Diotima into the scene of philosophy. Diotima was not there.

Nye argues that a woman like Diotima could have been an authority and thus we can consider the speech hers. By contrast, Irigaray reclaims Diotima from the priestess's absence. Irigaray uses the fact that Diotima was represented as an authority in her absence to bring the question of sexual difference to the *Symposium*. The uncertainty of what the *Symposium* presents us becomes an opportunity in Irigaray's hands to bring our concerns and needs to the text. *As though* Diotima were her interlocutor, Irigaray reflects what she hears in the speech, endorsing part and finding fault with part. Diotima's absence becomes an opportunity for Irigaray to bring the question of sexual difference to the materials at hand. Rather than appropriate Diotima's speech, either as the words of a woman in the history of European and Anglophone philosophy or as Plato's view or as Socrates's speech, Irigaray talks *with* the text. Under Irigaray's treatment, Diotima becomes an interlocutor, not on the basis of her reclaimed historicity, but through the love we can share with her.

Although Irigaray helps us move forward on a problem that Nye cannot dislodge—namely, Diotima's absence from the scene of philosophy—I am not arguing for Nye's contribution to be dismissed. Nye continues the dialogue with her response to Irigaray. Indeed, Nye's case that Diotima could have been Socrates's teacher helps to further establish her absence from the dialogue. That is, it was not unthinkable for a woman to have and teach views about love, but still Plato absents her, still we have no record of her and scant records of the words of her female contemporaries. Irigaray's theory of exclusion reveals that the inadequacy of the historical record, its absences and silences that cannot be filled through better empirical work, is a symptom and a means of sexual indifference. Irigaray may overread the *Symposium*—certainly by contemporary philosophical standards that would have us dismiss Diotima's philosophical authority, she does—but that overreading transforms philosophical authority.[52] Using Irigaray's approach, we can pry at cracks, "In which the stake is to wonder again and again. To steer incessantly toward the unpublished. Also to turn over everything that has already been impressed, printed, in order to liberate its impact and find its impetus on this side and beyond."[53] We can read with and against a tradition that has, to a degree we cannot fully account for, determined our possibilities for living and for thinking. We can read our history anew.

CONCLUSION

Irigaray provides reclamation with a radical diagnosis that makes the project of reclaiming women philosophers anything but straightforward. She does so with suggestions for and an example of how reclamation can move forward, not just illuminating the absences and silences, but using those absences and silences as openings for the creation of new forms of philosophical authority. There are also several concerns to raise about Irigaray's theorization of exclusion. By way of conclusion, I will sketch some of them here, not to argue against Irigaray as a resource for reclamation. Her work offers reclamation important provocations and insights. But the power of her analysis is, in part, derived from absences and appropriations that need to inform reclamationist use of her work.

Women have long been assumed to have been absent from European and Anglophone philosophy's history (this assumption is a crucial practice of exclusion) and Irigaray gives us a means of exploiting that assumption to reclamationist ends. Yet, Irigaray has a tendency to speak as though no women contributed to the history of European and Anglophone philosophy, and the absence of historical women from her texts is significant. Even if Irigaray would argue that any historical woman in European and Anglophone philosophy participated in the sexual indifference of its discourse, that is different than denying women's participation. But Irigaray neither makes that argument nor denies women's participation. Like Alain de Botton in the introduction, she simply does not engage women in the history of European and Anglophone philosophy. We must be cautious with Irigaray's approach not to become overly invested in women's absence. Women have not always been literally absent, though their work has certainly been excluded. Thus, we can argue for the sexual indifference of discourse, without thereby claiming that women have not philosophized. Indeed, we need to look for how women's philosophical work has contributed to the economy of the same. Rather than looking at how women's work has contributed to (and negotiated) the masculinization of reason, as Lloyd's analysis of exclusion recommends, Irigaray prepares us to look at how women's writing may, to borrow from the Deutscher quotation above, contribute to the overdetermination and repeated consolidation of exclusion against certain kinds of alternative possible identities.[54] But we can only engage women's work in this way if we are not already sure they are absent from philosophical history.

Further, Irigaray's troubling of what we are doing when we invoke the category of "women" offers an important intervention in a field that has often sought refuge, as I argued in the first chapter, in the category. Irigaray's critique unsettles the category of "women" within reclamation, and utilizes that unsettling to reconceive of philosophical authority through a reading of Diotima. But one of the risks of Irigaray's diagnosis that reclamation most needs to keep in mind is formulated succinctly by Judith Butler:

> Although Irigaray clearly broadens the scope of feminist critique by exposing the epistemological, ontological, and logical

> structures of a masculinist signifying economy, the power of her analysis is undercut precisely by its globalizing reach. Is it possible to identify a monolithic as well as monologic masculinist economy that traverses the array of cultural and historical contexts in which sexual difference takes place? Is the failure to acknowledge the specific cultural operations of gender oppression itself a kind of epistemological imperialism, one which is not ameliorated by the simple elaboration of cultural differences as "examples" of the selfsame phallogocentrism?[55]

This point is related to the problem of assuming women have been literally absent from the history of European and Anglophone philosophy. Irigaray's warning, "to speak *of* or *about* woman may always boil down to, or be understood as, a recuperation of the feminine within a logic that maintains it in repression, censorship, nonrecognition,"[56] should now receive a different emphasis. To speak *may* maintain those effects, but there are surely discursive moments and histories for which this diagnosis does not work. We must attend, as Irigaray has, to the power of discursive sexual indifference. But we cannot assume that all discourse has been arrayed against the same alternative identities; rather the specific forces of exclusion need to be diagnosed. Closely related to that concern is Deutscher's observation that "While [Irigaray] is aware that Asia has been appropriated and disregarded in the western tradition, she does not incorporate into her writing an appreciation of the way in which her own writing is part of the western tradition of which she is critical. This failure may be considered in the light of an overall feature of Irigaray's writing—its reluctance to analyze its own position as potentially appropriative."[57] The tradition that Irigaray so thoroughly critiques for its sexual indifference is also her tradition. And, as Deutscher makes clear by reading Gayatri Spivak's work with Irigaray's, European and Anglophone philosophy has consolidated itself through multiple exclusions.[58] Irigaray's emphasis on sexual difference licenses appropriations, such as of yoga,[59] that must be recognized and critiqued as appropriations. Reclamation already struggles to attend to the exclusions and appropriations it inherits and reinforces from European and Anglophone philosophy, and Irigaray has not developed a critical practice for attending to that mode of inheritance.

Finally, critiques of Irigaray's positive conceptions of sexual difference are highly salient for reclamation. Lisa Guenther provides a succinct account:

> The conviction that there are two and only two sexes marginalizes an experience of bodily multiplicity that is just as phenomenologically real and compelling as the experience of sexual duality. Irigaray's repeated suggestion that the only genuine encounter with difference can happen between the two sexes enforces a heterosexual paradigm that marginalizes same-sex relationships and makes it impossible for Irigaray to account for intersex or transsexual bodies without characterizing them as aberrant or unnatural.[60]

In critiquing the way European and Anglophone philosophy has constituted itself through the exclusion of women, we can and ought to attend to the way that exclusion produces belief in, experiences of, and commitment to duality. Rather than committing further to that duality, we can use feminist reclamation as a means to philosophically engage long histories of bodily multiplicity, seeking plurivocal philosophical authority.

My hope is that these problems will give us pause about the concept of love as a guide for reading practices. The pernicious possibilities of harm under the name of love are simply too well established within the history of feminist work.[61] Rather than turning away from Irigaray's work because of these problems, I want them to *pre*occupy reclamation. For attention to one mode of exclusion can consolidate others, and Irigaray's work offers a powerful example of the risks and the possibilities of love.

4

INSULTS AND THEIR POSSIBILITIES

In an observation that would be at home in the writing of Genevieve Lloyd or Luce Irigaray, Michèle Le Doeuff writes: "If you look at the history of philosophy you can find a pattern: on the one hand it would be all too easy to compile a big book based on the dreadful things voiced by philosophers on the subject of 'woman.' But those things could be summarized very briefly: she is said to be 'the Other.'"[1] Yet, Le Doeuff's critique and remediation of that history differ significantly from the thinkers I discussed in the preceding two chapters. Perhaps on no count is the difference more pronounced than in the way Le Doeuff's critique leads her to engage the writings of women throughout the history of European and Anglophone philosophy, beginning with pre-Socratics. Unlike the theorists I discussed in the previous two chapters, Le Doeuff has extensively engaged with women's work. But Le Doeuff did not start out with such a practice. Like Lloyd and Irigaray, Le Doeuff began by reckoning with the history of exclusion in European and Anglophone philosophy and the damage that it has done.

From early in her career, Le Doeuff has theorized that both women and the feminine, that is, both living women and woman as sign, have been drafted into the role of philosophical ameliorants. They have been used by men philosophers, thwarted in their quest for completion and wholeness through philosophy, to make the work more bearable. Le Doeuff argues that such completeness cannot be found in philosophy. Rather, the experience of radical lack that one encounters in philosophizing must be acknowledged and embraced as a necessary feature, a necessary disappointment, of philosophical thinking. Le Doeuff writes of this lack that it is "a radical lack which the Other cannot complete" and, crucially, "to my mind, forms the true starting-point of philosophy."[2] Rather than confronting this lack, Le Doeuff argues, philosophers and European and Anglophone philosophy as a corporate enterprise have used women and figurations of the feminine to paper over the disappointments that one desiring philosophical knowledge encounters. Thus, we must look for the ways women have been symbolically and actually relegated to roles of consolation and subordination in the history of European and Anglophone philosophy. We must interrogate philosophical history to understand how these sexist practices have unfolded, but moreover to reorient our own philosophical practices to embrace the radical lack of philosophical pursuit.

As part of that reorientation, Le Doeuff promotes openness to incompleteness and nondominating cooperation among thinkers. She asks, "Is it possible to make philosophy, or philosophical work, abandon its wish to be a speculation which leaves no room for lack of knowledge, to make it accept its intrinsic incompleteness and create a non-hegemonic rationalism, so that philosophy will no longer need a defence mechanism involving the exclusion of women—and children?"[3] While this remains a hypothesis, a question to be tested in her first book, *The Philosophical Imaginary*, from which the quotation comes, Le Doeuff's later writing both explores and models the possibility of philosophical work that abandons the hegemonic wish for completeness, as well as gives up sexism as a defense mechanism.

We seem to once again face a theory of exclusion that makes it possible for women to produce philosophy in the future—when philosophy has abandoned its hegemonic wish—but that does not hold much promise for finding historical work by women. Indeed, one of Le Doeuff's early theories from the *Philosophical Imaginary*, the Héloïse complex, could be read as an explanation for why women have not produced philosophy. The complex as Le Doeuff originally formulated it posits that a woman's admiration for a philosopher's work stymies her own philosophical development. Enthralled with the philosophy of a teacher or lover, a woman does not need to philosophize. So, the occasional woman who has left us apparently philosophical writings has left us with works of philosophical admiration, not philosophy proper.

Importantly for reclamation, Le Doeuff modifies the Héloïse complex as she begins more robust engagements with women thinkers, in her second text, *Hipparchia's Choice*. She makes a twofold modification: first, she notes that this venerating dynamic is a problem in philosophical practice more broadly; and second, women who have experienced this complex were not as thoroughly stymied as Le Doeuff initially believed. The first section of this chapter recounts how these modifications lead Le Doeuff to a new theorization of the relationship between philosophical practices and history. With this new theorization, Le Doeuff develops a robust reclamation practice, and provides a promising model.

A powerful tool of reclamation that Le Doeuff develops, uchronic history, is the focus of the second section. Uchronic history is the imaginative creation of alternative histories in which women's writings were not excluded from philosophical history and the projection of the possible contemporary consequences of those imagined histories. Through her interest in reorienting philosophical practice and her use of uchronic history, Le Doeuff creates a critical approach to philosophical practice and history that makes engagement with women's writing both possible and necessary. Indeed, Le Doeuff's aspiration to nonhegemonic philosophy and her willingness to experiment with history telling made it possible for her to claim the philosophical value of work that has gone unrecognized as philosophical in its own right.

The third section focuses on Le Doeuff's engagement with the writing of Harriet Taylor Mill and Penelope Deutscher's critical response to that work.[4] Deutscher raises important problems in Taylor's writing, problems she shows contemporary feminism to inherit even though it has not largely inherited Taylor's writings. Le Doeuff, motivated to understand and overcome the exclusion of women from European and Anglophone philosophy, creates the conditions of possibility for Deutscher's critique of Taylor. Yet, Deutscher's engagement with the problems of what we thereby bring into our range of hearing is essential to reclamation. Deutscher supplies a corrective to the major drawback of Le Doeuff's method: it tends to present the possibilities in women's historical work without sufficient attention to the problems. To return to the quotation from Tina Chanter, cited in second chapter: "In order to think about women's otherness, feminism also needs to take history seriously. Not only do we need to think through the history of women's otherness, but also the history of feminism itself. To do so is not to acquiesce to that history, but to appreciate both the limitations and the radicality of feminist theories by situating them in their theoretical, historical, and political context."[5] Le Doeuff tends to appreciate the radicality of women's work, while Deutscher helps us keep in view its limitations.

Finally, I consider the role of Diotima in Le Doeuff's corpus. Although Le Doeuff has not directly addressed Diotima's role in the *Symposium* or used the uchronic method to think through her speech, Le Doeuff's treatment of the priestess helps illuminate the structure of European and Anglophone philosophy that makes the uchronic method such a powerful approach to reclamation. *Pace* Michael Payne's tempting reading that Le Doeuff views Diotima as the female origins of European and Anglophone philosophy, I argue that Le Doeuff generally references Diotima as one example of European and Anglophone philosophy's scramble to define itself through exclusion. Through a uchronic approach to Diotima, we can begin to understand what it would mean to pursue philosophy by embracing its incompleteness. Diotima's attenuated contribution to European and Anglophone philosophical history can be interrogated subjunctively to illuminate how women's exclusion has operated and continues to operate.

THE HÉLOÏSE COMPLEX

Héloïse, Elisabeth of Bohemia, and even Simone de Beauvoir are defined, sometimes known only, by their connections to a recognized male philosopher. Chanter's charge, discussed in the second chapter, that even feminist readers of Beauvoir tend to attribute her interpretation of Hegel to Sartre's influence is one example of how a woman's philosophical authority can be undermined even as she is being engaged as a philosopher.[6] Le Doeuff's concept of the Héloïse complex seeks to explain this fate of women who did have access to a philosophical education: "a woman establishes herself as a philosopher's loving admirer; the situation is profitable to him and fatal to her. She sees the master's philosophy as complete in itself and does not therefore feel condemned to invent or to think something that has never been thought of before. He, on the other hand, benefits from her look, in which he sees his own thought as a perfection (as no thought is)."[7]

The situation Le Doeuff describes is one in which both the philosopher and the admirer are "saved" from the disappointments inherent in philosophical thinking by their relationship. The difference, of course, is that the admired has already encountered those disappointments and produced a philosophy that becomes a perfection under and through the gaze of the admirer. The admirer, in this account of it, succumbs to the power of bestowing perfection and fails to be disappointed in the way that Le Doeuff argues is crucial to philosophical work. Neither, though, can really be said to benefit philosophically from this relationship. For even though the admired has produced a philosophy, believing his own thought to be a perfection threatens to stall thinking and end his philosophical work. For the woman, however, the effects are truly grim: she does nothing but parrot the master's philosophy.

In her second book, however, *Hipparchia's Choice*, from which this quotation comes, Le Doeuff modifies the Héloïse complex with important consequences for how we understand philosophical history and the role of women in it.[8] The first modification connects this gendered dynamic to larger issues of philosophical practice: "the self-sacrifice a woman agrees to in her veneration of a mentor is part of a wider configuration: the mentor is seeking a general admiration (which is not commensurable with philosophical work) and wants not only to produce philosophy but also to be a philosopher."[9] In other words, veneration is not a problem only across gender lines, but in gendered configurations the bleakest effects are shown. So, the Héloïse complex could be observed in many kinds of philosophical relationships where these dynamics of subordination are at work, and where the aim of the subordination is the secure title of philosopher for the master.

We can begin to question what role the title "philosopher" has in the history of European and Anglophone philosophy. One reason such a move is important is that it allows us to find philosophical value in the writings of people who are given no credence as philosophers. Indeed, delinking the concept philosopher from the activity of philosophy is crucial to reclamation, since no one who confidently enjoys the title "philosopher" needs reclamation. Yet, with this first modification to the complex, we only make space for reclamation. Le Doeuff's second modification allows women's work to be addressed in the space of that opening.

Le Doeuff also moderates the consequences of the venerating relationship, again by undermining the importance of the idea of the philosopher. She writes: "The Heloise complex seems not to be so crippling[10] as I formerly meant it to appear. Can one escape it on the quiet and produce philosophy independently, on the condition of course that one does not attempt to pose as a philosopher? Producing philosophy unawares?"[11] This second modification acknowledges the power of the label "philosopher," even within Le Doeuff's own work. Le Doeuff questions the practice of identifying who is and who is not a philosopher and asks: Could it be that women produced philosophy that we cannot and do not recognize as such in the European and Anglophone tradition, that they themselves perhaps could not identify as such, because the qualifications for the title of "philosopher" have been in the way of our being able to appreciate philosophical thinking?

Le Doeuff notes that an interesting problem arises from this question. On the one hand, we might think that, since no author controls a text, commentators could declare something a work of philosophy that was never avowed as such by the author. Any number of women could have produced philosophy unawares. Or, on the other, one could take a more traditional route, in which the author is considered to be the founder of a text and our job is simply to understand it as the author intended. Thus, no woman who did not claim the mantle of philosophy (or who, like Beauvoir, denounced it) could authorize a philosophical work. On the one hand, we declare women of the past philosophers, despite their own intentions or desires. On the other, we pretty much agree that prior to the twentieth century women did not philosophize. Le Doeuff refuses to set up a dilemma.

Instead, she writes: "there is at least a third way of conceiving of philosophy and the history of philosophy: we can regard both as work, and thus as a dynamic, which can lead to and from each other. From this point of view, a philosophy is neither a monument nor an effect which is blind[12] to its origins and thus in relation to itself, but an effort to shift thinking from one state to another. . . . The advantage of this perspective is, among other things, that it regards the history of philosophy as a philosophical activity."[13] Le Doeuff proposes understanding the relationship of philosophical practice and the history of philosophy as work we undertake. Once again, Le Doeuff pushes aside the label of "philosopher" in preference to philosophical activity. Le Doeuff embraces as a space for creative action what Lloyd glimpsed—what the latter called the tension between contemporary feminism and past philosophy. While Irigaray gives us reclamation as love as a model by which to resist collapsing our own demands with that of the historical texts we encounter, Le Doeuff gives us a conception of philosophical history that compels us to seek out new archives and continually reassess what we think we know of our history.[14] Under Le Doeuff's conception, philosophical history is philosophical work.

Once Le Doeuff has amended the Héloïse complex to question the obscuring effects of titling people "philosophers," especially through the subordination of women and students, the pages of her work become crowded with the work of women thinkers. By making their writing our concern, Le Doeuff exposes not just how the silencing of their writing created our understandings and practices of European and Anglophone philosophy, but how reengaging their writing gives us critical perspective on our understandings and practices. In other words, Le Doeuff reads historical women's work to better apprehend the effects of its exclusion on us.

Le Doeuff's strategy is not enfranchising. She engages women's work not to argue for its status as philosophical, but to show how philosophical discourse has been shaped by exclusion, in multiple forms, of women's work. The exclusion thus becomes exposed as a practice, and women's work is engaged through new practices that seek to redress exclusion. History on this view is not memorialization, but the opportunity for philosophical practice to open toward works of all sorts and sources of all kinds. One of the primary ways Le Doeuff moves from identifying exclusion to actively redressing it is through uchronic history writing. What, she asks in the uchronic mode, would our lives be like had women's texts not been silenced? We must consider how to speak with texts that are formed by a history of having no voice and whose silence forms our history. One approach to that practice of consideration is to think through what might have been.

UCHRONIA

To understand what has been lost through the exclusion of women from philosophical history, Le Doeuff poses questions like the following: "If at school she had read Mary Wollstonecraft in English class, Anna Maria van Schurman in Latin, if a good history course had told her of the Anglo-American saga of women's right to vote, if in philosophy she had read Gabrielle Suchon and Harriett Taylor, if a popular edition of *The Book of the City of Ladies* had been available, would she have concluded her magnum opus as she did?"[15] The magnum opus in question is *The Second Sex*. Le Doeuff asks what Beauvoir might have written not only had she known about women in history (which *The Second Sex* amply shows that she did),[16] but also if women had been diversely represented throughout her society and education. Would Beauvoir have concluded with the suggestion that we all become brothers? Such a question is not merely an idle counterfactual longing in Le Doeuff's work. Rather, such a question makes an imaginative opening to a history in which women were not and are not ritually excluded.

Such questions are not mere counterfactuals because they have a historical end in Le Doeuff's work. She maintains: "It is a fairly futile mental exercise to seek to 'reclaim' a historical fact, unless one explicitly gives the attempt a uchronic form: let's imagine that we can start again and that I can draw the outlines of a reworked history on my blank paper."[17] In other words, Le Doeuff suggests that a historical fact in need of reclamation is one that has not been remembered, and creating the possibility of its being remembered, of its entering history, requires starting again with history.

That starting again has two intimately related parts: one imaginary, one practical. First, what if, for instance, we imagine that women had gained citizens' rights during the French Revolution? In the fourth notebook of *Hipparchia's Choice*, Le Doeuff meditates on what the effects of the establishment of such equality would have been on French society. She writes: "The phenomenon of battered women would long ago have disappeared, since it is basically a problem of married women who are economically dependent."[18] One of the possible historical agents of this imagined history is the French writer and provocateur Olympe de Gouges. Le Doeuff observes of the social contract that, in 1791, de Gouges proposed to replace the marriage contract: "This is a wonderful contract, for it preserves the rights of women and children and enables us to see, by contrast, how the real legislation at once sacrificed both women's freedom and children's interests to what is commonly called patriarchy."[19] De Gouges's contract is essentially a document for the protection of children, regardless of the legal status of the biological parents. Neither adult entering the contract gains legal rights over the other, but both are bound to provide for the children they produce either together or "as the result of any other inclination."[20] As Le Doeuff notes, such a contract requires the economic independence of women through establishing both parent's obligation to dependent children.

Though Le Doeuff's history is an imagined one, one in which de Gouges's writing influences the course of society and leads to the elimination of domestic abuse, it has the real consequence of engaging with the writing of a woman who has largely been excluded from philosophical history. The imagining of a world in which she was influential begins to suggest a different way of understanding how history has thus far been told and here the imaginary begins to tip over into the practical. Within that uchronic story of the French Revolution, Le Doeuff brings to the fore the importance of Olympe de Gouges's role in the history of the Revolution. Not merely one of the women guillotined in the course of the Revolution, de Gouges's was a voice silenced with consequences Le Doeuff's uchronic exercise now helps us to hear. Thus, the imaginative becomes grounds for a critical engagement with what occurred and a guide to retelling history. Le Doeuff's uchronic approach revivifies that silenced writing. The importance of that reawakened work is established through the imaginative exercise of constructing a history that the work was not able to inaugurate. Thinking through the effects that would have followed from the requirement of women's economic independence that follows from de Gouges's contract illuminates the dependence that the actual marriage contract has bred and required.

In other words, De Gouges's contract was a failure, but it is a failure worthy of lamentation. The idea of what might have been imparts value on what was and was silenced. It also acts as the guide for writing a different history, one that considers not how influential an idea or a thinker was, but what the world might be like if an idea had become influential; it gives us an opening to imagine the forms of life that were lost with the silencing of that work. Thus, Le Doeuff is not providing us with an alternative tradition. Her uchronic speculations give us critical perspective on the production of our forms of life. In a similar vein, Le Doeuff's uchronic method is not meant to be a mere corrective to philosophical history—that history was produced through women's exclusion, but our future, her method suggests, does not have to be. That is to say, on Le Doeuff's view, European and Anglophone philosophy does not just need to be more philosophical; we need to examine how our ideals of philosophical work have been predicated on exclusionary practices.

While in *Hipparchia's Choice* uchronic questioning motivates retelling history, by *The Sex of Knowing*, Le Doeuff reverses that order. The ethical force of Le Doeuff's uchronic question about *The Second Sex*, for instance, is deepened by the reclaimed history that leads to its asking. The women Le Doeuff lists, including the writer of *The Book of the City of Ladies*, Christine de Pisan, are part of the history at work in *The Sex of Knowing*. The introduction to *The Sex of Knowing* does not begin with the assumption that we are familiar either with Christine de Pisan or with her writing, but rather it begins with the story of why we are not, that is, it begins with the story of Christine's silencing. As a reader who did know about Christine and her work, I found this introduction thrilling. What had, prior to turning back the cover of Le Doeuff's book, seemed like a bit of arcana picked up in a questionable back alley of philosophical inquiry was suddenly before me as something important enough to silence and not just once, but through a series of repetitions by which Christine's writing was not engaged, but rather ritually avoided through calling Christine a "bluestocking."

Le Doeuff's question about Beauvoir does not appear until near the end of *The Sex of Knowing*, by which time Le Doeuff has tackled not only Christine's silencing, but also the silencing of Wollstonecraft, Schurman, Suchon, and Taylor. Whereas in *Hipparchia's Choice*, uchronic questioning was used to motivate and guide the reclamation of Olympe de Gouges's writing, in *The Sex of Knowing*, reclamation occurs throughout the text and motivates the uchronic questioning of a consummate text of twentieth-century feminism. The flexible relationship between uchronic thinking and reclamation that Le Doeuff demonstrates in her work suggests not only methodological flexibility for reclamation projects, but also the varied means by which the task of reclamation can be undertaken. The uchronic moment, the "what might have been," facilitates our reimagining of the history that has led to current practices and institutions, but, as the *Sex of Knowing* demonstrates, it does not have to precede the work of historical reclamation. The two together, however, make it more difficult for the silencing of women's work to appear as a mere historical curiosity or a fait accompli. In other words, uchronic history and reclamation together are more than a subjunctive exercise in what might have been. Reclamation undertaken with uchronic history shows us the damage that has actually been done and thus can motivate new practices moving forward.

Further, uchronic thinking and reclamation together build a case for reading women's writing in a way that does not repeat the criterion of exclusion as the criterion of inclusion. That is, Le Doeuff is not reclaiming these women because they are women. Indeed, Le Doeuff, in *The Sex of Knowing*, aims to reveal the long tradition of sexual differentialism in philosophical thinking and its importance in excluding women not only from philosophical practice but also from political life. In Le Doeuff's writing, the fact that a thinker has been dismissed—called a bluestocking, for instance, as Christine so often has been—becomes a reason for engaging with her writing. Each moment of silencing, each name-calling, each repetition of a rumor about a thinker is an opportunity for investigating what is being repudiated, disavowed, or effaced. The long philosophical history of othering *woman* is reason to engage the writing of women. Le Doeuff asks with and through her uchronic questioning, what possibilities were lost with the writing of these women? Le Doeuff gives us a model of reclamation as transformation of philosophical practice. Asking what might have been draws us into realms of thinking that have been excluded and, in so doing, helps us to understand what these thinkers may offer us now.

Olympe de Gouges envisioned a marriage contract that did not subordinate one person's economic status to another's, a contract that did not rely on a tradition of economic dependence of women and children to husbands and fathers. De Gouges sought to expand into the domestic sphere the restructuring of relationships of dependence that the French Revolution made possible, at least in the realm of thought. The next figure I will consider, Harriet Taylor Mill, denied sexual differentialism and affirmed women's ability to collectively agitate for political recognition and equal rights. Within philosophical history, however, we have access to her through a series of contradictory character assessments that largely agree on one thing: she is not worth our philosophical attention.[21]

HARRIET TAYLOR MILL

Le Doeuff reports that her main method for treating Taylor and John Stuart Mill as independent thinkers is to focus on points of disagreement between them. Le Doeuff endorses this approach in part because it helps to frame moments of agreement within their writings as part of a process of thinking together, rather than as the signs of a preestablished harmony.[22] The development of the Héloïse complex in Le Doeuff's work underlines the need for such a seemingly simple methodological commitment. Especially when there is a long history of established discourse claiming that a writer is nothing more than a parrot of an established philosopher, such a method of reclamation helps to counteract unwittingly doxastic readings. Focusing on points of disagreement underscores that, even if Taylor's primary access to philosophy was through Mill, such mediation did not make Taylor and Mill univocal.

Yet, once Le Doeuff begins to engage Taylor as an independent thinker, she finds another influence on Taylor's thinking, one that fed and strengthened the disagreement between husband and wife. Thinking for herself does not, in Taylor's case at least, mean thinking by herself.[23] Le Doeuff discovers that the conventions on women's rights inspired by the first Seneca Falls Convention in 1848 and its *Declaration of Sentiments* profoundly affected Taylor's thinking.[24] Taylor's review of the *New York Tribune* article that brought reports of the conventions to England testifies to the effect that the nascent movement had on her thinking. That review is what we now know as the essay "The Enfranchisement of Women." Le Doeuff lingers over how the historical reception transformed the review into an essay and what has been lost by that rebranding: "this transformation erased any sense that the essay had initially been the work of a female journalist or historian of the present reporting a current event she describes as historic, namely, that the issue of women's equal access to all rights and their enfranchisement in law and practice is no longer merely an idea, but now manifests itself in something hitherto unheard of—organized agitation."[25] In restoring the title of the review to "The Enfranchisement, " Le Doeuff restores a sense of the newness of what began at Seneca Falls, the surprise of the new possibilities, by situating Taylor's writing as a response to events unfolding. And it allows us to recognize that Taylor herself was a thinker changed by those events.

As Le Doeuff writes: "[Taylor] is pleased to learn that what she had believed impossible is in fact possible, pleased that History has shown the error of her earlier belief."[26] Until these women proved her wrong, Taylor believed that women required men to represent their political interests.[27] Post–Seneca Falls, Taylor no longer writes of sexual duality vis-à-vis mental faculties and she no longer thinks men are the necessary agents of women's political demands. Though it may not have been the intentions of the conventioneers to intervene in a philosophical problem, they did so.

In writing of the influence of Seneca Falls on Taylor, Le Doeuff states: "When some women and one woman establish themselves as subjects with the capacity to make judgments about reality and rights, instead of situating themselves among the objects on which people can expound ad libitum, this is a major political-intellectual event that necessarily displaces the givens of discourse."[28] But only, I must insist, if they are heard. When that event is lost to history, when it is written out, no displacement can occur. In other words, Le Doeuff's engagement of these historical events makes possible the displacement she attributes to the historical event. Of course, any displacement that Le Doeuff's engagement effects depends upon the historical events these women caused by establishing themselves as judging subjects. By reexamining those events, Le Doeuff brings into philosophical discourse the political-intellectual event of women working together to change reality and rights. By paying attention to what has been submerged or dismissed, Le Doeuff pulls at the thread of Taylor's essay, discovers that it's actually a review, and sees that it had tremendous effects on Taylor's thinking. What if we pay attention to this history? What if we treat philosophical work and philosophical history as a dynamic that leads to and from each other?

One of the points that Le Doeuff emphasizes in her project of disengaging Taylor from the discourse on Mill is that Taylor surpassed Mill in her thinking about sexual difference. Mill, Le Doeuff argued, vacillated in his thinking about sexual difference and never fully rejected some notion of fundamental sexual difference, as Taylor did. In particular, Mill never seemed to abandon the view that a woman could be the source of philosophical inspiration, but not its elaborator. Thus, Le Doeuff strikes this cautionary tone about Mill: "A male philosopher willing to recognize civil rights for women is still a historical rarity. But the fact that Mill does not want to recognize our capacity to think without a man is also reminiscent of a common historical practice."[29] This passage is very close to the end of *The Sex of Knowing* and Le Doeuff is returning us to the exclusion of women from European and Anglophone philosophy.

Indeed, without the epilogue, the arc of the book is from silencing to exclusion. The silencing of Christine would lead, through a book of reclamations, to the story of how Mill's work colluded in the exclusion of women, including his much loved wife, from the realm of philosophy. The epilogue, however, extends a different ending to her readers. There, Le Doeuff suggests that Taylor and Mill might be a model to us, after all. A man and a woman, "these two romantics," can speak to us of tolerating the unpredictability that comes with each of us gaining a bit more freedom from the stereotypes that define us. Though it is largely now forgotten, or passed over too quickly, these two thinkers disagreed and yet loved each other. Tolerance, Le Doeuff suggests, is necessary if we are going to keep thinking, for thinking surely breeds disagreements and, not to be underestimated, disappointments. Mill may not be the feminist that we wish he were, but in his work he promotes a notion of tolerance that we can extend to him.

We do well to keep that suggestion in mind as we turn to consider the disappointments that await us in Taylor's writing. For, as Penelope Deutscher has well argued, there are many. Deutscher's engagement with Taylor begins with a critique of Le Doeuff's work that results in the opening up of a very different Taylor from the one presented in *The Sex of Knowing*. Deutscher argues that Le Doeuff stabilizes the ambivalences and contradictions in Taylor's work and thereby occludes the problematic inconsistencies that are integral to Taylor's feminist arguments and conclusions. Moreover, Deutscher warns, we risk repeating those argumentative tensions, rather than learning from them, if we similarly stabilize the inheritance that we receive from earlier feminists. In Deutscher's reading of Taylor, the ambivalences and contradictions she exposes not only resist such stabilization, but bring us into dynamic contact with Taylor's thinking. Deutscher treats the history of philosophy as philosophical work to be done, as Le Doeuff has urged. Thus, Deutscher reads Taylor both with and against Le Doeuff and thereby offers an important critical turn in this reclamation model.

In brief, Deutscher analyzes the narrative of progress that Taylor interweaves into her feminist arguments and that is in tension with her ideas of equality. Deutscher is clear: "The point is not to condemn Taylor Mill for a race elitism and hierarchy that was common in the nineteenth century, but neither should a reading of Taylor Mill look away from it. We do need to fold into our understanding of her writing the ways in which such hierarchies were *points of appeal in her feminism*, as it was tightly interconnected with notions of the barbarous, the ignorant, the primitive, progress, the high and the low."[30] The concern that Deutscher expresses can fairly be characterized as a reclamationist one. Taylor is an important feminist source, but all the more reason for seeing the ways that her feminism was intertwined with and depended upon problematic notions of hierarchy. In other words, Deutscher's interest in reading Taylor critically is to read her in philosophical and feminist history.

Part of Deutscher's importance for this project is that her concern is not only with Taylor's work, but with Le Doeuff's reclamation of it. Deutscher writes: "it is true that *this* 'differentialism,' the aspect that decried women, and indeed, the contradictory aspect that revered women's intuition, is largely missing from Taylor Mill's work. But to stop there is to overlook other hierarchies fundamental to her feminism, many of which she shared with Mill."[31] Le Doeuff overlooks other hierarchies in order to return to one of her earliest preoccupations, and a central theme of *The Sex of Knowing*: the exclusion of women from European and Anglophone philosophy. Le Doeuff, rather than continuing to develop a more complex account of Taylor's thinking, returns to a critique of Mill and the philosophical corporation that sustained his disbelief about women's capacity for thinking in his philosophy. Le Doeuff does so to suggest that such disbelief still operates in the field of philosophy today. In other words, Le Doeuff has, at that point in her text, a limited interest in Taylor's thinking that is restricted to the influence of Seneca Falls and sexual differentialism. Le Doeuff's focus shares the aim of Deutscher's broadening of perspective on Taylor's writing: both Le Doeuff and Deutscher are relating the prejudices of contemporary thinking to philosophical history and suggesting, further, that engagement with that history is the critical work that will expose those ideological underpinnings in an effort to shift thinking.

There are important reasons for Le Doeuff to read Taylor in this way. The case for reading Taylor carefully, closely, and well is not yet sufficiently established within philosophical practices. That is to say, Le Doeuff's return to the exclusion of women from European and Anglophone philosophy is a move that is still needed for women's writing to be reclaimed. The risk of Taylor's work being silenced in philosophical discourse is still very high, given that philosophical practices still so heavily depend on the exclusion of women.

However, Deutscher's move is also crucial to reclamation. While Deutscher's critical move relies on a context of reclamation, it does not allow the difficulties of reclamation to overwhelm the critical interrogation of what is being reclaimed. Deutscher makes the argumentative appeal at several points in the essay that feminists need to examine the writings they are reclaiming with a commitment to understanding what is silenced in those reclaimed texts. Those appeals indicate an ethical motivation to the essay that her conclusion makes explicit: "Is it possible to look another, or one's own, imaginary in the face? How to avoid a clearly impossible ideal of transparency? Could one nonetheless formulate, as an ethical stance, the patient amplification of the locus of the oversights generative of a project, the willingness to articulate costs, exclusions, rhetorical conditions, and blind spots?"[32] Deutscher is already working in a context of reclamation in which she is highlighting the importance of issues like transparency and oversight. Taylor's work must already be in the field of discourse, it must count as philosophy, for Deutscher to raise these issues. But Deutscher's critical project is as important to reclamation as Le Doeuff's work to expose how philosophical discourse was framed by the exclusion of Taylor's work. Le Doeuff shows how Taylor's exclusion, and, in particular, the exclusion of her rejection of sexual differentialism, was productive of the transmissions of Mill's philosophy. Deutscher shows us how a rejection of sexual differentialism can itself produce exclusions that are, as she says, points of appeal.

Le Doeuff inspiringly writes of the Seneca Falls organizers: "They had found their vision of what had to be done to change the destiny of women, and a language in which to articulate their plan. Not only the right to speak, civil rights, the right to vote, eligibility, access to all occupations including religious ministry, to all levels of education, and so on, but also a technique that would allow them to translate these wishes into political reality: the mass movement."[33] Le Doeuff presents Seneca Falls as a political event that shifted and can shift philosophical thinking; with Deutscher, we can also look for the ways it failed and fails to do so. Deutscher does not so much offer the Disuchronia to Le Doeuff's Uchronia. Rather, Deutscher returns us to the limits of counterfactual analysis. We must reckon with what did happen. The difficulty, of course, is that what did happen is not a stable datum from which to work. It has been constructed and we are heirs of those practices of construction. The uchronic moment allows us to think about how we construct history through imagining differently, according to different norms. But even our imaginations are shaped by what we have inherited. In the final chapter, I return to this work of historical construction to consider the *Declaration of Sentiments* in more detail to appreciate the issues at stake for the mass movement it inaugurated. To conclude this chapter, let's pick up the thread of Diotima's story to appreciate what Le Doeuff can offer us by way of reclamation.

DIOTIMA

While Le Doeuff mentions Diotima throughout her oeuvre, she tends to do so primarily as a nod to European and Anglophone philosophy's poor treatment of the priestess. For instance, Le Doeuff writes in "Ants and Women, or Philosophy Without Borders" that "when philosophers insist on the idea that myth or fables are 'old wives' tales,' nanny lore, at best the inspired voice of a Diotima, they are also emphasizing the fact that there is a big difference between philosophy and myth."[34] Diotima's role as a conduit of inspired knowledge has served European and Anglophone philosophy's project of distinguishing itself from myth. Much later, Le Doeuff writes of approaches to interpreting the *Apology*: "For my part, and experimentally, I would like to give it a structural reading mixed with a pinch of suspicion, and to hypothesize that the author is willing to imagine that female persons could be capable of thought and the contemplation of truth, but only when it would be of no consequence: as for example on the model of divine inspiration, in the case of Diotima."[35] The permissive prohibition of Diotima's role allows that women might be capable of philosophy, but it does not matter. That is, women's philosophical authority need not be contemplated.

Le Doeuff has understood Diotima to occupy a permissively prohibited role at least as far back as the article "Women and Philosophy," published in 1977, which would later be incorporated into *The Philosophical Imaginary* as its sixth chapter. In that essay, Le Doeuff wrote:

> And the man/woman difference is invoked or conscripted to signify the general opposition between definite and indefinite, that is to say validated/excluded, and opposition of which the logos/mythos couple represents one form, for the mythos is "an old wives' tale," or at best the inspiration of a Diotima. But in so far as the activity of separation, of division, is philosophically creative (the field is created by its exclusions), philosophy creates itself in what it represses, and, this object of repression being essential to it, is endlessly engaged in separating, enclosing and insularizing itself. And the old wives' tales and nannies' lore are always "obscuring" the clear light of the concept—not because the repressed in general might be overwhelming by nature, but because the finite stock of admissible procedures is never sufficient.[36]

Here Le Doeuff identifies Diotima's knowledge as part of the opposition European and Anglophone philosophy produces to define itself. As an object of ongoing repression, Diotima is essential to philosophy, guaranteeing a border that the admissible practices of philosophy could not possibly secure.

Does this mean that Le Doeuff thinks we ought not to take Diotima seriously? After all, she represents Diotima as having merely divinely inspired knowledge to share. If Le Doeuff were interested in shoring up the borders of the discipline, then we would be right to read Le Doeuff as endorsing the denigration of Diotima. But Le Doeuff's point is, of course, that philosophy must accept its lack. On the issue of lack, Michael Payne suggests an important role for Diotima in "Women and Philosophy."[37] Payne writes: "A major thread that runs though that essay is Le Doeuff's tracing of efforts by modern (male) philosophers to suppress the female origins of philosophy in Diotima's teaching of Socrates as set forth in Plato's *Symposium*. Diotima bequeaths to philosophy the celebration of a lack: insofar, she writes, 'as the activity of separation, of division, is philosophically creative (the field is created by its exclusions), philosophy creates itself in what it represses.'"[38] Payne describes Diotima as the female origin of philosophy in Le Doeuff's essay. Further, according to Payne, Diotima celebrates the lack that generates philosophical creativity.

I cannot find textual support for Payne's view. Certainly, Le Doeuff is arguing that the activity of repression is the means of European and Anglophone philosophy creating itself as a discipline. But to give Diotima the status of the repressed origin fixes her as *the* object of repression in a way that Le Doeuff seems at pains to avoid. Indeed, recall the quotation from the beginning of the chapter in which Le Doeuff calls the insurmountable incompleteness of knowledge the lack that is the starting place of philosophy. The excluded may be "at best the inspiration of a Diotima," but even in that phrasing it is not Diotima in particular, but Diotima as an example of European and Anglophone philosophy's constructed other. Nor do I read the role of the *Symposium* in the essay as Payne does. Le Doeuff does not mention it by title, as she does the *Apology* and *Phaedrus*, nor does she connect Diotima to Plato or Socrates.

In contrast to Payne's view, I contend that Diotima's importance for Le Doeuff is as a member of the repressed. Diotima does not stand at the beginning for Le Doeuff; rather, the priestess is part of the process of repression. We can ask: What if Diotima was a real woman? But perhaps more importantly, we can ask: What if Plato has presented us with Diotima's teaching? Then, we might both gain from her vision of love and critique the hierarchy that Diotima establishes with that concept of love. Diotima does not have to have founded anything. The fact that Diotima's historicity has been the subject of speculation with varying degrees of evidence is, with Le Doeuff's method, reason enough to reconsider her works and ask: What if she had been heard? With Deutscher we can wonder to what extent Diotima's hierarchy of rational procreation over physical procreation would have reinforced other hierarchies. With Le Doeuff, however, her entire speech becomes a resource for feminist thinking. What if we had, from the beginning of European and Anglophone philosophy, a theory of love and knowledge handed down to us from a woman? What might we do with history like that?

I suggested in the last chapter that Irigaray overreads Diotima's speech, and that this was a strength of her approach. Le Doeuff offers another method of overreading through imagining what might have been had a text not been excluded.[39] Additionally, with Le Doeuff's delinking of the activity of philosophy from the label "philosopher," her method opens much more readily to sources that have not made it into the tradition of European and Anglophone philosophy. Texts that philosophers have dismissed as nonphilosophical, either by traditional canonical figures or by people who are dismissed as possible sources of philosophical authority (including women, children, and, importantly for the last chapter, people who could not read or write), become opportunities for speculative engagement.

CONCLUSION

With the theories of exclusion provided by Lloyd and Irigaray, we must seek out women writers who their methods will not help us find. Le Doeuff's transformation of her own understanding of exclusion into a reclamationist practice means that we already have guidance on how to find women writers. Indeed, all it takes with this method is one snide comment about a thinker and we are on alert—insults indicate where to dig. Yet, a different problem arises with Le Doeuff's method and it is directly related to uchronic thinking. By setting up historical women's writing as an ideal from which we construct an imaginative history, we risk losing the critical skepticism with which ideals must be treated. The tendency in Le Doeuff's work is for historical women to appear as benevolent benefactors of a liberatory vision. She tends not to address how these women, through the very same work, can strengthen the practices that underwrote the political order they aspired to participate in, including colonization, slavery, and genocide.

Uchronic history is a starting point for engaging women's writing, but we cannot become enthralled with only the hopeful, inspiring, transformative possibilities. Thus, in the final chapter, when I return to Seneca Falls, I use a critical uchronic practice that looks not just for the hopeful, but also for what needs to be overcome in the visions left to us by historical women. That critical uchronic reading of the *Declaration* leads me to Sojourner Truth's contemporary critique of some of the problematic hierarchies of the early women's movement and her speculations on freedom in one speech in 1851. Before we follow Le Doeuff's method back to 1848 and then 1851, let's examine the strengths of Le Doeuff's approach from another angle, through comparison with the approaches of Lloyd and Le Doeuff.

5

FROM EXCLUSION TO RECLAMATION

Our methods of reclamation are dependent on our theories of exclusion. My aim thus far has been to highlight that dynamic. First, I inventoried different strategies of reclamation to show that, even if only implicitly, every reclamation operates from a theory of exclusion. I found four basic modes of claiming women's work as philosophically authoritative, and I argued that only one strategy adequately attends to how the norms of exclusion that have shaped European and Anglophone philosophy also shape feminist philosophy. That strategy, transformative reclamation, can transform philosophical and feminist practice through engaging historical women's philosophical authority.

The next three chapters then looked at three influential feminist theories of women's exclusion to consider their potential for guiding reclamation. While Genevieve Lloyd, Luce Irigaray, and Michèle Le Doeuff have each offered theories of exclusion that make possible methods of reclamation, those three chapters also suggested that Le Doeuff's theory motivates the most transformative approaches, evidenced in part by her readings of historical women's work. In this chapter, I argue more explicitly for the advantages of Le Doeuff's approach. In a nutshell, Le Doeuff attends to what has been excluded in and through philosophical practice to create open-ended speculative engagements with historical texts. We can employ her speculative practices to heighten our awareness and strengthen our critiques of how we think and know. The goal of such speculative reclamation is not the right version of history or the correct canon of philosophy. Rather, the goal of this method is an ongoing critical engagement with how our thinking has been made possible, particularly by exclusions, and how we can think differently. The rest of this chapter examines the strengths of Le Doeuff's approach in detail, comparing her approach with those of Lloyd and Irigaray.

I begin by comparing how each theorist can respond to concerns about historical accuracy using the example, explored in the first chapter, of R. M. Dancy's critique of Mary Ellen Waithe's reclamation of Diotima. Such a starting point is necessary because reclamation depends on careful historical work, but feminist reclamation does not and should not, I argue, limit its scope to such work. To use the example of Diotima, because the archive available for establishing her historicity is limited, we cannot currently, and likely will not be able to, prove her historicity conclusively. And it is even less likely that we will find any other record of her words than the one supplied by Plato. Rather than dismiss her authority, I suggest we engage with it speculatively. In my comparison, I show that Lloyd does not enter into these debates, but rather treats Plato's account as the words of a woman. Irigaray and Le Doeuff, by contrast, both provide imaginative responses to this problem that highlight the formative power of women's exclusion. Thus, both thinkers draw our attention to how the dearth of evidence about Diotima is not an accident of history or the archive, but is rather part of the process of undermining women's philosophical authority. In developing creative responses to a paucity of evidence in Diotima's case, Irigaray and Le Doeuff turn the demand for historical accuracy into questions about how the archive has come to have the voices of so few.

There are limits to reclamationist imagination intimately tied to the limits of our archives. While Diotima's voice has been dissipated by the tradition that has transmitted her, we have a purported version of her speech. The archives to which reclamation can turn to read creatively, speculatively, and excessively are shaped and restricted by the violent exclusion of the thoughts of millions.[1] One structure of exclusion was chattel slavery, enabled by racist practices that are alive and well, if in new forms. In the next section, I argue that although reclamation cannot change the practices of violence that ensured few records of the thoughts of those who were enslaved, it must attend to how this limit shapes our understanding of history and, thus, of our present. Reclamation cannot redeem this history of destruction. But it should not turn away from how our archives have been constricted. We must attend to how the shape of our archives indicates the shape of our contemporary practices of philosophy. How, for instance, does the erasure of black thought and life central, not incidental, to the production of the archives of European and Anglophone philosophy shape who is engaged as philosophically authoritative now?[2]

I follow another avenue for addressing that question in the next section. What more can we do with the texts we do have? How can we engage historical texts, those traditionally considered philosophical and those that have not been, to gain perspective on contemporary practices of authority? I compare the practices of imaginative engagement—overreading—that Irigaray and Le Doeuff develop. While both thinkers offer productive methods for reclamation, Irigaray's focus on the impossibility of sexual difference already focuses reclamation practices on questions of subjectivity. Le Doeuff's revivification of failed ideals does not have a similar narrowing tendency. In other words, Le Doeuff's approach gives us more latitude to engage with historical texts in order to problematize our contemporary practices.

Le Doeuff's theory of exclusion led her to read women across European and Anglophone philosophical history. For quite different reasons, which I analyze in the next section, Lloyd and Irigaray reproduce traditional histories of European and Anglophone philosophy from which women are largely absent. For Lloyd, there is a natural connection between men and masculinizing symbol use. While symbolic gender can be analytically separated from biological sex, Lloyd ultimately understands the masculinization of reason as a natural outcome of a tradition of men thinkers. Irigaray focuses on traces of the repression of feminine subjectivity as a generative site for feminist work but one that does not often lead her to sustained engagements with women's work. While Irigaray's theory predicts that women also practice(d) philosophy predicated on the disavowal of feminine subjectivity, she does not engage women in the history of philosophy, even to show that this is the case. One of reclamation's aims is to give the lie to the idea that the history of European and Anglophone philosophy has been a history of men's work. Through the histories they construct, and as a result of their theories of exclusion, Lloyd and Irigaray further entrench the belief that there have been no women in the history of philosophy.

Finally, Le Doeuff has been charged with a loyalty to philosophy that makes her commitment to feminism suspect, so I spend some time addressing these charges to show how they miss the mark. Primarily I clarify Le Doeuff's conception of the relationship between feminism and philosophy. Le Doeuff conceives of both as practices of withdrawing from commonly held belief, and thus kindred, pursuits. She is also critical of both families of practice when they fail to engage in this critical pursuit, most often turning feminist critiques on European and Anglophone philosophical history and practice. Ultimately her aim is to illuminate the historical possibilities for how we think and know in the present in order to think and know differently. My defense is not that Le Doeuff's work is perfect or offers a perfect performance of feminist critique. It isn't and it doesn't. Her work does, however, take seriously the philosophical authority of historical women thinkers in order to give us critical purchase on our contemporary modes of thinking. Le Doeuff does not supply all the answers for reclamation; she rather gives a method that eschews pursuing answers in favor of thinking.

Although this chapter is an argument for transformative reclamation that employs Le Doeuff's methods, the point, again, is not that Le Doeuff's work is above critique or a perfect guide. Far from it. There are many advantages to Le Doeuff's approach that I highlighted in the chapter devoted to her work and seek to clarify here. But, as I also argued in that chapter, there are serious limitations to her approach. In the final chapter, I employ Le Doeuff's method with attention to its limitations in order to work past some of them. In other words, some of the problems with Le Doeuff's approach become a guide to my readings of the *Declaration of Sentiments* and Sojourner Truth's speech from 1851. The work of reclaiming the speculative possibilities of these texts is not thereby finished, but rather, I hope, begun anew.

DEMANDING HISTORICAL ACCURACY

Diotima has been a central thread of this project, and I have shown the different means for engaging her that are enabled by Lloyd, Irigaray, and Le Doeuff. Irigaray offers the most thorough reclamation of Diotima, but in chapters 2, 3, and 4, I showed that all three thinkers can help us engage her as a philosophical authority. I have not yet addressed the concern about the accuracy of the historical record that Dancy raised in the first chapter. While Dancy's critique was directed to Waithe's project, it is a concern that could extend to the methods of reclamation discussed here. To reiterate, Dancy wrote: "Perhaps Diotima was a historical person. If so, she may have held the theory of forms we associate with Plato, if what Plato makes Socrates makes her say in the *Symposium* is true to her, she certainly did. But we have been given no reason whatever for supposing that she must have been a historical person, or that, if she was, she held the views put into her mouth in the *Symposium*."[3] In other words, if Diotima was a real person whose speech Plato accurately records, then she held the theory of the forms. None of the issues of historicity can be decided, however, based on the evidence we have or on evidence we can hope to attain. How can these theorists of exclusion help us with this problem?

Lloyd does not engage with questions of the priestess's historicity. Moreover, Lloyd presents Diotima's words as her own and as representing an advancement in Plato's view of reason, a view that Lloyd seems to endorse. While, as I argued in the second chapter, Lloyd has resources for critiquing the hierarchy of reason over body that she finds in the speech, ultimately Lloyd has the least defense against Dancy's criticism. If we accept the speech as the words of a woman, then Lloyd gives us a powerful method for analyzing the concepts Diotima employs. Lloyd does not help us to establish Diotima as part of the historical record, either in her absence like Irigaray or in our uchronic rendering like Le Doeuff. Indeed, Lloyd's lack of a means to imagine a different history may be related to why she chose to reproduce a traditional philosophical history. While Lloyd certainly urges new histories, she is most helpful with the analysis of figures once they are identified as philosophers.

So what about Irigaray? In Dancy's criticism of Waithe's disregard for the careful historical work already done on Greek philosophy, we can recognize something akin to Nye's objections to Irigaray. As Dancy did in relationship to Waithe's work, Nye uses established historical facts about ancient Greek culture of that period to reject Irigaray's approach. In both cases, the authority of the historical record is invoked to challenge the feminist reclamation proposed, although each invocation has different aims. Dancy argues that Waithe overattributes importance to Diotima, either as a historical figure or as a philosophical authority, and thus argues against the possibility of a feminist reclamation of Diotima. Nye, by contrast, seeks to bolster Diotima's authority using the historical record while dismissing Irigaray's reclamation as fatally ahistorical.

As I argued in the third chapter in response to Nye's critique, Irigaray's method counters concerns about Diotima's historicity by engaging her speech *as though* she were a woman speaking. Irigaray looks for the traces of sexual difference, here given to us through Plato's attribution of the words to Diotima. Diotima becomes Irigaray's interlocutor through the love Irigaray shows her words. This love is admiring and hopeful, and it is also imaginative. Irigaray finds a beautiful vision of immortality—immortality as something developed between us through engaging one another. No source can be so degraded, according to Irigaray's method, as to prevent us from treating it with love and sometimes even finding a lesson of love in it.

Irigaray's approach exposes the power of Dancy's seemingly simple demand that any change of the historical record must take into account the work already done. The record thus far has been generated through the disavowal of sexual difference. We do not just happen to lack records of Diotima or other women of the ancient world. The record has been constructed through their absenting. But the absenting has been incomplete; we have traces. While the question of the historical veracity of Plato's rendering of Diotima's speech must be suspended, because we lack the evidence to answer it, we can still move forward with the project of introducing the question of sexual difference. We can introduce it with our engagement of the traces. Thus, Irigaray's method delinks historical accuracy from philosophical authority. This delinking opens up possibilities for thinking with historical texts, which does not negate the importance of the historical work Nye and Dancy advocate, but it does not narrow our engagements to that kind of work.

Finally, there is Le Doeuff, in whose work Diotima arises in an apparently cautionary fashion: as a woman who is only allowed to speak through a man, and as the teacher of divine inspiration, but whose knowledge does not originate with her. Yet, Le Doeuff's project makes us reconsider whatever we have been told is not worth our attention. Le Doeuff gives us the method of uchronic questioning with which to approach these denigrated figures and texts. We can ask: What if Diotima was a woman who taught Socrates about love? As uchronic history is counterfactual practice, it is already suspending the norms of traditional history, which Dancy is invoking, to imagine what might have been had an excluded voice been heard. Indeed, with Le Doeuff's approach, we can ask what philosophical history might have been like if Plato had made Diotima present at the *Symposium*. What if Plato had put a theory of love and knowledge in the mouth of a woman?

Beyond offering a satisfying exercise in what might have been, Le Doeuff helps us to understand that our archive has been shaped through practices of exclusion that shape what we can know. We do not have a reliable record of this priestess that Nye gives us evidence to believe had some authority to speak in public in that time and place. Indeed, we have a scant history of any women speaking in public in many cultures, and much of the record has been established in the last two centuries. The point is not merely to lament the loss of excluded voices, though that is an important part of uchronic history writing, but also to understand how our ways of thinking have been shaped by their exclusion. Thus, calls for historical accuracy get reframed through uchronic questioning. The lack of evidence supports our curiosity and investigation, not because we can fill in the gap with data, but because we can ask: Why isn't there a good record of Diotima's teachings? How have our epistemes, our practices, our senses of what is properly philosophical, and our senses of history been shaped not just by this gap, for which we have a rather substantial trace, but by other exclusions about which we do not have even an inkling?

In contrast to Lloyd, Irigaray and Le Doeuff offer illuminative defense against Dancy's criticism. They illuminate how silencing and exclusion shape the possible archives upon which we can draw. Both warrant imaginative work in response to the problems of a canon built on the exclusion of women. Before comparing those imaginative responses, there is a limit to our possible archives of speculation that needs our attention.

VIOLENT ARCHIVAL LIMITS

Texts by or attributed to survivors of chattel slavery have sometimes been employed as a means of resolving the horrors of slavery by purporting to grapple with and transcend them. In the next chapter, I critically explore the feminist history of such readings of Sojourner Truth's work, in part to make transformative readings possible. But I want to underscore that transformative reclamation does not attend to historical violences to achieve remediative inclusions. As I showed in the first chapter, that sort of enfranchisement approach to reclamation maintains the tradition of exclusion. By acknowledging a limit to reclamation, in the form of vast silences all but present in the archives to which we can turn to read about the lives and thoughts of those enslaved, I hope not just to amplify grief and anger about these silences, as well as facilitate such attunements to them. I also aim to show how these silences are the work of the present. Facing the archival limit of chattel slavery, and the impossibility of overcoming or remediating it, is particularly important in this project that reads the word of someone who stole herself from slavery. That reading cannot undo the violence that made it all but impossible to inherit Truth's words.

Saidiya Hartman has extensively theorized the limits to our ability to engage with the lives and thoughts of those turned property through chattel slavery. I pick up her analysis in the essay "Venus in Two Acts." In that piece, Hartman grapples with the desire to say more about those erased in the violent construction of the archive(s) of slavery.[4] Hartman finds mere traces of "a *dead girl*," sometimes called Venus, in a legal indictment for murder.[5] These traces offer us very little with which to render a historically accurate picture. "We stumble upon her in exorbitant circumstances," Hartman writes, "that yield no picture of the everyday life, no pathway to her thoughts, no glimpse of the vulnerability of her face or of what looking at such a face might demand. We only know what can be extrapolated from an analysis of the ledger or borrowed from the world of her captors and masters and applied to her."[6] Because we do not have access to what Venus thought, along with almost all other aspects of her lived experience and existence (we only know of her particular existence through a faint archival trace), we could simply look away. What can we say when the archive will not yield up any more information?

Yet, Hartman does not turn away for many reasons, not least of which is the way our present is shaped by this history. In resonance with the theories of exclusion from Irigaray and Le Doeuff, the gaps, silences, and traces are telling us something not just about the archive, but about what we can know, do, and understand *because* this is our archive. Hartman writes: "The archive of slavery rests upon a founding violence. This violence determines, regulates, and organizes the kinds of statements that can be made about slavery and as well it creates subjects and objects of power."[7] We are, to return to Hortense Spillers's formulation cited in the introduction, grappling with how the construction of "the paradox of non-being" has formed our archives.[8] Rather than accept this limit, Hartman has developed a counterhistorical practice of critical fabulation:

> By playing with and rearranging the basic elements of the story, by re-presenting the sequence of events in divergent stories and from contested points of view, I have attempted to jeopardize the status of the event, to displace the received or authorized account, and to imagine what might have happened or might have been said or might have been done. By throwing into crisis "what happened when" and by exploiting the "transparency of sources" as fictions of history, I wanted to make visible the production of disposable lives (in the Atlantic slave trade and, as well, in the discipline of history), to describe "the resistance of the object," if only by first imagining it, and to listen for the mutters and oaths and cries of the commodity.[9]

Again, Irigaray's and Le Doeuff's approaches to reclamation resonate: the displacement of authorized accounts; re-presenting elements in new ways to illuminate what has not been attended to; and responding in an imaginative mode to suggest what might have happened, been said, or been done.

As compelling as I find these connections between Hartman, Irigaray, and Le Doeuff, there are risks to such a comparison. There are risks to suggesting that Diotima and Venus are similar cases. Such a move levels out, for instance, the difference between a dialogue by Plato and an indictment for murder. Yet, in bringing these problematics together, at least insofar as to claim both as the work of reclamation, I am suggesting that feminist reclamation that does not consider what structures the limitations of our archives fails to sufficiently grapple with the power of exclusion, and thereby risks fortifying this limit. This violent archive is also the archive of European and Anglophone philosophy. That the history of European and Anglophone philosophy does not appear so formed is an effect of the violent exclusions to which Hartman attunes us. Reclamation should be so attuned.

Venus is not like Diotima. We do not even have a ventriloquized record of Venus's words. When Venus and "girls who share her circumstances"[10] show up in the archive, "the stories that exist are not about them, but rather about the violence, excess, mendacity, and reason that seized hold of their lives, transformed them into commodities and corpses, and identified them with names tossed-off as insults and crass jokes."[11] The *Symposium* certainly has crass jokes, and perhaps Diotima is one of them, but she is called a priestess, and a teacher, and she laughs at Socrates. For Venus, "the archive is . . . a death sentence, a tomb, a few lines about a whore's life, an asterisk in the grand narrative of history."[12] Diotima and Venus do not share a situation. And philosophy has no place for the philosophical authority of either. By suggesting they are both women excluded from the history of European and Anglophone philosophy, I seek not to make them alike, but rather I seek methods of reclamation that can acknowledge these different situations. And further, I seek the transformation of a philosophical tradition that has retained highly circumscribed traces of the first and has largely not even been aware that the second was absent. As Spillers observes, "Having encountered what they understand as chaos, the empowered need not name further, since chaos is sufficient naming within itself."[13] Reclamation ought not accept such practices of naming, even if the reclaimed fragments do not allow us to establish other, rightful names.

Hartman faced with the faintest traces, overwritten with violence, suggests that at such a limit, we face the impossibility of reclaiming a voice:

> The intent of this practice is not to *give voice* to the slave, but rather to imagine what cannot be verified, a realm of experience which is situated between two zones of death—social and corporeal death—and to reckon with the precarious lives which are visible only in the moment of their disappearance. It is an impossible writing which attempts to say that which resists being said (since dead girls are unable to speak). It is a history of an unrecoverable past; it is a narrative of what might have been or could have been; it is a history written with and against the archive.

Reclamation cannot overcome an archive that leaves us so little to read of Venus's life, let alone her thoughts. The paradox of nonbeing constructed through the Atlantic slave trade cannot be dissolved through reclamation practices. But the creation of that paradox, the historical work of slavery, can be attended to by reclamation in order "to imagine a *free state*, not as the time before captivity or slavery, but rather as the anticipated future of this writing."[14] In other words, reclamation must theorize practices of exclusion "to illuminate the intimacy of our experience with the lives of the dead" and "to write our now as it is interrupted by this past."[15] Reclamation must contend with the possibilities for philosophical authority created and sustained by practices of exclusion that did not stash redeeming texts in secret repositories or even in between the lines of a ledger.

Because this work of exclusion is part of "a past that has yet to be done," we need reclamation not to fill in what is missing, but to transform philosophical authority in "the ongoing state of emergency in which black life remains in peril."[16] European and Anglophone philosophy has been created through anti-black racism, and we cannot redeem that history through reading Venus's thoughts, regardless of how speculative we are willing to be. Reclamation must recognize this constitutive limit as noteworthy, problematic, and irreconcilable with the desire to bring back what has been lost. And reclamation can critically consider how historical readings strengthen, transform, or undermine contemporary practices. Mary Warnock, to use an example from the first chapter, clearly sought to strengthen dismissals of feminist philosophical work through reclamations of historical women's texts. While Warnock offers a particularly blatant example of reclamation used to entrench practices of exclusion, the subtler means of exclusion, such as Green's appeal to the sameness of women's experience, also analyzed in the first chapter, are also powerful. Reclamation must consider how it perpetuates, works against, and transforms these practices. My reading of Truth's Akron speech in the final chapter will return to this problematic through Nell Painter's account of writing Truth's biography. For now, I want to emphasize that while we cannot fathom what has been lost, we can identify and castigate philosophical practices that would have us pretend these violences are not at work.[17]

In considering what cannot be brought back—whose authority has not been permissively prohibited but systematically and violently prohibited—Le Doeuff's practice of attending to insults and epithets can again be useful. Le Doeuff finds in these moments of denigration indicators of excluded possibilities, possibilities excluded in order to legitimate others. To use Hartman's language, Le Doeuff recognizes that "Infelicitous speech, obscene utterances, and perilous commands give birth to the characters we stumble upon in the archive."[18] These insults are at work. Spillers has made clear that these epithets are at work not only in our history, but in our present, through her own litany of names: "Let's face it. I am a marked woman, but not everybody knows my name. 'Peaches' and 'Brown Sugar,' 'Sapphire' and 'Earth Mother,' 'Aunty,' 'Granny,' God's 'Holy Fool,' a 'Miss Ebony First,' or 'Black Woman at the Podium': I describe a locus of confounded identities, a meeting ground of investments and privations in the national treasury of rhetorical wealth. My country needs me, and if I were not here, I would have to be invented."

Le Doeuff points to the meeting ground of investments and privations to show how a discipline has been built. While reclamation cannot undo that history, it can adopt methods that work with and against it. Venus was made into property, under a name conferred by practices of slavery, in a history of massive exclusion that usually only appears, if it leaves a mark at all, as an insult. Feminist reclamation can mark the limit of historical archives and the need for new practices of constructing authority that do not maintain this limit in the present. There were lives and thoughts completely erased from any possible engagement, and that destruction was ancillary to the project of making money from flesh. The *hope* of reclamation must be dashed against the limit of our archives so that we find our work in the present. Reclamation, bereft of historical work at this limit, can prompt us to ask: Whose thoughts continue to be dismissed in order to maintain a certain tradition of philosophical practice?

OVERREADING

Within the limits of our archives, there are texts, sometimes fragmentary and sometimes of no apparent philosophical significance. It is these texts that David Kazanjian, in conversation with Hartman's work, proposes to overread for their speculative potential: "I want to suggest that the structural impossibility Hartman describes can actually lead us to a productive possibility: to reading what archives we do have more speculatively, for their theoretical work rather than just for their empirical content."[19] Put another way, Kazanjian suggests that we read for philosophical authority in texts that do not present themselves as works of philosophy or, perhaps more accurately, that we in the European and Anglophone tradition have not inherited as philosophy. In the chapters on their work, I suggested that both Irigaray and Le Doeuff have developed practices of overreading. Now I compare their methods.

In claiming overreading as a practice, Kazanjian utilizes a term usually wielded as a critique of immoderate, excessive readings. In Kazanjian's description of this charge, we can recognize something akin to Dancy's critique of Waithe's reclamation of Diotima or Nye's critique of Irigaray's: "The charge of overreading presumes a strict separation between historically contextualized reading and ahistorical reading, which in turn presumes that one can adequately determine the context in which a text was written and linger in that context with the text in a kind of epistemic intimacy."[20] If we do not presume an epistemic intimacy with a text, if we treat historical texts, instead, as work to be done, then the practice of overreading points to new possibilities. Kazanjian writes: "By *embracing* the practice of overreading such texts, perhaps we could offer an unverifiable but textually coherent account of this archive of slavery's speculative reflections, just as we would read any nineteenth-century philosophical treatise on freedom."[21] Overreading does not presume to give the correct reading, but a reading that moves our thinking nonetheless. As Kazanjian writes: "By *speculative work* I mean that which might not be the expression of a subject's will, desire, intention, or voice but might still be readable to us, today, as a powerfully political text."[22] Tailoring this point to reclamation, we can say, speculative work might not give us the expression of a woman's will, desire, intention, or (to displace a metaphor that circulates widely in the reclamation literature) voice but it might still be readable to us, today, as a powerfully political text.

Irigaray and Le Doeuff have both created speculative approaches to historical texts that prompt reading them for their powerful political work. Yet, Irigaray reads for subjectivity, while Le Doeuff reads for what throws off accepted modes of thinking. Irigaray's reading for subjectivity is certainly aimed at disrupting the powerful sexual indifference she has diagnosed as a highly acceptable mode of thinking. However, Kazanjian's characterization of speculative work that does not purport to represent something attributable to a subject, but that is still powerful, points to an important difference in Irigaray and Le Doeuff's methods. Irigaray's readings can be enormously surprising for the way sexual indifference functions, and for the glimpses of other possibilities she raises. But the way forward is narrow. By attending to the traces left by a certain mode of exclusion, Irigaray seeks to put history to work in the present. But, and this relates to the critiques of her work I raised at the end of chapter 3, this method of speculative overreading is limited by the organizing desire for the past to speak and to speak of sexual difference.

To come at this from another angle, consider Michelle Walker's characterization: "Luce Irigaray, Genevieve Lloyd and Michèle Le Doeuff investigate the systematic silencing of both woman and women from the discourse of Western philosophy. They understand silence as involving an absence of women's voices from the dialogues that constitute the philosophical enterprise as a tradition."[23] As a summary statement that gestures at similarities in the projects of these three thinkers, the quotation points to the field of concern. Yet, it seems that voice is a less apt metaphor for Le Doeuff's work than for the others. Le Doeuff reads constellations of thinkers to expose the discourses that sustain their arguments, as well as for the way the arguments of individual thinkers point to powerful political possibilities. Le Doeuff seems less interested in unearthing the subjectivity of a text—its metaphorical voice—and more in its potential for thinking.

I suggested in the last section that Le Doeuff, through her attention to insult, offers a way for feminist reclamation to identify where the possibility for philosophical authority has been systematically and violently denied. That method also points us toward exclusions less thoroughly rendered, exclusions that have left us texts. Le Doeuff's uchronic method revivifies failed ideals by reading historical texts that have survived into the present. Part of what I find compelling about this approach is that it does not purport to an authentic reading or offer us a historical "voice." With Le Doeuff's uchronic reading, we are clearly engaged in an imaginative practice to understand our own situation and its antecedents. What possibilities can we imagine through our encounter with these texts? What problems can we now see?

THE HISTORY OF EUROPEAN AND ANGLOPHONE PHILOSOPHY

I have also gravitated to Le Doeuff's approach because of the kinds of histories she builds. The extraordinary nature of Le Doeuff's engagement with women's work becomes clearer if we look at the relative dearth of such engagements in Lloyd and Irigaray. While Lloyd and Irigaray have importantly different reasons for construing the history of European and Anglophone philosophy as the work of men, the net result in both of their work is the exclusion of women. In this section, I explore in more detail how these invested theorists of women's exclusion became agents of it.

In glossing Irigaray's work, Lloyd writes:

> What does it mean to say that women are outside the symbolic structures? In one sense it is, of course, clearly true. It is not women but men who have created the symbolic structures we have inherited in the philosophical tradition. Men have conceptualized reason through Woman, symbolizing what is opposite to maleness and, to that extent, what is opposite to themselves as men. The symbolization of reason as male derives historically from the contingent fact that it was largely men—to the literal exclusion of women—who devised the symbolic structures. This is a symbolism appropriate to men as exclusive symbol users.[24]

Lloyd's explanation is causal and a reiteration of her view that the history of European and Anglophone philosophy comprises only men. Symbolic structures are masculine because men created them—Lloyd will later argue, "Sexual difference provided the symbolism."[25] As I argued in the chapter on her work, Lloyd's account of the history of European and Anglophone philosophy is too totalizing because she moves from arguing that reason is masculinized to arguing that only men have practiced philosophy.

The reason for that totalizing move makes more sense when Lloyd later clarifies her understanding of metaphor. She theorizes an interaction between what she refers to as "gender identity" and what she refers to as "symbolic gender." What grounds gender identity in Lloyd's account is biological sex. In other words, for Lloyd, there is a truth of the matter, "real men and women," upon which gender plays.[26] While Lloyd is analytically interested in symbolic gender, for her there is a necessary, if complex and attenuated, relationship between gender identity and symbolic gender, because both arise from biological sex, even if both can also somehow affect biological sex. Hence, in the above quotation, Lloyd speaks of the *appropriateness* of the symbolization of reason as male. Such symbolization is dictated by the maleness of those who philosophize.

Lloyd's notion of symbolization here is strikingly different from Irigaray's. Irigaray argues that symbolic exchange has been predicated on the disavowal of the feminine, even among women. Whereas sexual difference is causative on Lloyd's account, it has been made impossible on Irigaray's. Indeed, in the chapter on Irigaray, I raised a concern that stems from her view that feminine subjectivity has not yet spoken. Namely, if feminine subjectivity has not spoken, then perhaps women philosophers can only give us access to masculine discourse. Perhaps there is no good feminist reason to reclaim women's work. I argued that Irigaray engages philosophical discourse because the disavowal of the feminine occurs within the texts of European and Anglophone philosophy and leaves there the marks of the work of repression. Hence, philosophical history has value for feminist philosophers as a site for us to take up the position assigned to the feminine and jam the machinery from within discourse. Now, I want to say something more in light of Lloyd's critique and her position on the symbolic.

European and Anglophone philosophy, Irigaray showed us with Diotima, is more than just the site of repression. We can also read for the work of repression and can perhaps, as Irigaray did with Diotima, exploit those traces as resources for reclamation. From whence do those resources come? Is there something special about women that supplies these hoped-for resources? That does not seem to be Irigaray's position. Rather, Irigaray's reading of Diotima takes the fragments of a disavowed imaginary available in Plato's speech and presents them as possibilities for how we might (re)conceive of the world. Notably, these fragments of a repressed imaginary come to us via the writing of a man. This reading suggests that there is not a prediscursive ground that one can express. There is not an *appropriate* symbolism arising from one's sex. Instead, Irigaray shows us how to read for the repressed imaginary at work in a man's text. That is not to denigrate the importance of the attribution of the speech to a woman, but instead it requires that we read with the complications of the text, rather than looking for the biological cause of the disruption the text presents in an attempt to remedy a tradition that has mostly tried to eliminate the disruption. Irigaray identifies the conflict of imaginaries, the mark of the work of repression—Diotima's absent appearance as a woman—as the feminist entry point into philosophical history.

Yet, as powerful as this mode of reading is, we should not let go of the concern that Irigaray does not engage women thinkers. To grasp why, let's turn to a story from Eileen O'Neill. This story is helpful because the absence of women philosophers from Irigaray's work is unremarkable from the point of view of the dominant tradition she is critiquing. O'Neill helps make Irigaray's conservativism on this point strange. In "Early Modern

Women Philosophers and the History of Philosophy," O'Neill writes:

> In the mid-1990s a publishing company decided to produce a supplement for one of its reference works on philosophy. Since the original version of the reference tool had included pitifully few entries on women philosophers, a feminist philosopher who was on the editorial board had encouraged the press to include in the supplement a number of entries on women philosophers. But despite the feminist editor's many suggestions, in the end the press chose to add entries only on the following figures: one woman from the ancient world, Hypatia; one from the Middle Ages, Hildegard of Bingen; one from the Renaissance, Marie de Gournay; one from the seventeenth century, Anne Conway; and one from the eighteenth century, Mary Wollstonecraft; plus Anscombe, Arendt, and Beauvoir from the twentieth century. It was never explained to me why Conway was chosen but not Mary Astell; why Wollstonecraft was selected but not Emilie du Châtelet; and why no women philosophers from the nineteenth century were included.
>
> Since the press wasn't going to budge on the issue of adding more entries on individual women, I asked if the supplement couldn't at least include an overview essay. After some negotiations, I was asked to write a 1500-word article on "Women in the History of Philosophy," to which I agreed on the condition that the length of the bibliography for the article would not be restricted. I continue to be pleased about the fact that the bibliography of primary sources alone is about the length of the article to which it is appended. Although I was allowed no space in which to speak about the importance of the women's philosophical contributions, the sheer volume of the titles of the women's publications stands as a type of monument. The bibliography

> seems to shout, "Here is the material that within this reference work remains buried and silenced. Here is the material about which we are not permitted to speak. But by all means, find these titles and read them for yourself."[27]

Of the many striking things about this story, not least of which is the exclusion of any women philosophers in the nineteenth century, is O'Neill's characterization of her bibliography as a monument. One can imagine a reader encountering the bibliography within the reference work as a list of figures too insignificant to garner their own entries. Hypatia, Hildegard of Bingen, Marie de Gournay, Anne Conway, Mary Wollstonecraft, Anscombe, Arendt, and Beauvoir would all have an elevated status in relation to the monumentalized women. There are, maybe the open-minded reader will think, eight women worth our attention in the history of European and Anglophone philosophy and a crowd of others that might be interesting for specialists.

O'Neill's story gives a different interpretative frame for the monument. The women chosen for entries were not selected through a considered process that yielded a well-justified or apparently justifiable set of thinkers to include.[28] Instead, O'Neill exposes the lack of a coherent approach and the apparent arbitrariness of the attempt to solve the lack of women's representation. By showing that women constitute a problem for reference works on the history of European and Anglophone philosophy, O'Neill helps foster readers who will be alert to this issue when referring to such works.

But O'Neill is also clear that it is impossible for even those curious readers, *as individual readers*, to make up for the deficit. As O'Neill observes: "Determining the philosophical value of a text requires that we first understand the context in which a text was written, what its philosophical goals are, what the argumentational strategies are, and so on. Accomplishing all this in the absence of any preexisting critical and historical literature on the text is very difficult. It typically takes many scholars, working hard for some time, before we can properly interpret, and thus be in a position to evaluate the philosophical significance of, a text."[29] The accumulation of scholarship, interpretive disagreements, and a great deal of contextualization are necessary for a figure to be appreciated. A bar to establishing that appreciation, O'Neill notes, is the presupposition that "if there were women who contributed in significant ways to early modern philosophy, well-educated scholars would already know about them."[30] O'Neill exposes the difficulties that exclusion presents for accumulating adequate scholarship. We can read Irigaray as potentially contributing to this problem through her theory of exclusion, and even in her engagement with Diotima. For when Irigaray acknowledges a woman in this history of European and Anglophone philosophy, it is one who is all but absent—one whose words we cannot know. What about all the women who have left some record of their thinking? If one's feminist source on the history of European and Anglophone philosophy is Irigaray, then one might not think to look for these women. We are back to Alain De Botton's description of the philosophical cocktail party I referenced in the introduction: the lovers of wisdom have been a small group of men.

THE MENACE OF PHILOSOPHY

The importance of Le Doeuff's engagements with historical women has to some extent been occluded by concerns about her loyalty to philosophy. Meaghan Morris, for instance, writes in the *Pirate's Fiancée*:

> The other question that concerns me is that through *L'Imaginaire philosophique*, the most explicit argument used to urge the practice of philosophy is in fact the argument by menace. To say that certain feminisms of difference, for example, run the risk of reproducing the schemas they presume they are renouncing, is to invoke the classically philosophical threat of entrapment *by* philosophy for those who do not pay heed. It would be excessive, as well as parasitic on Michèle Le Doeuff's own arguments, to read in this a trace of the paternalism of reason. The problem is rather the accompanying absence of *other*, positive arguments for the value of philosophy to feminism.[31]

Authors such as Elizabeth Grosz and Michelle Walker echo Morris's concern that Le Doeuff fails to provide arguments for philosophy and only menaces feminism with the force of philosophical tools. In this section, I explore these critiques, to offer defenses against them, but more importantly to clarify how Le Doeuff conceives of the relationship between European and Anglophone philosophy and European and Anglophone feminist theory and practice.

Grosz, who quotes Morris, writes: "One is left with a suspicion that, rather than render Irigaray's insights in her critique of philosophical phallocentrism historically and textually specific, as her comments may imply, Le Doeuff is instead acting as feminine preserver and commemorative historian of masculine wisdom."[32] Michelle Walker draws on both Morris's and Grosz's work, though she does not quote their reservations about Le Doeuff's allegiance to philosophy. Walker, however, clearly echoes them: "I am concerned that Le Doeuff's project of salvaging rationality runs the not inconsiderable risk of silencing those who reject her belief that reason is in fact gender-neutral. Le Doeuff works against herself when, in the final analysis, her own voice enacts a closure of those discourses attempting to speak in logics other than the dominant rationality of the logos."[33] There are some reasons to think these charges do not stick. First, and as something of an aside, the reading that Morris suggests, but does not develop, would not be parasitic on Le Doeuff's arguments. That is, Le Doeuff does not think that reason has a paternalistic character. Le Doeuff is certainly interested in how it has been conceived as masculine and why that has been a characterization with such a long life, but nowhere does Le Doeuff argue that paternalism is a feature of rationality.

Second, and more to the point, Morris reveals a misunderstanding of Le Doeuff's project when she suggests that Le Doeuff lacks an explicit argument for the value of philosophy for feminism. Le Doeuff's view of the relationship between philosophy and feminism is rather more complicated. Take, for instance, the following from *Hipparchia's Choice*: "If we make a link (as least as a hypothesis) between thinking philosophically and self-assertion through thought, or the individual withdrawal from generally held beliefs, then 'thinking philosophically' and 'being a feminist' appear as one and the same attitude: a desire to judge by and for oneself, which may manifest itself in relation to different questions."[34] Yet, as Le Doeuff repeatedly documents, the history of European and Anglophone philosophy fails to bear out this complicity. Indeed, feminism appears in many different ways in Le Doeuff's texts as a spur to European and Anglophone philosophy to deepen its practices of critique; thus there is a corrective inflection to Le Doeuff's concept of the relationship between European and Anglophone philosophy and feminism. But, as I argued in the chapter on Le Doeuff, her method is more than corrective in that she argues that even the ideals of European and Anglophone philosophy have been shaped by women's exclusion. Thus, even our ideals for European and Anglophone philosophy need to be transformed. Le Doeuff does not accept the tradition of exclusion as the proper tradition of philosophy. Le Doeuff does not need an argument for the value of philosophy for feminism because she recognizes and aims to foster productive conflict between these modes of withdrawal from generally held beliefs.

Now to Grosz's concern "that there is a certain reverence and respect, a propriety in her patient, meticulous, restricted readings, almost as if she were to claim that if philosophy is misogynist, this can be confined to those imaginary elements she has been concerned to reveal."[35] In these comments, a category is implicitly at work that Grosz employs in *Jacques Lacan: A Feminist Introduction*: the dutiful daughter. The dutiful daughter, Grosz explains, is "one who submits to the Father's Law."[36] Grosz suggests here that Le Doeuff submits to the law of philosophy, one form of the Father's Law.

By way of response, let's look to Penelope Deutscher's essay "'Imperfect Discretion': Interventions Into the History of Philosophy by Twentieth-Century French Women Philosophers." There, Deutscher reminds us of Le Doeuff's argument in "Long Hair, Short Ideas" that women have been admitted to philosophical history as commentators and thereby excluded from importance as canonical figures. Deutscher, responding to Le Doeuff, suggests:

> To undermine the marginal status attributed to the woman commentator, we could ask what women have achieved as creation and innovation within the crevices of philosophical commentary. We can, strategically, read the commentator in more interesting ways. Perhaps it is impossible to be successfully dutiful, really faithful, really reproductive, not distorting? In writing, as in life, acts of fidelity are often acts of passive aggression and

> resistance. If dutiful commentary often displaces that to which it is ostensibly faithful, we might renegotiate our understanding of the texts of figures who are coded as "faithful."[37]

Deutscher suggests the powerful move of reevaluating what we have been taught to disregard. We can, in a move familiar from Le Doeuff, look at what we have been told not to look at and consider what has been denigrated. Perhaps we will find there speculations we need.

Deutscher's suggestion, which she carries through to wonderful effect with the work of Clémence Ramnoux, Nicole Laraux, and Barbara Cassin, among others, is important here for two reasons. First, she highlights something that Grosz and Morris seem to have disregarded in their apprehensions that Le Doeuff is first a disciple of philosophy and only secondarily a (much compromised) feminist. Deutscher highlights Le Doeuff's critique of philosophical practice for privileging the image of the philosopher over the effort to shift thinking. Thus, Deutscher helps us to understand that Grosz and Morris misread Le Doeuff's appreciation and utilization of philosophy's ability to move thinking with an allegiance to a male pantheon. That is, Grosz and Morris tend to conflate practices of philosophy with dominant conceptions of European and Anglophone philosophy's history.

Second, Deutscher's interest in revaluing commentary suggests that Grosz's concern—that Le Doeuff's reverence and respect for philosophical texts undermine her critical ability—may be part of the denigration of commentary. Where Le Doeuff appears merely dutiful to Grosz, Deutscher asks us to look for displacements and resistance. One caveat to that second point: I think Grosz exaggerates the faithful nature of Le

Doeuff's writing. That is not to elevate Le Doeuff's work for being something other than commentary and, thus, subtly effecting the denigration that Deutscher argues against. It is just that if Le Doeuff's writing has a tendency, it seems to me to be toward the polemical, not a style common to commentaries, and, moreover, her polemical intent seems to change depending on whether she is critiquing feminist writing or philosophical writing. Thus, at the very least, if we are searching for an epithet for Le Doeuff's work it might be "traitorous," for her allegiance to philosophy usually seems to be in the service of feminism. I offer that label with the hope it will draw the attention that Le Doeuff would have given to any name-calling.

Finally, to Walker's concern that Le Doeuff silences those who do not agree with her that reason is gender-neutral. I am not sure where Walker thinks Le Doeuff argues for a gender-neutral conception of reason. *The Sex of Knowing*, the title of which points to questions of gender and reason, is, if nothing else, an exposé of how ideas about the gendered nature of reason developed, took hold, and persist—in both philosophical and popular discourse. Le Doeuff responds to what would amount to a hilarious history of rumor, innuendo, prejudice, and power grabs, except for its dire and enduring consequences, not by arguing for a gender-neutral conception of reason. Instead, Le Doeuff brings diverse resources to bear, including and especially the philosophical writing of many women in European and Anglophone philosophy's history, to move our thinking not just about reason, but also about a concept that I think may have greater importance in Le Doeuff's writing and thinking: judgment. Le Doeuff writes, for example: "Not all the conditions that affect the exercise of judgment are derived from knowledge: not all are rational."[38] Le Doeuff continues in this passage to suggest that there is an important parallel between Christine de Pisan's thinking and Arendt's. Le Doeuff writes: "If we take Christine de Pisan and Hannah Arendt together, we can begin to see, not that the thinking subject can be marked by gender, but—and this is more important—that every subject is caught up in an imaginary network of self-representations, authorizations, or inhibitions more significant than the mere intellectual conditions of thought, and error can result from too many of these just as easily as from too few."[39] Le Doeuff is not interested in whether reason is gendered or neutral; she is interested in understanding how that became a compelling framing of an issue in European and Anglophone feminism and philosophy. Further, she is interested in moving beyond that debate that has acted like a barricade to further consideration of women's thinking and the cultivation of everyone's judgment.

It is obviously unfair to address Walker's criticism with passages taken from a work published after the criticisms were made. While *The Sex of Knowing* is Le Doeuff's most developed exploration of how knowledge is produced and how we can gain critical leverage on that production, on this point it does not break with her earlier work. From *The Philosophical Imaginary* on, Le Doeuff shows her readers how we have come to "know" that women are not philosophers and that men are the reasonable sex. Further, her work is full of suggestions for what should happen once we are aware of that history, but she has never counseled the adoption and promotion of gender-neutral conceptions of reason. Walker erroneously reduces Le Doeuff's thinking to debates about reason's gendering. Le Doeuff's work to expose the pervasiveness of that way of framing reason throughout feminist and philosophical debates has been ongoing, and perhaps helps us understand why Walker makes such a move.

CRITICAL RECLAMATION

Regardless of how one assesses Le Doeuff's allegiance to philosophy, her engagement with women in its history sets her apart from most people working in European and Anglophone philosophy at any point in the history of that tradition of philosophy. And Le Doeuff has given us a powerful mode of engagement to further the project of reclamation. Again, Le Doeuff has not offered us a perfect form of reclamation. Deutscher points out that Le Doeuff tends not to follow up on the problematic hierarchies that operate within historical women thinker's work, even as they are making (proto)feminist arguments. That tendency is a weakness endemic to the uchronic method, inasmuch as the method leverages these ideals in contrast to our own time. The problematic hierarchies shared by the ideals and our own times may not come into relief. As Deutscher has shown, we must question the scaffolding of these ideals, and that is part of my project in reading the *Declaration of Sentiments* in the final chapter.

Put differently, in our interest to transform European and Anglophone philosophy through attention to women's work, we must also consider the limitations of attending to this category of exclusion. Le Doeuff is again helpful. In one of her most cited essays on women and European and Anglophone philosophy, "Long Hair, Short Ideas," she observes: "Up to and including today, philosophy has concerned only a fringe—minimal, indeed evanescent in certain periods—of what was itself a minority class. Sexist segregation seems of slight importance compared with the massive exclusion that has caused philosophy to remain the prerogative of a handful of the learned."[40] Le Doeuff's point is not that sexism is unimportant, but that it is only one strategy that European and Anglophone philosophy has used. If we construe this exclusion narrowly, as feminist reclamation has tended to do, then we strengthen the power of philosophy as a practice of exclusion and risk even the goal of reclaiming a few women's philosophical authority. If, however, we comprehend sexist exclusion as a method within a larger history of massive exclusion, then we can forge methods of reclamation that engage women's philosophical authority as part of a transformation of European and Anglophone practices of philosophy. Because this massive exclusion has had degrees of success, prohibitively permitting some, while successfully excluding others, we must be imaginative in our engagement with history. Sometimes we face insurmountable historical limits, and we must grieve them. We must also face those insurmountable limits to understand how they may be structuring our contemporary practices—how does our history shape who can be an authority now? About what? And how do we know? And how are we judging? I turn now to the *Declaration of Sentiments* and Truth's speech in Akron, Ohio, in 1851 to explore these questions.

6

INJURIES AND USURPATIONS

On July 19 and 20, 1848, a crowd of around three hundred people met in the Wesleyan Methodist Church in Seneca Falls, New York, "to discuss the social, civil, and religious condition and rights of women."[1] At the meeting, they signed a document, the *Declaration of Sentiments* (see appendix A), and passed resolutions that had begun to take shape during an earlier planning session between Elizabeth Cady Stanton, Mary Ann M'Clintock, and probably her daughters Elizabeth and Mary Ann Jr.[2] Using the *Declaration of Independence* as their model, they submitted "to a candid world" the facts of the "repeated injuries and usurpations on the part of man toward woman."[3] As did the drafters of the *Declaration of Independence*, the drafters of the *Declaration of Sentiments* list the grievances that constitute their reasons for seeking a new political order. Also like the drafters of the *Declaration of Independence*, they offer a solution to their grievances. Unlike those first drafters, however, their solution is not to dissolve the bands that have connected them and those they identify as the perpetrators of their grievances. Instead, with the *Declaration of Sentiments*, they seek to transform the bands that have connected them into bands of equality.

On May 29, 1851, in Akron, Ohio, Sojourner Truth delivered a speech at the Women's Convention, one of many conventions called to discuss what it meant to expand the rights of women in the United States in the wake of the Seneca Falls meeting. We have many versions of the speech (see appendix B), including one authorized but not written by Truth, and the one most commonly cited is the least likely to present what Truth actually said. Given, however, the legendary status of Truth's speech in Akron, and despite (or perhaps because of) the lack of an authoritative text, it is easy to believe we are already familiar with Truth's message. Thus, a simple summary of Truth's speech is harder to render than one of the text adopted at Seneca Falls. Even with these difficulties, it is clear that Truth recognizes possibilities in the women's rights movement that she hopes to shape.

Far from being silenced, the *Declaration* and Truth's speech are well known. The gathering at Seneca Falls and Sojourner Truth even have monuments and parks dedicated to them. Why spend time on texts that may have had little impact on European and Anglophone philosophy, but that are certainly not historically obscure? Part of my impetus comes from the reclamation work Michèle Le Doeuff has already done on the *Declaration* in relation to Harriet Taylor, discussed in chapter 4. Here, I extend Le Doeuff's analysis to draw out the problematic hierarchies that operate within the *Declaration*. I thereby put into practice the critical uchronic method urged by Penelope Deutscher's critique of Le Doeuff's work. That uchronic reading is also in service of another, even more pressing aim: to complicate a powerful story of the women's movement that casts Truth's speech in 1851 as an important step forward in the progress narrative begun at Seneca Falls. My uchronic reading illuminates the complex context of the political possibilities and white supremacist entrenchments of the early women's movement that

Truth was negotiating. On my reading, Truth's speech offers an incisive challenge to the women's movement as a white supremacist project and develops different resources for thinking through the political project of freedom.

In other words, part of what stands in the way of philosophical engagements with the *Declaration* and Truth's speech are the mechanisms by which both texts have been rendered toothless by their legends—by which they could become the subjects of monuments and parks. The *Declaration* is treated as primarily and most importantly a demand for women's suffrage. The other demands of the text, and the complex vision of political change developed through the juxtaposition of these demands, are thereby occluded. Truth's authority, in a different process, is often distilled to a question, variously rendered as "Ar'n't I a woman?" or "Ain't I a woman?" In this rendering, Truth corrects a women's movement prone to construing its organizing categories too narrowly. One goal of this chapter is to contest these seductive and simplistic readings of both texts. In both cases, the reduction of these texts to simple demands for inclusion blocks consideration of the more challenging arguments available in them. By reading these texts together and uchronically, I hope to revivify them, and their conflicts, for contemporary philosophical work. I hope to open them to speculative engagements that help us to problematize our own times.

To breath new life into these texts, I first develop a critical uchronic reading of the *Declaration*. The people gathered at Seneca Falls had a vision of political change that went far beyond extending the suffrage to women. Through a uchronic reading, I imagine what our lives might be like if the many ideals of that document, including suffrage, had become widely operative in 1848. While my aim is to show the importance of aspects of this vision for our contemporary times, I also show how their radical vision depended on problematic hierarchies with which we still struggle. Thus, I develop a critical uchronic reading, attending not just to the ideals, but also to their limitations. Even as the document argues against the civil death of wives, for instance, it remains silent on those who are born to civil death as slaves. The *Declaration* uses an analogy, no less problematic for its prevalence in the history of feminist thought, of wives to slaves. My reading appreciates the importance of claims to citizenship for married women, at the same time as it appreciates the manner in which that citizenship remains dependent, metaphorically and literally, on enslavement. Attention to such moves can help us think about how contemporary feminism continues to set up and rely on such hierarchies. While analogies to slavery are still sometimes deployed, even more pressing is the alignment of women's rights with white supremacy. For example, the reliance of mainstream domestic violence on state violence, especially imprisonment, reflects an ongoing and consequential reliance of feminists on a system widely acknowledged to be racially biased, if not a central mechanism of racism.[4] Reclamation can aid in the work, primarily done by feminists of color, to show how this history shapes our present.

In the second section, I consider how to engage the authority of Truth given that we do not have an authoritative record of her thoughts. Rather than try to determine the correct text to represent her thoughts or turn away from the project, I argue reclamation ought to highlight and engage the difficulties of establishing a text for Truth. My reading is more concerned, ultimately, with our contemporary ability to engage with Truth as a thinker than it is with establishing *the* authoritative text for Truth's speech. I examine how Nell Irvin Painter's authority, in particular and as an example, is, in part, constrained by a legendary version of Truth. What appears as Painter's trouble—that is, she faces persistent resistance to offering evidence that Truth's legend is false and less interesting than what the historical record suggests Truth said and did—illuminates the work of the past in the present. Truth's legend becomes a means of stifling her speculations on freedom and Painter's engagement with them, speculations that can help us think freedom anew now. By questioning the authority of the legendary version of Truth's speech, I hope less to suggest the correct version of the speech than to model speculative engagement with a historical thinker in order to move our thinking in the present.

A UCHRONIC READING OF THE *DECLARATION OF SENTIMENTS*

Le Doeuff suggests that with the *Declaration of Sentiments* the women at the convention established themselves as judging subjects, as did Harriet Taylor Mill in her response to it. I have argued that for those subjects to be established as subjects *to us* we must be able to hear and engage them. At issue is how Seneca Falls becomes part of our philosophical history. How do we engage this text as one with philosophical authority?

First, we can appreciate that Le Doeuff's analysis in *The Sex of Knowing* resists the common practice of reducing the *Declaration* to a demand for suffrage. That later analysis builds on one she began in an article for the *New Left Review* in 1993 where she elaborated happiness as a political theme.[5] After quoting the *Declaration*'s preamble and first resolution,[6] Le Doeuff observes: "what they found in this juridico-political thematization of happiness was a language making it intellectually possible to oppose in a specific way the absolutist oppression to which they were subjected."[7] Le Doeuff does not take her reflections in a uchronic direction in this article, though she developed the method of uchronic history prior to it. She does, however, offer us a frame for applying her method. Le Doeuff writes: "our friends at Seneca Falls added a list of all the legal or social dispositions which they thought ran counter to women's happiness."[8] With this framing, Le Doeuff invites a reading that looks beyond the theme of suffrage to a broader and arguably even more freighted theme of happiness.[9]

Second, we can ask some uchronic questions: What might the world, or at least the United States, be like if those legal and social dispositions had been remediated? What if women's happiness had been valued? We can look to the list of grievances to imagine a world in which they had been redressed. This document also takes us further than the grievances, for it is not just a list of grievances, a valuable sort of list in itself. The *Declaration* also contains resolutions with remedies for the grievances within the current political body. Thus, the resolutions prescribe some of our imaginative work. But because the document uses, to return to Deutscher's language, race elitism and hierarchies as points of appeal, we must also critically examine the possibilities suggested by this text.

In her critique of Taylor and Le Doeuff's reclamation, Deutscher does not discuss the Seneca Falls Convention beyond making an allusion to it. I follow the thread back to the *Declaration* in order to excavate what hierarchies were at work in this influential text. Deutscher notes that for Taylor the equality of women was a matter of racial progress: "That the enfranchisement of women was in America a matter of public meeting was an indication of what was occurring in the 'most civilized and enlightened' portion of the United States."[10] What hierarchies did the women's movement in the United States rely upon, produce, and reinforce?

Because the resolutions seek to remediate the existing political body, it is a document fundamentally different than the *Declaration of Independence*. As Le Doeuff puts the point, "their discourse was not separatist."[11] The *Declaration of Sentiments* did not seek to dissolve political bands. Rather, it sought to transform them. The conventioneers were enlisting men and women alike to reject the rights and claims of sovereignty by one class of subjects over another as the basis for organizing political and social life. The *Declaration* charges that men have been engaged in the project of establishing "absolute tyranny" over women and the grievances are the evidence to establish this problem as one that must be addressed.[12] Yet, as we will become clear, even this vision of tyranny is problematically narrow.

The first grievance, the most contentious, and the one to which the *Declaration* is most often reduced is women's lack of access to the franchise. It reads: "He has never permitted her to exercise her inalienable right to the elective franchise."[13] The *Declaration* returns to this issue in the fourth grievance when it states: "Having deprived her of this first right of a citizen, the elective franchise, thereby leaving her without representation in the halls of legislation, he has oppressed her on all sides."[14] Intervening are two related grievances. First, "He has compelled her to submit to laws, in the formation of which she had no voice."[15] In other words, the lack of enfranchisement is directly linked to being under laws to which one has had no say, through representation or otherwise.

The second intervening grievance between the enfranchisement grievances reads: "He has withheld from her rights which are given to the most ignorant and degraded men—both natives and foreigners."[16] In a sense, this is a reiterative grievance. It underscores that women have been denied access that men have been granted. But the grievance makes this point by highlighting that even foreign and degraded men have been granted civil rights. Here is a hierarchizing point of appeal. There are educated and nondegraded women, the grievance implies, who are being ranked below men of ignorance and degradation in access to civil rights. I return to this grievance and its importance below.

The *Declaration* describes voting as the first right of citizens and connects that right to representation. The *Declaration of Independence* said of the right of representation that it was "formidable to tyrants only." Although we are still far from universal suffrage—children and many felons, even those who have served their time, do not have access, for instance—it may still be difficult to appreciate the radical nature of this grievance. There is no longer any robust public debate about whether women ought to have the right to vote.[17] Imagine, however, if women had been given the right to vote in 1848. What might have happened?

We could wonder how women's votes might have affected the makeup of the Congress that created the Compromise of 1850.[18] Perhaps civil war would not have been delayed and there would have been a war on the heels of the Mexican War. Without the eleven years of industrialization in the North, the outcome of the conflict might have been quite different.[19] This is not, however, the sort of counterfactual speculation that Le Doeuff's method invites. When we ask with Le Doeuff's method what might have happened if women had been granted the vote in 1848, the level of questioning is not about how specific events might have changed. Rather, as when Le Doeuff connects de Gouges's contract to the elimination of domestic abuse, the most salient questions are about how a historically available theoretical innovation in the way we organized our life in common might have changed the structures by which we live.

If voting rights had been granted in 1848 we can imagine, for instance, the expansion of the concept of citizen to account for bodies with the potential to bear and feed infants. There are, nearly one hundred years after the expansion of the suffrage, far from perfect protections for parental leave (or any sort of leave for the care of family members), but the Family Medical Leave Act of 1993 was, in part, the result of women agitating for protections as workers and family members.[20] Had the women in 1848 had their way, industrialization would have taken place in a United States where political bodies would have had to take into account not just women workers, but women voters. There is no guarantee that the most politically powerful women would have prioritized the rights of less powerful workingwomen. Indeed, there is a great deal of evidence from what did happen that they would not.[21] But there would have been many more workers with the right to vote.

Note that the resolutions do not have a one-to-one correspondence with the grievances. Indeed, what takes the conventioneers fifteen grievances to enumerate takes them twelve to resolve. In the ninth resolution, the *Declaration* resolves "that it is the duty of the women of this country to secure to themselves the sacred right of the elective franchise."[22] The franchise is the first among the list of grievances, but not among the first resolved. We have reason to pause over the role that enfranchisement played at the convention and in the women's rights movements.[23] Popularly, First Wave feminists are often portrayed narrowly, as suffragists, with the resulting neat resolution of their cause by the Nineteenth Amendment. But the uchronic method allows us to situate suffrage within a complex conceptualization for social and political change in the *Declaration of Sentiments*.

The eight resolutions that precede the duty to fight for enfranchisement enumerate demands that we are still struggling to meet. Take, for instance, resolution four: "Resolved, that the women of this country ought to be enlightened in regard to the laws under which they live, that they may no longer publish their degradation by declaring themselves satisfied with their present position, nor their ignorance, by asserting that they have all the rights they want."[24] The Equal Rights Amendment would, most likely, have been unnecessary in a world in which the grievances of the *Declaration of Sentiments* had been redressed. Yet, it is worth noting, the antifeminist arguments and activism of people like Phyllis Schlafly, who argued that women would lose privileges if they were given rights equal to men's, were both familiar to the conventioneers and understood as an obstacles to women's true and substantial happiness.[25]

The first two resolutions speak against laws that limit women and thus raise the question of what laws need to be altered or eliminated. The fifth grievance tackles specifically the problem of the status of wives: "He has made her, if married, in the eye of the law, civilly dead."[26] The limitations on wives' ability to own property, have bank accounts, and sign contracts—all marks of civil death—were issues tackled by late-twentieth-century feminists; imagine for a uchronic moment what the world would have been like if these issues had been redressed in 1848. Perhaps the most startling example of civil death, and one that is taking an almost inconceivably long time to address, is the nonrecognition of marital rape.[27] The civil invulnerability of wives to rape was not redressed in all fifty states of the United States until 1993.[28] Naming the civil death of wives while repeatedly avowing men and women's equality creates a basis for laws protecting women's civil rights. That naming and avowal also demand that we consider how women's inequality has been established by and operated through laws. In this grievance, we also face another hierarchizing point of appeal. While white women could experience civil death through marriage, there is not a grievance about women who are born civilly dead because enslaved (indeed, because of their status as civilly dead, these women are not recognized by the state as capable of marrying).

In the seventh grievance, the *Declaration* acknowledges that equality will require greater moral responsibility for wives. That grievance begins: "He has made her morally, an irresponsible being, as she can commit many crimes with impunity, provided they be done in the presence of her husband."[29] In this grievance, however, the conventioneers directly link that lack of moral responsibility to the authority that husbands are granted over their wives. "In the covenant of marriage," the second part of the grievance reads, "she is compelled to promise obedience to her husband, he becoming, to all intents and purposes, her master—the laws giving him power to deprive her of her liberty and to administer chastisement."[30] The *Declaration* clearly links the assumption of moral responsibility with authority. The grievance hedges, "to all intents and purposes," marking a limit to the analogy with the slave master's authority. At work is a common analogy utilized by white women for women's rights that women are treated *like* slaves. The most straightforward problem with this rendering, at least in the absence of another grievance stating this outright, is that some women do have masters, with literal absolute authority. By treating women's situation as analogous to slavery, the *Declaration* positions enslaved women as outside its ambit. As Louise Michele Newman puts the point, "While they might not have believed in black equality, white women's rights activists generally opposed slavery, and they regularly compared 'women's status' (the women here were also assumed to be white) to the 'Negro's' (assumed to be men), leaving out of these comparisons altogether the specific experiences and conditions of black women, both free and enslaved."[31]

Showing an appreciation for the paradoxes of women's subjugation, the *Declaration* demands that men be held to the same high moral standards as women, writing: "Resolved, that the same amount of virtue, delicacy, and refinement of behavior that is required of woman in the social state also be required of man, and the same transgressions should be visited with equal severity on both man and woman."[32] So, while the drafters recognize that wives gain some license in marriage to violate laws—the amount allotted left to the discretion of husbands—the drafters also recognize that women's social behavior is policed to a greater extent than men's. Women are held to a higher standard of decorum. Indeed, in the resolution before, the conventioneers used the attribution of moral superiority to women to claim expanded roles in religious assemblies, thereby turning a means of limiting women's activity into the grounds for expanding it.[33] When the *Declaration* insists that men and women are equal and that there has been a massive failure of the state to enact and protect that equality, they are not simply demanding that women be treated like men. What the *Declaration* demands is a thorough assessment of sexual difference at all levels of public and private life with the understanding that adjustments will have to be made in the expectations everyone faces.[34] The conventioneers directly link that assessment to expanded roles in religious life, as well as employment opportunities, pay, public assemblies and public life more generally, and education.[35]

The right of women to speak in public deserves special attention, for unlike unequal pay for equal work, this may seem like an issue that has been resolved in the course of time. The fact that women spoke in public at the Seneca Falls Convention was, itself, a radical action. Sue Davis devotes a chapter of her book *The Political Thought of Elizabeth Cady Stanton: Women's Rights and the American Political Traditions*, titled "Gatherings of Unsexed Women: Separate Spheres and Women's Rights," to the power of the prohibition on women having a public role in political life. To gather together in public assemblies to hear women speak about anything, let alone women's rights, was scandalous in the mid-nineteenth century.[36] Harriet Beecher Stowe, for instance, advocated for women's suffrage, but maintained that women ought not to speak in public.[37] The *Declaration* specifically addresses this prohibition and its selective application with the seventh resolution: "Resolved, that the objection of indelicacy and impropriety, which is so often brought against women when she addresses a public audience, comes with a very ill grace from those who encourage, by their attendance, her appearance on stage, in the concert, or in feats of the circus."[38] The conventioneers were performing their refusal to be bound by the prohibition on public speaking, thereby exposing the use of the prohibition in preventing the achievement of women and men's equality, but not in preventing women from serving as entertainment.

Try now to imagine the 2008 U.S. presidential election if the *Declaration* had been able to inaugurate a society in which women could not only speak in public, but also publicly act without reflexive censure.[39] Would Hilary Clinton have found her voice only after several decades into her career as a highly visible public person?[40] Would Michelle Obama have been repeatedly described as angry?[41] Would there have been continual discussions, fueled by her own reversals on the issue, of whether or not Sarah Palin was a feminist?[42] While presidential politics may not be exemplary of any other part of life, the rhetorical and analytical habits used during presidential campaigns are. A uchronic analysis of the *Declaration* allows us to think more deeply about the effects of equal access to publicness and equal acceptance of men and women acting in public. Again, the point is not to think the outcomes would have been different, but to highlight how the shaping of women's appearance in public leads to some possibilities and forecloses others. Indeed, the women's movement's role in claiming public forums for women seems to be at the heart of the debate about whether Sarah Palin was a feminist: Perhaps only women who are feminists would speak publicly?

While the conventioneers do not offer a radical reframing of the marriage contract in the manner of their feminist foremother in rewriting declarations, Olympe de Gouges, they were aware that the dissolution of a marriage could be as devastating to a woman's rights as marriage itself.[43] They grieve: "He has so framed the laws of divorce, as to what shall be the proper causes, and in case of separation, to whom the guardianship of the children shall be given, as to be wholly regardless of the happiness of women—the law, in all cases, going upon a false supposition of the supremacy of man, and giving all power into his hands."[44] The conventioneers bring to light how the law unequally distributes protections for relationships of men and women with their dependent children. We can, perhaps, then wonder if divorce reform in the spirit of the *Declaration* could have helped to bring about the sort of protections for dependent children that Le Doeuff imagined as a result of marriage contract reform with de Gouges's critique.

Even without an exhaustive reading of the *Declaration of Sentiments*, the uchronic method helps us bring into focus many aspects of our current social and political structures that perpetuate and depend upon the subordinate treatment of women. Indeed, one of the strengths of the method is that even short forays of the imagination are critically fruitful. The efficacy of this method is directly linked to the extent to which we feel the loss of the *Declaration* as a historical antecedent. By encountering that loss, we are given new ways of framing our narratives about history in which what has been deemed as important, right, or necessary can be seen as the contingent results of political and historiographical contestations about what ought to be the case.

One of the powers of uchronic thinking, like that of utopic thinking, is that for as long as the exercise lasts, our ideals can determine the nature of the world. The danger, however—and this returns us to Deutscher's critique—is that imaginative freedom can obscure the need to think critically about the negative consequences of our ideals. With this warning in mind, let us return to the third grievance of the *Declaration*: "He has withheld from her rights which are given to the most ignorant and degraded men, both natives and foreigners."[45] There are women whose place of birth, education, and refinement are being ignored while less deserving men are civilly recognized. As Angela Davis writes: "The inestimable importance of the Declaration of Sentiments was its role as the *articulated consciousness of women's rights* at midcentury. . . . However, as a rigorous consummation of the consciousness of white middle-class women's dilemma, the Declaration all but ignored the predicament of white working-class women, as it ignored the condition of Black women in the South and North alike."[46] The *Declaration*, while claiming to speak on behalf of women in the United States, Davis observes, hardly reflects the lives of all those women. One way to interpret Davis's claim is that the document does not make explicit demands for improvements for differently situated women, on behalf of slaves, for instance. In fact, Davis writes: "While at least one Black man was present among the Seneca Falls conferees, there was not a single Black woman in attendance. Nor did the convention's documents make even passing reference to Black women. In light of the organizers' abolitionist involvement, it would seem puzzling that slave women were entirely disregarded."[47] Indeed, the document nowhere refers to race. But I think it would be wrong to narrowly interpret Davis's claim to mean that the document's failure was its failure to refer. These conventioneers, at least the ones who were actively involved in abolitionist organizations, knew something about unequal treatment based on race in the United States. The problem that Davis identifies is that the conventioneers failed to imagine, within the *Declaration*, all sorts of differently situated women being denied rights. That is not because these women, many of whom were abolitionists, were unaware of slavery.

Further, this was *Seneca* Falls. Sally Roesch Wagner gives compelling evidence that direct (and documented) experiences of conventioneers with the people and the organizations of the six nations of the Iroquois confederacy were a crucial source for "*a vision not of band-aid reform but of a reconstituted world completely transformed*."[48] The people at Seneca Falls not only saw possibilities for life in common unavailable in their own lives, Wagner argues; they were witness to the erosion of these forms of lives.[49] The conventioneer Matilda Joslyn Gage, for instance, wrote an editorial supporting the Council of Chiefs decision to oppose American citizenship for Iroquois men, linking the government's treatment of the Iroquois and U.S. women.[50] The people gathered at Seneca Falls were not just aware that race mattered deeply in the United States; they were directly involved, sometimes politically, with *how* race mattered. Yet, in a document of grievances, the differences between the grievances of women in different situations went unarticulated.[51]

Indeed, the *Declaration* employs the following construction: "in view of this entire disfranchisement of one-half the people of this country."[52] Much, much more than one-half of the people in the United States were de jure disenfranchised. Large numbers of people, including men who were owned and most men who were indigenous, did not meet the qualifications of citizenship.[53] To that point, we can return to the ninth resolution—"that it is the duty of the women of this country to secure to themselves the sacred right of the elective franchise"—and ask if this was a duty for women who were not recognized as persons, that is, for women whose civil death did not begin at marriage, but at conception. To reiterate Davis's point, the *Declaration* seems to best articulate the claims of women who could, through meeting the myriad qualifications, expect the rights of citizenship but for the fact that they were women.

To paraphrase Deutscher, the point is not to condemn the *Declaration* for a race elitism and hierarchy that were common in the nineteenth century, but neither should a reading of the *Declaration* look away from it. It is worth noting, as Davis does, that organized agitation on the part of women working in factories had been going on for decades prior to the convention and the Grimké sisters, Sarah and Angelina, had long been chastising abolitionist movements for their failures to involve black women and consider their suffering.[54] These facts help us lament a failure of a different kind. If the uchronic exercise helps us to lament the opportunities that were lost with women's voices, then reflection on the uchronic exercise helps us to lament the failure of those voices to articulate a more completely transformed world. There were resources for the drafters of and signatories to the *Declaration* to propose an even more radical vision than they did. We must continually ask: What appears with the radical vision? What undergirds it and makes agitation for the vote, for instance, possible?

We can ask what the connection is, for instance, between contemporary voter suppression and the way early women's rights articulated demands not just for the vote, but also for a changed political structure. How is it that women could gain the vote at the height of Jim Crow segregation, but that change had little meaningful impact on voting access for black men and women? How does that disconnection between dominant articulations of women's rights and black enfranchisement—or, perhaps more pointedly, the connection between dominant articulations of women's rights and white supremacy—continue to operate in contemporary feminist work? To take but one famous example, did Hillary Clinton merely misstep morally, if not at the time politically, in talking about superpredators, or is she also the inheritor of a long-developing understanding that women's rights mean white women's rights?[55]

Before turning to Sojourner Truth, I want to note that Lloyd's method would not set up this two-part process of critical reflection for reclamation. Lloyd understands every thinker as part of a conceptual history that cannot be escaped with even the most rigorous criticism. The conventioneers cannot be the source of a radical break, according to Lloyd's method, because they are bound to think by the metaphors of their times. Those metaphors can be criticized. So, the *Declaration* must be read as a document that shares in the history of the concepts it wields, even as it lodges protests against that history. Thus, Lloyd's approach does not risk obscuring the problems of the document with a focus on critical possibilities it engenders, inasmuch as every document is heir to the problems of its concepts.

The oft-remarked irony about the *Declaration of Independence* is that a slave owner wrote that all men are created equal. There are several strategies for dealing with that irony, including dismissing the entire U.S. American project as one of, to put it mildly, unrepentant hypocrisy. Lloyd offers us a different compelling strategy: namely, by engaging with the vicissitudes of the conceptual history of equality we can avoid a few problems and perhaps think differently than we did before. Lloyd does not offer us a way out of the reliance of conceptualization on metaphor or the accumulation of history in the operation of concepts.

Rather, Lloyd helps us keep those limitations of critique at the forefront of our reading.

"AIN'T I A WOMAN?"

In turning to Truth's Akron speech, I risk reinforcing a long-standing practice within feminism of making arguments through her authority, rather than engaging with her as an authority in her own right. As Roseann M. Mandziuk and Suzanne Pullon Fitch argue, Truth has been transfigured into a metonym.[56] "The metonymic representation heightens the power of Truth as cultural symbol," they argue, "but only when she is used as a narrow container for meanings devoid of specificity."[57] Because of this history, reclamation risks contributing to "the deadly metonymic playfulness" that characterizes Truth's reception for over one hundred years.[58] Through attention to the processes by which metonymic engagements have developed and dominated, however, we can foreground these risks in order to activate other possibilities. Further, we can appreciate how reclamation must always contend with modes of reception that seek to contain and deflect attention away from the speculations of historical actors. In other words, by facing the irreducible risks of ventriloquizing and neutralizing historical texts, we can read for unexpected speculations. We also remain aware that what was once startling and conducive to new thoughts can be worn into confirmation of widely held beliefs.

Feminists have a long history of using Truth's words. As Cheryl Harris has written, "Truth's illiteracy means that the functions of author and writer are split in ways not often contemplated under knowledge systems dominated by writing: Truth was the author but not the writer; they were the writers but not the authors." The "they" in this case are the white women Olive Gilbert, who was Truth's amanuensis for the 1850 edition of the *Narrative of Sojourner Truth*, and Frances Titus, who edited editions of the *Narrative* through the 1870s and 1880s. Harris is referring to the *Narrative* here, but the list of people who wrote Truth's words or represented her speech in her lifetime is quite extensive, including Harriet Beecher Stowe[59] and, of particular importance for my analysis, two people who authored accounts of the Akron speech, Marius Robinson and Frances Dana Gage. John Ernest has called the *Narrative* a fluid text, a term from John Bryant that refers to "any literary work that exists in more than one version."[60] Truth's Akron speech as Gage rendered it is part of the larger fluid text of the *Narrative*, but also functions as an independent fluid text. Robinson's account of the speech, published in the *Anti-Slavery Bugle* in Salem, Ohio, within a month of the Akron meeting, was not included in the *Narrative*, but has been argued to be more authoritative, particularly by Carleton Mabee, Susan Mabee Newhouse, and Nell Painter. This conflict of versions gives us clues to how our archives have been formed, and can feed our speculative engagement, rather than causing us to seek certainty about the most authentic version. And it is worth noting that while my reclamation focuses on the speech as a fluid text, there is much more work to be done on the speech as part of the larger fluid text of the *Narrative*.[61]

Her words have come to us through the hands of many, and to her has been attributed a line so famous that she may not appear in need of reclamation. That line is part of the production of a false intimacy with Truth. In an article written contemporaneously with her biography of Truth, Painter describes the effect of our understanding of this historical actor: "Within the figurative construction of Sojourner Truth, the knowledge she took from slavery seems to reach late twentieth-century audiences directly. It would seem that she spoke and automatically entered historical memory permanently, so that we still hear her a century and a quarter later through her own originating force."[62] While this version of Truth is powerful, Painter describes her as a metonym for "*the* black woman in American history" who has "no education beyond her experience of slavery."[63] So rendered, her power serves a containing acknowledgment that black women have been involved in the history of the United States, but once we have heard the words of a woman enslaved we need look no further.[64]

There is undeniable power in this version of events. Perhaps the most compelling rendering comes from Angela Davis:

> When this Black woman did rise to speak, her answer to the male supremacists also contained a profound lesson for the white women. In repeating her question "Ain't I a Woman?" no less than four times, she exposed the class-bias and racism of the new women's movement. All women were not white and all women did not enjoy the material comfort of the middle classes and the bourgeoisie. Sojourner Truth herself was Black—she was an ex-slave—but she was no less a woman than any of her white sisters at the convention. That her race and economic condition were different from theirs did not annul her womanhood. And as a Black woman, her claim to equal rights was no less legitimate than that of white middle class women.[65]

Davis's analysis has Truth claim the women's movement as her movement, and deny narrower interpretations of "woman," like that supported by the *Declaration of Sentiments*. "Woman" is not just that propertied person being taxed without representation, if single, or losing her property, if married. "Woman" is also that person who was property and, in some places, could not become a wife because she could not be recognized as a person capable of consent. On this reading, as Truth links the claims of the enslaved and formerly enslaved to those of the women's movement by claiming her place within the women's movement, she puts pressure on the concept of citizen at work in the *Declaration*.

How this version of events was available to Davis is important for feminist reclamation to consider carefully. Davis relies on *A History of Woman Suffrage* for the speech, in which Gage's article from 1863 about what happened twelve years earlier is essentially reprinted. Yet, no account of the speech contains that phrase until Gage's article from 1863.[66] In other words, Gage introduces the phrase that Davis takes to be Truth's. Mabee and Mabee Newhouse argue that "The 'Ar'n't I a Woman?' expression, as Gage reported it, was undoubtedly an adaptation of the motto, 'Am I not a Woman and a Sister?,' which had for many years been a popular antislavery motto."[67] To support this claim, Mabee and Mabee Newhouse note that, in addition to the fact that none of the contemporaneous reports of what Truth said contains the phrase, Truth is never reported to have repeated the rhetorical device in her other speeches.[68] Further, Mabee and Mabee Newhouse observe that Gage, not Truth, was given to rhythmic repetitions.[69] Thus, the famous question arises from a white woman's use of Truth's speech.

Davis presents a familiar heroic image of Truth when she writes: "Sojourner Truth single-handedly rescued the Akron women's meeting from the disruptive jeers of hostile men."[70] That is the image most often replicated in late-twentieth-century accounts of Truth's speech at the Women's Convention in Akron, Ohio. Mabee and Mabee Newhouse's research shows that "In fact, none of the twenty-seven descriptions published at the time, despite their many different points of view, gives the impression, as Gage did twelve years later, that there were 'mob-bish' opponents of women's rights present, much less that the convention or its leaders were ever 'staggering,' or about to panic, or about to be overwhelmed by these opponents."[71] Again, the image of a hostile meeting in which misogyny and racism threatened to win the day but for Truth's speech seems to have its origins in Gage's article from 1863. Contemporary accounts, including Gage's and Truth's, do not reflect a tenor of hostility at the meeting, directed at either the women or Truth in particular.[72] Painter succinctly observes: "The antiblack setting, though crucial to latter-day users of Sojourner Truth the symbol, is Gage's creation."[73]

But Gage's version was not always assured such influence on later understandings of Truth. Other accounts of the meeting, including and especially Harriet Beecher Stowe's article from 1863 that seemed to prompt Gage to write her article, received more attention than Gage's account until the latter half of the twentieth century: "It was only in the 1970s and 1980s, in a period of heightened concern about both black and women's rights and the relation between the two, that references to Gage or her article for the first time exceeded references to Stowe or her article."[74] Davis's rendering of events at Akron is from that period of heightened concern. Mabee and Mabee Newhouse write: "As far as is known, no one has seriously attempted to check the accuracy of Gage's account until now."[75]

As compelling as Mabee and Mabee Newhouse's explanation for motivations to turn to Gage's account in the 1970s and 1980s is, the question for reclamation remains *how* that account could supersede those other accounts. Why was Gage's account ready to hand? As I noted above, Davis is relying on the reprint of Gage's article in *A History of Woman Suffrage.* That is one clue to the legitimation of the Gage account. Another is Truth's own apparent endorsement of Gage's rendering through its inclusion in the *Narrative of Sojourner Truth*. Mabee and Mabee Newhouse give two distinct possibilities for why Truth allowed Gage's report to be included in the *Narrative*. First, because Truth could not read she could not check the accuracy of the report. Second, Mabee and Mabee Newhouse speculate that Truth may have felt that the moral message of her speech was retained and "Truth often seemed willing to let friendly myths develop about her, myths that might make her a more fascinating advocate of the causes she supported."[76] The reasons that Mabee and Mabee Newhouse give for Truth's inclusion of Gage's version point to Truth's negotiations of the white supremacist order of her time. Truth's illiteracy and the marketability of slave narratives in the mid-nineteenth century were central factors to Truth dictating her *Narrative* to others, and both were effects of white supremacy.[77] We return, again, to the way the archives from which reclamation works have been shaped.

Which is not to say that Truth's support of friendly myths was not a canny move in a context where unfriendly myths about her were sure to flourish. As Harris observes: "In publicly speaking out against slavery before a white audience, Sojourner Truth marked herself as an exceptional woman. She was not the first to do so—that distinction belonged to Maria Stewart. But like those other few Black women who were allowed to come to voice, Truth too often spoke into a void constructed by prevailing ideologies of womanhood and of race which distorted her story and affected how it was told and understood."[78] Harris calls the white supremacist context into which Truth spoke a void, a description that resonates with "the paradox of non-being" that Spillers uses to describe "the structure of unreality that the black woman must confront."[79] Truth is remembered for words that likely are not hers, but remembered nonetheless. Given what

Davis, among many others, notably bell hooks, has done with the question, and given this project's investment in imaginative reclamation, perhaps there is not really a problem here.[80] Why question this powerful myth in the history of feminism and the United States? Why consider the void into which Truth spoke? Why call this question an effect of the paradox of nonbeing? And why read it all into a cautionary tale for reclamation?

Let's turn to the coda of *Sojourner Truth: A Life, a Symbol* to take one tack for understanding what might be made possible by undermining the authority of Gage's account. There, Nell Painter writes a history of the present that links two lessons she learned from her work on Truth's life and legend: "The symbol of Sojourner Truth is stronger and more essential to our culture than the complicated historic person; and the process that makes a black woman speaking firmly into a show-stopper has not come to an end. I can explain to you the making of the symbol of Sojourner Truth, the electrifying black presence in a white crowd. But I cannot talk you out of the convictions you need to get through life. The symbol we require in our public life still triumphs over scholarship."[81] Painter recounts numerous experiences in which the symbol of Truth triumphs not just over scholarship, but more particularly over Painter's ability to make an argument that her audience can hear. As she describes it, Truth's role as "an electrical presence who terminates debate"[82] is too deeply inscribed for audiences to hear Painter's arguments. The evidence that Painter can marshal for the inauthenticity of Gage's account cannot overcome her audiences' investments in Truth's ability not just to close the discussion with one question, but also to resolve what is at issue in the discussion.[83]

In a description that resonates with Irigaray's critique of teleological approaches to texts and people, examined in chapter 3, Painter writes: "Truth is consumed as a signifier and beloved for what we need her to have said."[84] There is not just intellectual resistance to Painter's argument, but a love for Truth's symbolic function that prevents other modes of engagement with Truth. Truth cannot be engaged as a lover, to use Irigaray's language, but only as an object of love, as beloved. Painter describes a process by which her own words—her arguments about the inauthenticity of Gage's account of Truth—are turned into an electrifying showstopper. The myth of Truth structures Painter's reception. Put another way, Painter records her inability on numerous occasions to overcome the intimacy her audience feels to "Ar'n't I a woman?" in order to speak with authority about Truth's life and thoughts.

Given Painter's narrative of her own experiences presenting her arguments—linking the role that Truth plays to the public space available for Painter to speak—I read the following quotation from Harris, already cited above, with something of a temporal confusion: "The question is how, if at all, does a Black woman, a former slave—a woman officially without a voice—traverse the ground from being an object of property to a subject position in which her voice is self-authenticating and recognized as hers without the seal of white authority? The position of the Black female subject occasions questions of authenticity and authority, because under racial patriarchy, the degree to which a Black woman is permitted to occupy a subject position at all is highly contested."[85] To use Hartman's language, Painter's history of the present in her coda "strives to illuminate the intimacy of our experience with the lives of the dead, to write our now as it is interrupted by this past, and to imagine a *free state*, not as the time before captivity or slavery, but rather as the anticipated future of this writing."[86] How can we read to reclaim Truth in such a way that we create the conditions for Painter's arguments to be heard? A uchronic reading might be helpful here, but of what text?

We cannot simply swap in Robinson's account of Truth's speech as the authentic one. We have reasons to consider it more authentic than Gage's, reasons given to us by the work of Painter and Mabee and Mabee Newhouse, among others, but the fact remains that we do not have a fixed text to rely upon. We have a fluid one. What ought feminist philosophical reclamationists do?

Carla Peterson, to pick one path forward, uses the lack of an authoritative text productively, by reading Robinson's version against Gage's. Robinson, but not Gage, reports that Truth observed: "man is in a tight place, the poor slave is on him, woman is coming on him, he is surely between a hawk and a buzzard."[87] Peterson writes:

> The figurative expression "between hawk and buzzard" is a colloquialism of the dominant culture that suggests a positioning between two sufficiently similar but unpleasant entities that can only lead to indecision or paralysis.[88] Yet "hawk" and "buzzard" are also figures from an African-American folktale in which the two vultures are seen as oppositional and come into conflict in a struggle for survival, the buzzard, a descendant of the powerful African "King Buzzard," always gaining the ascendency. To an African-American audience this colloquialism can be read as the site where the two cultures overlap without converging and makes it possible to see the position of "slave" and "woman" not as symmetrical but as divergent and possibly hostile, thus undermining the kind of coalition that Gage's later 1863 narrative worked so hard to build.[89]

The hawk and the buzzard offer less resolution than Gage's account. Gage concludes: "She had taken us up in her strong arms and carried us safely over the slough of difficulty, turning the whole tide in our favor."[90] In Robinson's version, rather than resolving the difficulties of the meeting, Truth suggests an alliance that does not dissolve the work that differences in women's positions demand. As Teresa Zackodnick glosses Peterson's analysis: "In Robinson's account, Truth asserts the 'difference' race makes within the women's movement. She thereby employs a double voiced strategy to argue that the interests of the 'slave' and 'woman' are often opposed, with the interests of African Americans frequently subordinated to woman's rights."[91]

Peterson's reading suggests there is not *a* woman's voice to be reclaimed in Truth's speech. Truth's speech is critical of the women's rights movement, and the Robinson version does not end in a safe embrace, as Gage's does. Thus, Truth does not simply add her voice to the women's movement. As Naomi Greyser argues of the famous question attributed to Truth by Gage: "This imagined question, posed by a white woman out of feeling for a woman of color, already contains its own reply. The resounding yes, absent textually but registered in the audience's portrayed conversion and the reader's presumed response, invokes a too quick sense of connection and mutual understanding for the sake of a posited white reader."[92] If the resolution is denied, then the gap between Truth's understanding of women's rights and that of the white women who position themselves as the managers of the movement remains open.[93] We have speculative moves within the early women's movement, rather than a woman's voice.

Further, Zackodnik reads Truth into a tradition of speaking that allows her to link women's rights and abolition and, *at the same time*, delink them. Through a double voice strategy, Truth offers a solidarity predicated on differences that are not resolved by the shared project of advocating for women's rights. Truth does not have *a* voice. This reading attends to the authority of Truth's intervention as a destabilizing plurivocality. Reading into the history of contestation over what Truth really said, we have much more than a cautionary tale for feminist reclamation. We have a theorist involved in (at least) two social movements offering, in a single image, an allegory of their tense coalition.[94] We have, as Kazanjian calls it, a speculation: "the comprehension or beholding of the ongoing, dynamic relationship between unities and distinctions."[95]

We should have been prepared for such speculation by the second line Robinson reports of Truth's speech: "I am a woman's rights."[96] Perhaps the material for Gage's famous question, it offers a far less easily resolved interpretive problem than that question. Rather than asserting her belonging to the category of "woman," Truth is much more elliptically claiming *to be* a woman's rights. While Stowe's and Gage's renderings of Truth support a dismissal of this sentence as an error of grammar, Kazanjian via Hegel suggests a disruption of a different sort: "from a speculative perspective the promise and posture of the subject of a sentence is continually 'shaken' or 'upheaved' by a 'movement' so forceful that the formal, grammatical distinction between the subject and the predicate breaks down—'the Subject has passed over the Predicate'—allowing for reconfigurations of the very meaning of any given subject as well as any given predicate."[97]

What if we read Truth's sentence as upheaving? Later, glossing Butler's reading of Hegel's "Substance is Subject," Kazanjian writes: "Speculative thinking, understood according to the figure of the sentence *and* enacted by rhetorical form itself, thus draws one away from the formal, the static, and the abstract, and toward the recursive, the reflexive, the cyclical, and the open."[98] Reading Truth as reconfiguring the "I" of the sentence suggests not only that she is aware of what Harris describes: "The position of the Black female subject occasions questions of authenticity and authority, because under racial patriarchy, the degree to which a Black woman is permitted to occupy a subject position at all is highly contested."[99] Truth also acts within the contest. Truth makes a speculative claim, which we can read uchronically. We can imagine our own time as heir to a different history in which Truth's authority was taken up not to secure the safety of the women's movement, but to think freedom without white supremacy. If Truth is a woman's rights, then maybe the category "wife" cannot be reconceived through analogy to slavery, but only through complex solidarity that points beyond these categories. We could imagine a women's movement in which "the slave" as a rhetorical resource for white women's claims to greater political power faltered when met with claims from those who had experienced enslavement or its continuous threat. To draw from Audre Lorde's metaphor, we can imagine a women's movement capable of giving up that master's tool in order to construct a different house.[100]

So, finally, for now, what if we imagine that Truth's speculation had allowed reconfigurations of the subject and the predicate? Would Gage have inserted herself as host of the proceedings in Akron such that the women's movement has long had a question with which to anesthetize itself from further speculation? Would Truth have been played with as a metonym that resolves the complexities of solidarity before they are allowed to shake or upheave a movement? Would, to pick one example, Ida B. Wells-Barnett have had other work to do as journalist? Could the women's movement have prevented or ended sooner the practice of lynching? As Wells-Barnett so clearly showed: "Crimes against women is the excuse, not the cause."[101] And yet, as Crystal Feimster observes: "white women were all too willing to accept the myth of black rape while ignoring the rape and murder of black women and men."[102] Again, a mirage of safety entranced the women's movement at the expense of the difficult work of freedom. Aligning with white supremacy looked like a path to freedom for some women. But if Truth is a woman's rights, then that path is clearly false. Not just treacherous, not just crooked, but not a path to freedom at all. If woman's rights and Truth as a speaking subject cannot be disentangled, then woman's rights cannot mean only white, born free, or literate. Truth's specificity disrupts the categories of "woman" and "rights," not just once and for all—ain't I a woman?—but in a continuous upheaval that calls us to think again and again about what it means that Truth is a woman's rights.

I am following one possibility opened by Truth's fluid texts. Painter offers another when she argues for reading the photos that Truth had taken of herself and sold as part of her income as providing a more authoritative, if still not unmediated, image. "She appropriated," Painter argues of Truth, "the power of the American gaze and used it in her own mimesis."[103] Painter's compelling reading of the images, which highlights Truth's use of costume, props, angle of gaze, and mode of production, uses Truth's mimesis against practices of metonymic reduction. In an important provocation for reclamation, Painter explains her turn to images: "Working on Sojourner Truth has taught me that if we are to write thoughtful biographies of people who were not highly educated and who did not leave generous caches of personal papers in the archives where historians have traditionally done their work, we will need to develop means of knowing our subjects, and adapt our subjects' ways of making themselves known, that look beyond the written word."[104] Those who have believed that Truth had ways of making herself known have been far less likely to ventriloquize her and far more likely to seek creative means of thinking with her.

CONCLUSION

To be honest, I started researching Sojourner Truth because I thought she thundered out, "Ain't I a Woman?!" to a hostile crowd where no one wanted her to speak, and in so doing she made the women's rights movement better. And I thought my analysis of the *Declaration of Sentiments* would be strengthened by this connection. Painter's *Sojourner Truth* initially read like a terrible setback in my research. Only through developing a more critical uchronic practice did I recognize the speculative gift of Painter's, and thereby Truth's, work. Feminist reclamation cannot will itself out of its history or the history it has inherited from the tradition of philosophy it critiques. As I have argued throughout this book, however, reclamation can critically engage its own practices, how it theorizes exclusion, and the consequences of that theorization for which texts are reclaimed and for how they are reclaimed. There are resources, within and outside feminist philosophy, to support, nurture, and supply methods for this critical work. But there is still an element of choice to taking complex responsibility for the aims and practices of feminist philosophy. The tradition of European and Anglophone philosophy provides an astonishing amount of cover.

By foregrounding the white supremacy of the early women's movement and the legacy of its productive power in shaping the reception of Truth's speech in 1851, I have followed literary scholars in developing a more complex responsibility for and in response to Truth's words. Truth resisted reconciliation. Her participation in the women's movement may have suffered reconciliation at the hands of others, but we have evidence of a much more thoughtful theorist of freedom. She could not, and cannot, guide feminist practice out of white supremacy. This desire is, at least in some forms, a desire of white supremacy, distilled into Gage's image of Truth sweeping white women up in her arms in order to save them. But if we do not engage the past to save us or to legitimate it, then much more speculative, incomplete, and provocative practices become possible. Reclamation becomes a project of making choices about how to engage with the conflicted and complex archives we have, as well as how these archives are limited. By continually seeking to redress exclusions that have and do define the field, reclamation can be a force of transformation. The goal is not, then, arriving at the right interpretation of Truth's work or figuring out her proper place in history. Interpretation and history are ongoing communal practices. Through these communal practices, we can understand our present differently and take responsibility, together, for its continuity with injustices that have made it possible.

Not many people think Truth was a philosopher.[105] Truth, as far as I can tell, never thought about whether or not she was a philosopher. Nor did the women at Seneca Falls, again, as far as I can tell. Le Doeuff first made me aware that securing the title of philosopher, for oneself or someone else, was a powerful mode of distraction from thinking philosophically. Yet, being recognized as a philosopher matters a lot in the discipline in the United States as I am writing this book. For instance, it means being able to work in the field one spent years studying and practicing. But those very real practical concerns do not mean we must endorse the preoccupation. We can imagine philosophy practiced differently. Ladelle McWhorter has recently asked: "Might philosophy be better served if its academic avatar were abolished? Might philosophy flourish if conservative, increasingly corporatized neoliberally politicized academic institutions no longer held it under their control? Instead of focusing on resisting eradication from the academy, perhaps philosophy should seek refuge outside it."[106] Perhaps these questions are not where reclamations of Truth's speech, the *Declaration of Sentiments*, and work by many others who have not been considered philosophers will lead us, but the hopeful prospect, to my mind, is that they could. We could think radically, even if the steps we are able to take practically, at least at the moment, are rather modest.

"How might philosophical living," McWhorter goes on to ask, "including training for it, be best accommodated in light of the prevailing networks of power and levers for resistance and transformation? . . . Where is philosophy livable? And how?"[107] What if we do not foreclose answers to the first question by how the second two must be currently answered? That is, what if we do not let the possibilities for how philosophy might be lived be dictated by where and how European and Anglophone philosophy is currently livable? I have argued that we can think differently—live philosophy in new ways—through treating the work of disregarded historical thinkers as philosophical. Truth imagined life lived differently, through a transformation of injustices that determined where and how life was then livable. Reclaiming Truth can mean more than admiring her as a model; it can mean imaging life lived differently, with and against the thinking she left us.

CONCLUSION

Reclamation and exclusion are intimately linked. Not only has the historical and ongoing exclusion of women from European and Anglophone philosophy made reclamation necessary, but reclamation can also function as a mechanism of exclusion. Reclamation that seeks to transform European and Anglophone philosophy, however, can attend to these dynamics of exclusion. Such attention is necessary for understanding our own times, how we frame our current struggles, and how we could frame them differently through engaging with past thinkers. At the same time, feminist philosophy cannot fully reveal to itself what it owes to its relationship with European and Anglophone philosophy, what metaphors, hierarchies, and norms make feminist philosophy intelligible as philosophy. While we cannot labor under what Penelope Deutscher terms "clearly impossible ideals of transparency," we can seek philosophical engagements that trouble our discussions, that make things uncomfortable and reveal, if only in our defensiveness, what we are holding too close to examine.[1]

We can use reclamation as a practice of problem-finding. Through attention to thinkers excluded, we can become more aware and more critical of how we think. But if we rely on dominant norms and practices of European and Anglophone philosophy to certify a woman as a philosopher, we hone tools of exclusion under the guise of inclusion. Some women's texts might make it onto a syllabus or garner a mention in an encyclopedia. Perhaps a new professional society will be formed. With the good intention of diversifying European and Anglophone philosophy, feminist philosophers can secure the inclusion of some (mostly white) women, while shoring up other modes of exclusion. This pattern is all too common in the history of feminism. I have shown different ways we can recognize and interrupt this pattern to engage in new practices of speculative engagement with historical thinkers. But reworking the past is never done.

Because that reworking is never done, I risk concluding with an incomplete gesture. I begin to take some account of a process of violent exclusion upon which this book is built: settler colonialism. In the last chapter, I read Sojourner Truth's Akron speech in 1851 as a philosophical authority in the early women's movement with vital speculations on the nature of freedom. Now, we need to look at a central problem within her thinking on freedom. During Reconstruction, Sojourner Truth advocated for western lands for freed slaves.[2] Nell Irvin Painter describes Truth's search for relief from the desperate circumstances of the refugee freedpeople she saw and worked with in Washington, DC: "The federal government, she knew, had allotted millions of acres to Indian tribes and railroad companies. Why not put some of this land at the disposition of needy freedpeople, where they could 'work and earn their own living?'"[3] Painter's framing of Truth's solution is telling. Put this way, the U.S. federal government has rightful sovereignty over land it dispenses to Indian tribes, corporations, and now, perhaps, people freed from slavery. "Indian tribes" become another entity upon which land as property can be conferred.

The settler colonialism of Truth's vision and that of Painter's description are linked. Even as each works to envision freedom from within slavery and its afterlife, the territory of freedom is conceived as empty and allottable by the United States at its discretion.[4] That conception of land as property is the sine qua non of settler colonialism. Eve Tuck and K. Wayne Yang write:

> Within settler colonialism, the most important concern is land/water/air/subterranean earth (land, for shorthand, in this article). Land is what is most valuable, contested, required. This is both because the settlers make Indigenous land their new home and source of capital, and also because the disruption of Indigenous relationships to land represents a profound epistemic, ontological, cosmological violence. This violence is not temporally contained in the arrival of the settler but is reasserted each day of occupation. This is why Patrick Wolfe emphasizes that settler colonialism is a structure and not an event. In the process of settler colonialism, land is remade into property and human relationships to land are restricted to the relationship of the owner to his property. Epistemological, ontological, and cosmological relationships to land are interred, indeed made pre-modern and backward. Made savage.[5]

We can understand why Truth and Painter retain this vision of freedom, since that vision of freedom through the ownership of land is central to the dominant settler colonial contexts in which they struggle for justice. But in our philosophical engagements, we must attend to this replication of colonial violence in the demands of those fighting slavery and its afterlives.[6] We can question visions of freedom that conceive of the territory currently occupied by the United States as properly the domain of the United States. We can point to the ongoing work of genocide in that conception. And we can envision not just the abolition of academic philosophy in the United States, suggested in the last chapter, but also the abolition of the United States.[7]

I would rather Truth had gotten everything right and that we just needed to read her carefully enough to understand how to practice freedom. Like us, however, Truth drew on imperfect resources to speculate on freedom. And her speculative practice made powerful demands for justice that also recapitulated modes of injustice. Many records we have of Truth's words suggest that she understood, as Tuck and Yang write, that "Solidarity is an uneasy, reserved, and unsettled matter that neither reconciles present grievances nor forecloses future conflict."[8] Indeed, part of my privileging of Robinson's account of the Akron speech in 1851 was the clear resistance to reconciliation Truth offered in it. But Truth, at least so far as we know, did not appreciate the incommensurability of dreaming of land as freedom, on the one hand, with the struggle against settler colonialism, on the other, that "requires the abolition of land as property."[9] That is, it appears that Truth's speculations on freedom were not so unsettled as to be decolonial. The point, to repurpose Deutscher's quotation once more, is not to condemn Truth for a settler colonial imagination that was common in the nineteenth century, but neither should a reading of Truth look away from it.[10]

This critique of Truth's vision extends to a critique of Painter's mode of engaging with Truth. In the last chapter, I emphasized Painter's struggle to engage with Truth beyond the legend in part to illustrate how dominant modes of telling the past can prevent us from reading texts more speculatively or listening to others when they engage in such speculations. We need, I argued, these speculative engagements so that we can think freedom differently now. The question of my conclusion is, how can we critique those speculations for the problems and hierarchies upon which they depend? I am repeating the move of critical reclamation that structured my reading of the *Declaration of Sentiments*. Because we cannot merely look for the inspiring ideals, but must also seek what makes the ideals possible, we must, again, upheave our understanding to pursue "the ongoing, dynamic relationship between unities and distinctions."[11] That is, we must speculate.

One place to look for decolonial reclamation is Sarah Deer's work. In her book on ending sexual violence in Native America, Sarah Deer recounts the formation of an archive of Mvskoke law through federal colonial policy. Deer does not claim that this version of the law is a pure artifact of precontact law making. The fact that the law was written down is already an indication that the Mvskoke are negotiating invasion.[12] Rather she seeks clues to precolonial ways of life through these records in order to strengthen practices that will end sexual violence in Native America.[13] Deer also resists romanticizing precolonial forms of life as feminist ideals to which we should try to return.[14] Rather, Deer is reclaiming precolonial resources, and examining contemporary tribal court practices that draw on native traditions, to develop new responses to gendered violence. Deer characterizes this work as an "ethic of decolonization" that reclaims and builds indigenous feminisms.[15]

It may be that what Deer is doing amounts to what Tuck and Yang call "settler harm reduction," which "is to reduce the harm that white supremacy has had on white people, and the deep harm it has caused non-white people over generations."[16] With her analysis of tribal court practices that draw on indigenous epistemic and legal resources, Deer is "resuscitat[ing] . . . practices and intellectual life outside of settler ontologies."[17] But Tuck and Yang are clear: "Until stolen land is relinquished, critical consciousness does not translate into action that disrupts settler colonialism."[18] In other words, to disrupt and dismantle settler colonialism, we must not only understand it and envision its demise, but land as property must also be abolished, along with the settlements that build on that ontology. Deer's engagements offer one model for how feminist reclamation can engage in decolonial critique and the resuscitation of other possibilities, not instead of abolishing land as property, but perhaps as steps in that undertaking.

There is no easy reconciliation of Truth's dream of land for freedpeople and the ethic of decolonization developed and being developed by Deer, Tuck, Yang, and many others.[19] "Reconciliation," Tuck and Yang argue, "is about rescuing settler normalcy, about rescuing a settler future."[20] As I have argued throughout the book, we may be tempted to produce apparent reconciliations, the way paved by others before us. In legends of people no longer here to insist that their strong arms will not carry us over the slough of difficulty, we can anesthetize ourselves against the ongoing conflicts that are the work of freedom. But feminist philosophical reclamation can choose a more complex responsibility through engagements with historical texts that upheave not only how we practice European and Anglophone philosophy, but also how we conceive the goals of feminism. The possibilities are, as Tuck and Yang insist, literally unsettling. To paraphrase Hortense Spillers, only from certain points of view are these possibilities understood as chaos.[21]

Appendix A

THE DECLARATION OF SENTIMENTS AND RESOLUTIONS

When, in the course of human events, it becomes necessary for one portion of the family of man to assume among the people of the earth a position different from that which they have hitherto occupied, but one to which the laws of nature and of nature's God entitle them, a decent respect to the opinions of mankind requires that they should declare the causes that impel them to such a course.

We hold these truths to be self-evident: that all men and women are created equal; that they are endowed by their Creator with certain inalienable rights; that among these are life, liberty, and the pursuit of happiness; that to secure these rights governments are instituted, deriving their just powers from the consent of the governed. Whenever any form of government becomes destructive of these ends, it is the right of those who suffer from it to refuse allegiance to it, and to insist upon the institution of a new government, laying its foundation on such principles, and organizing its powers in such form, as to them shall seem most likely to effect their safety and happiness.

Prudence, indeed, will dictate that governments long established should not be changed for light and transient causes; and, accordingly, all experience has shown that mankind are more disposed to suffer, while evils are sufferable, than to right themselves by abolishing the forms to which they were accustomed. But when a long train of abuses and usurpations, pursuing invariably the same object, evinces a design to reduce them under absolute despotism, it is their duty to throw off such government and to provide new guards for their future security. Such has been the patient sufferance of the women under this government, and such is now the necessity which constrains them to demand the equal station to which they are entitled.

The history of mankind is a history of repeated injuries and usurpations on the part of man toward woman, having in direct object the establishment of an absolute tyranny over her. To prove this, let facts be submitted to a candid world.

He has never permitted her to exercise her inalienable right to the elective franchise.

He has compelled her to submit to law in the formation of which she had no voice.

He has withheld from her rights which are given to the most ignorant and degraded men, both natives and foreigners.

Having deprived her of this first right as a citizen, the elective franchise, thereby leaving her without representation in the halls of legislation, he has oppressed her on all sides.

He has made her, if married, in the eye of the law, civilly dead.

He has taken from her all right in property, even to the wages she earns.

He has made her morally, an irresponsible being, as she can commit many crimes with impunity, provided they be done in the presence of her husband. In the covenant of marriage, she is compelled to promise obedience to her husband, he becoming, to all intents and purposes, her master—the law giving him power to deprive her of her liberty and to administer chastisement.

He has so framed the laws of divorce, as to what shall be the proper causes and, in case of separation, to whom the guardianship of the children shall be given, as to be wholly regardless of the happiness of the women—the law, in all cases, going upon a false supposition of the supremacy of man and giving all power into his hands.

After depriving her of all rights as a married woman, if single and the owner of property, he has taxed her to support a government which recognizes her only when her property can be made profitable to it.

He has monopolized nearly all the profitable employments, and from those she is permitted to follow, she receives but a scanty remuneration. He closes against her all the avenues to wealth and distinction which he considers most honorable to himself. As a teacher of theology, medicine, or law, she is not known.

He has denied her the facilities for obtaining a thorough education, all colleges being closed against her.

He allows her in church, as well as state, but a subordinate position, claiming apostolic authority for her exclusion from the ministry, and, with some exceptions, from any public participation in the affairs of the church.

He has created a false public sentiment by giving to the world a different code of morals for men and women, by which moral delinquencies which exclude women from society are not only tolerated but deemed of little account in man.

He has usurped the prerogative of Jehovah himself, claiming it as his right to assign for her a sphere of action, when that belongs to her conscience and to her God.

He has endeavored, in every way that he could, to destroy her confidence in her own powers, to lessen her self-respect, and to make her willing to lead a dependent and abject life.

Now, in view of this entire disfranchisement of one-half the people of this country, their social and religious degradation, in view of the unjust laws above mentioned, and because women do feel themselves aggrieved, oppressed, and fraudulently deprived of their most sacred rights, we insist that they have immediate admission to all the rights and privileges which belong to them as citizens of the United States.

In entering upon the great work before us, we anticipate no small amount of misconception, misrepresentation, and ridicule; but we shall use every instrumentality within our power to effect our object. We shall employ agents, circulate tracts, petition the state and national legislatures, and endeavor to enlist the pulpit and the press in our behalf. We hope this Convention will be followed by a series of conventions embracing every part of the country.

RESOLUTIONS

Whereas, the great precept of nature is conceded to be that "man shall pursue his own true and substantial happiness." Blackstone in his Commentaries remarks that this law of nature, being coeval with mankind and dictated by God himself, is, of course, superior in obligation to any other. It is binding over all the globe, in all countries and at all times; no human laws are of any validity if contrary to this, and such of them as are valid derive all their force, and all their validity, and all their authority, mediately and immediately, from this original; therefore,

Resolved, that such laws as conflict, in any way, with the true and substantial happiness of woman, are contrary to the great precept of nature and of no validity, for this is "superior in obligation to any other."

Resolved, that all laws which prevent woman from occupying such a station in society as her conscience shall dictate, or which place her in a position inferior to that of man, are contrary to the great precept of nature and therefore of no force or authority.

Resolved, that woman is man's equal, was intended to be so by the Creator, and the highest good of the race demands that she should be recognized as such.

Resolved, that the women of this country ought to be enlightened in regard to the laws under which they live, that they may no longer publish their degradation by declaring themselves satisfied with their present position, nor their ignorance, by asserting that they have all the rights they want.

Resolved, that inasmuch as man, while claiming for himself intellectual superiority, does accord to woman moral superiority, it is preeminently his duty to encourage her to speak and teach, as she has an opportunity, in all religious assemblies.

Resolved, that the same amount of virtue, delicacy, and refinement of behavior that is required of woman in the social state also be required of man, and the same transgressions should be visited with equal severity on both man and woman.

Resolved, that the objection of indelicacy and impropriety, which is so often brought against woman when she addresses a public audience, comes with a very ill grace from those who encourage, by their attendance, her appearance on the stage, in the concert, or in feats of the circus.

Resolved, that woman has too long rested satisfied in the circumscribed limits which corrupt customs and a perverted application of the Scriptures have marked out for her, and that it is time she should move in the enlarged sphere which her great Creator has assigned her.

Resolved, that it is the duty of the women of this country to secure to themselves their sacred right to the elective franchise.

Resolved, that the equality of human rights results necessarily from the fact of the identity of the race in capabilities and responsibilities.

Resolved, that the speedy success of our cause depends upon the zealous and untiring efforts of both men and women for the overthrow of the monopoly of the pulpit, and for the securing to woman an equal participation with men in the various trades, professions, and commerce.

Resolved, therefore, that, being invested by the Creator with the same capabilities and same consciousness of responsibility for their exercise, it is demonstrably the right and duty of woman, equally with man, to promote every righteous cause by every righteous means; and especially in regard to the great subjects of morals and religion, it is self-evidently her right to participate with her brother in teaching them, both in private and in public, by writing and by speaking, by any instrumentalities proper to be used, and in any assemblies proper to be held; and this being a self-evident truth growing out of the divinely implanted principles of human nature, any custom or authority adverse to it, whether modern or wearing the hoary sanction of antiquity, is to be regarded as a self-evident falsehood, and at war with mankind.

Appendix B

PRINTED VERSIONS OF SOJOURNER TRUTH'S SPEECH AT THE WOMEN'S RIGHTS CONVENTION IN 1851 IN AKRON, OHIO

SOJOURNER TRUTH'S SPEECH AS REPORTED BY MARCUS ROBINSON IN THE ISSUE OF THE *ANTI-SLAVERY BUGLE* FROM JUNE 21, 1851

I want to say a few words about this matter. I am a woman's rights. I have as much muscle as any man, and can do as much work as any man. I have plowed and reaped and husked and chopped and mowed, and can any man do more than that? I have heard much about the sexes being equal. I can carry as much as any man, and can eat as much too, if I can get it. I am as strong as any man that is now. As for intellect, all I can say is, if a woman have a pint, and a man a quart—why can't she have her little pint full? You need not be afraid to give us our rights for fear we will take too much,—for we can't take more than our pint'll hold. The poor men seems to be all in confusion, and don't know what to do. Why children, if you have woman's rights, give it to her and you will feel better. You will have your own rights, and they won't be so much trouble. I can't read, but I can hear. I have heard the bible and have learned that Eve caused man to sin. Well, if woman upset the world, do give her a chance to set it right side up again. The Lady has spoken about

Jesus, how he never spurned woman from him, and she was right. When Lazarus died, Mary and Martha came to him with faith and love and besought him to raise their brother. And Jesus wept and Lazarus came forth. And how came Jesus into the world? Through God who created him and the woman who bore him. Man, where was your part? But the women are coming up blessed be God and a few of the men are coming up with them. But man is in a tight place, the poor slave is on him, woman is coming on him, he is surely between a hawk and a buzzard.[1]

THE SPEECH AS REPORTED IN *NARRATIVE OF SOJOURNER TRUTH* BASED ON THE ACCOUNT IN FRANCES GAGE'S *NATIONAL ANTI-SLAVERY STANDARD* ARTICLE FROM MAY 2, 1863

The leaders of the movement trembled on seeing a tall, gaunt black woman, in a gray dress and white turban, surmounted by an uncouth sun-bonnet, march deliberately into the church, walk with the air of a queen up the aisle, and take her seat upon the pulpit steps. A buzz of disapprobation was heard all over the house, and such words as these fell upon listening ears:—

"An abolition affair!" "Woman's rights and niggers!" "We told you so!" "Go it, old darkey!"

I chanced upon that occasion to wear my first laurels in public life as president of the meeting. At my request, order was restored and the business of the hour went on. The morning session was held; the evening exercises came and went. Old Sojourner, quiet and reticent as the "Libyan Statue," sat crouched against the wall on the corner of the pulpit stairs, her sun-bonnet shading her eyes, her elbows on her knees, and her chin resting upon her broad, hard palm. At intermission she was busy, selling "The

Life of Sojourner Truth," a narrative of her own strange and adventurous life. Again and again timorous and trembling ones came to me and said with earnestness, "Do n't let her speak, Mrs. Gage, it will ruin us. Every newspaper in the land will have our cause mixed with abolition and niggers, and we shall be utterly denounced." My only answer was, "We shall see when the time comes."

The second day the work waxed warm. Methodist, Baptist, Episcopal, Presbyterian, and Universalist ministers came in to hear and discuss the resolutions presented. One claimed superior rights and privileges for man on the ground of superior intellect; another, because of the manhood of Christ. "If God had desired the equality of woman, he would have given some token of his will through the birth, life, and death of the Saviour." Another gave us a theological view of the sin of our first mother. There were few women in those days that dared to "speak in meeting," and the august teachers of the people were seeming to get the better of us, while the boys in the galleries and the sneerers among the pews were hugely enjoying the discomfiture, as they supposed, of the "strong minded." Some of the tender-skinned friends were on the point of losing dignity, and the atmosphere of the convention betokened a storm.

Slowly from her seat in the corner rose Sojourner Truth, who, till now, had scarcely lifted her head. "Do n't let her speak!" gasped half a dozen in my ear. She moved slowly and solemnly to the front, laid her old bonnet at her feet, and turned her great, speaking eyes to me. There was a hissing sound of disapprobation above and below. I rose and announced "Sojourner Truth," and begged the audience to keep silence for a few moments. The tumult subsided at once, and every eye was fixed on this almost Amazon form, which stood nearly six feet high, head erect, and eye piercing the upper air, like one in a dream. At her first word, there was a profound hush. She spoke in deep tones, which, though not loud, reached every ear in the house, and away through the throng at the doors and windows:—

"Wall, chilern, whar dar is so much racket dar must be somethin' out o' kilter. I tink dat 'twixt de niggers of de Souf and de womin at de Norf, all talkin' 'bout rights, de white men will be in a fix pretty soon. But what's all dis here talkin' 'bout?"

"Dat man ober dar say dat womin needs to be helped into carriages, and lifted ober ditches, and to hab de best place everywhar. Nobody eber helps me into carriages, or ober mud-puddles, or gibs me any best place!" And raising herself to her full height, and her voice to a pitch like rolling thunder, she asked. "And ain't I a woman? Look at me! Look at my arm! (and she bared her right arm to the shoulder, showing her tremendous muscular power). I have ploughed, and planted, and gathered into barns, and no man could head me! And ain't I a woman? I could work as much and eat as much as a man—when I could get it—and bear de lash as well! And ain't I a woman? I have borne thirteen chilern, and seen 'em mos' all sold off to slavery, and when I cried out with my mother's grief, none but Jesus heard me! And ain't I a woman?"

"Den dey talks 'bout dis ting in de head; what dis dey call it?" ("Intellect," whispered someone near.) "Dat's it, honey. What's dat got to do wid womin's rights or nigger's rights? If my cup won't hold but a pint, and yourn holds a quart, wouldn't ye be mean not to let me have my little half-measure full?" And she pointed her significant finger, and sent a keen glance at the minister who had made the argument. The cheering was long and loud.

"Den dat little man in back dar, he say women can't have as much rights as men, 'cause Christ wan't a woman! Whar did your Christ come from?" Rolling thunder couldn't have stilled that crowd, as did those deep, wonderful tones, as she stood there with out-stretched arms and eyes of fire. Raising her voice still louder, she repeated, "Whar did your Christ come from? From God and a woman! Man had nothin' to do wid Him."

Oh, what a rebuke that was to that little man. Turning again to another objector, she took up the defense of Mother Eve. I can not follow her through it all. It was pointed, and witty, and solemn; eliciting at almost every sentence deafening applause; and she ended by asserting:

"If de fust woman God ever made was strong enough to turn de world upside down all alone, dese women togedder (and she glanced her eye over the platform) ought to be able to turn it back, and get it right side up again! And now dey is asking to do it, de men better let 'em." Long-continued cheering greeted this. "'Bleeged to ye for hearin' on me, and now ole Sojourner han't got nothin' more to say."

Amid roars of applause, she turned to her corner, leaving more than one of us with streaming eyes and hearts beating with gratitude. She had taken us up in her strong arms and carried us safely over the slough of difficulty, turning the whole tide in our favor. I have never in my life seen anything like the magical influence that subdued the mobbish spirit of the day and turned the jibes and sneers of an excited crowd into notes of respect and admiration. Hundreds rushed up to shake hands, and congratulate the glorious old mother and bid her God speed on her mission of 'testifying again concerning the wickedness of this 'ere people.[2]

NOTES

INTRODUCTION

1. Alain de Botton, *The Consolations of Philosophy* (New York: Vintage, 2000), 7–8.
2. There is a growing literature in this area, some of the highlights include Sally Haslanger, "Changing the Ideology and Culture of Philosophy: Not by Reason (Alone)," *Hypatia* 23, no. 2 (2008): 210–223; Jennifer Saul, "Implicit Bias, Stereotype Threat, and Women in Philosophy," *Women in Philosophy: What Needs to Change* (2013): 39–60; Molly Paxton, Carrie Figdor, and Valerie Tiberius, "Quantifying the Gender Gap: An Empirical Study of the Underrepresentation of Women in Philosophy," *Hypatia* 27, no. 4 (2012): 949–957; Peggy DesAutels, "Is the Climate Any Warmer for Women in Philosophy?," *APA Newsletter for Feminism and Philosophy* 11, no. 1 (2011): 4–7.
3. Michèle Le Doeuff, *The Philosophical Imaginary* (London: Continuum, 2002), 102.
4. Le Doeuff, 103.
5. While the term "blind spot" refers to a part of a seeing eye where the optic nerve attaches, the metaphor relies on the association of blindness with something undesirable. The implication of the metaphor is that the problem with philosophical practice is where it fails to operate normatively. Alcoff's point, however, is that the norms of philosophy are the problem. In other words, the metaphor marginalizes people with disabilities while also misconstruing Alcoff's point.

   Disability scholars, such as Vivian May, Beth Ferri, Sami Schalk, and Amy Vidali, have critiqued the use of metaphors in feminist scholarship that align disability with what is undesirable or in need of overcoming. Vivian M. May and Beth A. Ferri, "Fixated on Ability: Questioning Ableist Metaphors in Feminist Theories of Resistance," *Prose Studies* 27, nos. 1–2 (2005): 120–140; Sami Schalk, "Metaphorically Speaking: Ableist Metaphors in Feminist Writing," *Disability Studies Quarterly* 33, no. 4 (2013): 1–21; Amy Vidali, "Seeing What We Know: Disability and Theories of Metaphor," *Journal of Literary and Cultural Disability Studies* 4, no. 1 (2010): 33–54. As Schalk argues: "feminists should strive to develop ways in which to talk and write about the damage done by patriarchy that do not simplistically, negatively, and detrimentally associate and even conflate that 'damage' with disability" (4). I try to mark all such metaphors in the quotations I use, as well as endeavor to employ nonableist metaphors, in recognition of this history within feminism and as a small step in redressing these exclusionary practices.

6. Linda Alcoff, "Is the Feminist Critique of Reason Rational?," *Philosophic Exchange* 26 (1996): 62.
7. Hortense Spillers, "Interstices: A Small Drama of Words," in *Black, White, and in Color: Essays on American Literature and Culture* (Chicago: University of Chicago Press, 2003), 159.
8. See also Joan Wallach Scott, *Gender and the Politics of History* (New York: Columbia University Press, 1999); Judith Butler, "Against Proper Objects. *Introduction*," *differences: A Journal of Feminist Cultural Studies* 6, nos. 2–3 (1994): 1–26; and Biddy Martin, "Sexualities Without Genders and Other Queer Utopias," *Diacritics* 24, nos. 2–3 (Summer-Autumn, 1994), 104–121.
9. I have thought many times that this book should argue for giving up the term "reclamation" for a word that has never meant "The action of civilizing a people considered wild or savage; the removing or saving of a people *from* a way of life considered as uncivilized." The word has also meant "The action of protesting, objecting, or of expressing disapproval; opposition, disagreement; an instance of this, *esp.* a formal objection. ("reclamation, n.," *OED Online*, June 2017, Oxford University Press, http://o-www.oed.com.skyline.ucdenver.edu/view/Entry/159603?redirectedFrom=reclamation). Rather than having a settled view, I have used the term I found when I began this research.
10. Spillers, "Interstices," 158.
11. Indeed, the scope of this book is almost entirely limited to work from Europe and the English-speaking world. While some reclamationists

in the Western tradition have engaged women philosophers from beyond this narrow range of traditions—Therese Boos Dykeman, whose work I discuss below, for instance—the scope of reclamation in European and Anglophone philosophy has been consequentially shaped by this Eurocentric boundary setting. Reclamation, I am rather lately coming to understand, can and should be a force for questioning this boundary and dismantling it. Jay L. Garfield and Bryan W. Van Norden argue that philosophy departments in the United States systematically neglect traditions of philosophy from the vast majority of the world, and in the face of the intractability of many departments to do something about this, they counsel: "let's be honest, face reality and call departments of European-American Philosophy what they really are." Jay L. Garfield and Bryan W. Van Norden, "If Philosophy Won't Diversify, Let's Call It What It Really Is," *The Stone* blog, *New York Times*, May 11, 2016. Given the shape of reclamation so far, I have opted to talk about European and Anglophone philosophy in this book, rather than philosophy.

12. Ethel Smyth is represented by a grand piano. Truth's place setting shows three faces, as well as a raised hand and breasts.
13. Spillers, "Interstices," 156.
14. Spillers, 157.
15. Spiller, 156.
16. Indeed, it is not clear that by creating a vulva place setting for Truth, Chicago could attend to Spiller's critique. Or rather, it seems clear such a place setting could not, given the still potent historical practices of displaying black women's bodies as chattel.

    Further, the use of a party of vulvas as a metonym for women risks underwriting a longstanding patriarchal norm of female embodiment that trans and disability theory has shown to be a significant means of limitation and control. For a discussion of *The Dinner Party* specifically, see Kim Q. Hall, "Queerness, Disability, and *The Vagina Monologues*," *Hypatia* 20, no. 1 (2005): 99–119.

    Thank you to Nicole A. Spigner for discussion of, as you put it, "a very intricate set of complications."
17. Audre Lorde, "The Master's Tools Will Never Dismantle the Master's House," in *Sister Outsider: Essays and Speeches by Audre Lorde* (Freedom: Crossing, 1984), 111.
18. Luis E. Navia, *The Socratic Presence: A Study of the Sources* (New York: Garland, 1993), 144.

19. A. E. Taylor, *Plato: The Man and His Work* (London: Methuen, 1969), 224.
20. Taylor, 225. Waithe argues that Taylor is wrong in treating Diotima's speech in such a manner. Waithe argues against Taylor's reading strategy to claim not only Diotima's historicity, but her philosophical authority. To do so, as mentioned above, Waithe reconstructs argumentative differences between Diotima and both Plato and Socrates.
21. Martha C. Nussbaum, *The Fragility of Goodness: Luck and Ethics in Greek Tragedy and Philosophy* (Cambridge: Cambridge University Press, 2001), 177.
22. Hunter here alludes to the oft-made observation that Diotima's arguments respond to the views earlier expressed in the dialogue by Aristophanes. Thus, if we are to believe that Socrates is giving us an accurate account of Diotima's speech, she anticipated Aristophanes's views by a quarter century. David Halperin, for instance, argues: "The textual strategies of the *Symposium* reveal Diotima's fictionality as much as they conceal it. Plato hints that Sokrates has—if not simply invented Diotima out of whole cloth—at least shaped the doctrine he ascribes to suit the needs of the present occasion. . . . He . . . has Diotima rebut the view of *eros* that Aristophanes had articulated a few minutes earlier, on the same evening as his own speech (205d–206a)." David Halperin, "Why Is Diotima a Woman? Platonic Eros and the Figuration of Gender," in *Before Sexuality: The Construction of Erotic Experience in the Ancient Greek World*, ed. David Halperin, John Winkler, and Froma Zeitlin (Princeton: Princeton University Press, 1990), 292. That Socrates or Plato may have taken liberties with Diotima's view in this context is an important complexity for reclamation to address, and one that I will argue can only be met through imaginative engagement with Diotima's philosophical authority.
23. Richard Hunter, *Plato's Symposium* (Oxford: Oxford University Press, 2004), 81.
24. The concept of resilience I am relying on here comes from Kristie Dotson, who describes a kind of oppression arising not solely from social or political factors, but also from epistemological systems that resist changes, despite evidence of significant gaps in the system. See Dotson, "Conceptualizing Epistemic Oppression," *Social Epistemology: A Journal of Knowledge, Culture, and Policy* 28, no. 2 (2014): 130.
25. Margaret Urban Walker, "Diotima's Ghost: The Uncertain Place of Feminist Philosophy in Professional Philosophy," *Hypatia* 20, no. 3 (Summer 2005): 155.

26. As Penny A. Weiss observes of the abundance of historical women who wrote political theory: "What we are faced with is not the absence of writings—they exist in gratifying abundance. The seemingly intractable problems include, instead, failure to keep works by women theorists in print, paucity of academic commentary on the texts, an unmistakable pattern of underestimation and careless analysis in the few judgments on those cases scholars have rendered, and omission of women philosophers in standard college courses." Weiss, *Canon Fodder: Historical Women Political Thinkers* (University Park: Pennsylvania University Press, 2009), xiii.
27. The way I develop the concept of transformation throughout this book is deeply indebted to Elizabeth Minnich, *Transforming Knowledge* (Philadelphia: Temple University Press, 2005).

1. RECLAMATION STRATEGIES

For this chapter, I have drawn freely on material published as "From the Exclusion of Women to the Transformation of Philosophy: Reclamation and Its Possibilities," in *Metaphilosophy* 45, no. 1 (January 2014): 1–18. Used with permission.

1. Waithe is often credited by feminist philosophers for making the pioneering contribution to the field of reclamation. See, for example, Linda Lopez McAllister, "On the Possibility of Feminist Philosophy," *Hypatia* 9, no. 2 (1994): 188–196, 192; Eileen O'Neill, "Early Modern Women Philosophers and the History of Philosophy," *Hypatia* 20, no. 3 (Summer 2005): 185–197, 188; Karen J. Warren, *An Unconventional History of Western Philosophy: Conversations Between Men and Women Philosophers* (Lanham, MD: Rowman and Littlefield, 2009), xiii. In *Historical Dictionary of Feminist Philosophy*, Catherine Gardner notes that Waithe's volume is "incomparably the best" for information on women in the history of philosophy. Catherine Villaneuva Gardner, *Historical Dictionary of Feminist Philosophy* (Lanham, MD: Scarecrow, 2006), 240.
2. In *The Blackwell Guide to Feminist Philosophy*, Eileen O'Neill's "Justifying the Inclusion of Women in Our Histories of Philosophy: The Case of Marie de Gournay," offers a particularly good overview of these projects. O'Neill, "Justifying the Inclusion of Women in Our Histories of Philosophy: The Case of Marie de Gournay," in *The Blackwell Guide to Feminist Philosophy*, edited by Linda Martín Alcoff and Eva Feder Kittay, 17–42 (Malden, MA: Blackwell, 2007).

3. Mary Ellen Waithe, *A History of Women Philosophers*, vol. 1 (Dordrecht: Kluwer Academic, 1987), xii.
4. Mary Warnock, *Women Philosophers* (London: Orion, 1996), xxx.
5. Waithe, *A History*, xviii.
6. Warnock, *Women Philosophers*, xxxiii. I take it that Warnock uses this term as a gesture to the genealogy of feminist questions, rather than a historical conflation of periods in the negotiations of the category of "women."
7. Waithe, *A History*, x.
8. Waithe, xix.
9. Waithe, x.
10. Waithe, xii.
11. Waithe, xi.
12. Waithe, x.
13. Waithe, xii.
14. Waithe, xii.
15. Waithe, xii.
16. Waithe, xiii.
17. Waithe, xviii.
18. Waithe, xviii.
19. Waithe writes: "I was never going to include Diotima in these volumes. Everyone knew that she was a fictional character in a platonic dialogue. Then, I decided to try and find out. After all, what if everyone were wrong? . . . We are philosophers, and questioning, doubting, is what we are supposed to do well. In this one area, we haven't done it at all while other disciplines have done it for us—although not as well as we might have done it had we done it." Waithe, xx.
20. Waithe, xiv.
21. Mary Ann Warren, "Feminist Archeology: Uncovering Women's Philosophical History," review of *A History of Women Philosophers*, vol. 1, by Mary Ellen Waithe, *Hypatia* 4, no. 1 (March 1989): 157.
22. Warren, 159.
23. Warren, 158.
24. R. M. Dancy, "On *A History of Women Philosophers*, Vol. I," review of *A History of Women Philosophers*, vol. 1, by Mary Ellen Waithe, *Hypatia* 4, no. 1 (March 1989): 169.
25. Dancy, 165.
26. Dancy, 166. Dancy's view that Diotima holds Plato's theory of the forms is contentious on a number of levels, not least of which is the

long history of disagreement about how, exactly, to understand Plato's theory of the forms. More to the point in this context, how to read Diotima's speech in relation to Plato's philosophical views is also a rich area of disagreement. In *Erotic Wisdom*, Gary Alan Scott and William A. Welton begin their exploration of these issues with the following observation: "The decision about how to understand Diotima's role—in particular, whether we should understand her teaching about *Eros* as a conception endorsed by Plato or as offered in some way for criticism—is a key question to be wrestled with by readers of the *Symposium*. Unfortunately, there is no way to know at the outset which answer is the true one. But there are certain obvious features of Diotima's role in the dialogue that probably should guide its audience." Alan Scott and William A. Welton, *Erotic Wisdom: Philosophy and Intermediacy in Plato's Symposium* (Albany: State University of New York Press, 2008), 89–90.

The reading they develop using this method is a careful and fruitful engagement with the speech attributed to Diotima. Martha Nussbaum in *The Fragility of Goodness* is similarly careful and fruitful, yet she assumes at the outset that Diotima is a fiction. Scott and Welton leave that question open.

27. Dancy, "On *A History of Women Philosophers*," 165.
28. As an anthology evidencing the participation of women throughout women's history in, for instance, Penelope Deutscher, "'Imperfect Discretion': Interventions Into the History of Philosophy by Twentieth-Century French Women Philosophers," *Hypatia* 15, no. 2 (Spring 2000): 160–180; as primary source writing by women philosophers in Jacqueline Broad, *Women Philosophers of the Seventeenth Century* (Cambridge: Cambridge University Press, 2002); on the diversity of women in the history of philosophy in Lilli Alanen and Charlotte Witt, eds., "Feminist History of Philosophy," in *Feminist Reflections on the History of Philosophy* (Dordrecht: Kluwer Academic, 2004); as a source on the exceptions of the entirely male history of philosophy in Iddo Landau, *Is Philosophy Andocentric* (University Park: Pennsylvania State University Press, 2006); as a source for Mary Whiton Calkins in Dorothy Rogers, "The Other Philosophy Club: America's First Academic Women Philosophers," *Hypatia* 24, no. 2 (Spring 2009): 164–185.
29. Warnock, *Women Philosophers*, xxix–xxx.
30. Warnock, xxx.

31. Warnock, xxxiii.
32. Warnock, xxxiii.
33. Warnock, xxxiii.
34. Warnock, xxxiii.
35. McAllister, "On the Possibility of Feminist Philosophy," 2.
36. McAllister, xxxiii.
37. It seems that the quotation marks around "voice" serve a different function than those around "women's." In the first case, the marks seem to indicate the metaphorical status of voice. The second set of marks seems to be putting into doubt the aptness of the label for the subjects under consideration. That second set can be read as containing a sort of feminist impulse: it is prejudicial to assume that some subjects are gendered. Of course, the passage is concerned with why feminist writing is rightfully omitted from the volume, and so it is difficult to know if such a reading of the second set of marks is fair.
38. Warnock, *Women Philosophers*, xlvii.
39. Warnock, xxxvii.
40. See Eileen O'Neill, "Early Modern Women Philosophers and the History of Philosophy," *Hypatia* 20, no. 3 (Summer 2005): 185–197; and Stella Gonzalez Arnal, review of *Women Philosophers*, by Mary Warnock, *British Journal for the History of Philosophy* 6, no. 2 (1998): 306–308.
41. Karen Green, *The Woman of Reason: Feminism, Humanism, and Political Thought* (Cambridge: Polity, 1995), 26.
42. Andrea Nye, *Philosophia: The Thought of Rosa Luxemborg, Simone Weil, and Hannah Arendt* (New York: Routledge, 1994), xi.
43. Nye, 235.
44. Denise Riley notes of metaphors of leavening vis-à-vis women: "There was nothing innovatory about the conception of women as improvers. Some Enlightenment theorists had advanced their own versions of it; Millar's *Origin of the Distinction of Ranks* in 1771 had included 'women as indices of civilisation, as a kind of social leaven.'" Denise Riley, *"Am I That Name?": Feminism and the Category of "Women" in History* (Minneapolis: University of Minnesota Press, 1988), 48.
45. Nye, *Philosophia*, 234.
46. Nye, xix.
47. Nye, 228.
48. Nye, 235.
49. Nye, xviii.
50. Nye, 225.

51. Nye, 225.
52. Nye, 226.
53. Nye, 225.
54. Nye, xvi.
55. Nye, xx.
56. Green, *Woman of Reason*, 3.
57. Green, 19.
58. Green, 3.
59. Green, 9.
60. Green, 20.
61. While the etymology of "beyond the pale" suggests a geographic demarcation within Ireland, I invoke it here to underscore the imbrication of racial and gender norms in determining who is a legitimate target of violence and who must be protected at all costs.
62. Riley, *"Am I that Name?,"* 1–2.
63. Green, *The Woman of Reason*, 21.
64. Green, 7.
65. Green, 8.
66. Janet Kourany, "Philosophy in a Feminist Voice?," in *Philosophy in a Feminist Voice: Critiques and Reconstructions*, ed. Janet Kourany (Princeton: Princeton University Press, 1998), 3.
67. Kourany, 3–4.
68. With the emphasis that Kourany places on voice, it is interesting to note her use of visibility in this quotation. Kourany is likely reflecting the metaphor of invisible ink that O'Neill uses to describe women's writing in the history of philosophy.
69. Kristie Dotson, "Conceptualizing Epistemic Oppression," *Social Epistemology: A Journal of Knowledge, Culture, and Policy* 28, no. 2 (2014): 116.
70. Dotson, 129.
71. Dotson, 130.
72. Therese Boos Dykeman, *The Neglected Canon: Nine Women Philosophers: First to the Twentieth Century* (Dordrecht: Kluwer Academic, 1999), xi.
73. Dykeman, xv.
74. Dykeman, xv.
75. Dykeman, xvi.
76. Dykeman, xv.
77. Hortense Spillers, "Interstices: A Small Drama of Words," in *Black, White, and in Color: Essays on American Literature and Culture*, 152–175 (Chicago: University of Chicago Press, 2003), 167.

78. Spillers, 167.
79. Catherine Villaneuva Gardner, *Rediscovering Women Philosophers: Philosophical Genre and the Boundaries of Philosophy* (Boulder: Westview, 2000), 1.
80. Gardner, 1.
81. Jane Duran, *Eight Women Philosophers: Theory, Politics, and Feminism* (Urbana: University of Illinois Press, 2006), x–xi.
82. Gardner, *Rediscovering*, 2.
83. Gardner, 3.
84. Gardner, 3.
85. Gardner, 3.
86. Gardner, 4.
87. Gardner, 4.
88. Gardner, 10.
89. Charlotte Witt, "Feminist History of Philosophy," in *Feminist Reflections on the History of Philosophy*, ed. Lilli Alanen and Charlotte Witt (Dordrecht: Kluwer Academic, 2004), 2.
90. Witt, 5.
91. Witt, 5.
92. Witt, 7.
93. Witt, 7.
94. Witt, 7.
95. Witt, 7.
96. Witt, 9. Witt's characterization of feminist canon revision is, of course, contestable given the work done in Africana, Latin American, and Indigenous philosophies, for instance, which do not select from "an already established list of male philosophers" or at least not the same one that Witt references.
97. Witt, 10.
98. Witt, 10, emphasis mine.

2. CONCEPTUAL EXCLUSION

1. Genevieve Lloyd, *The Man of Reason: "Male" and "Female" in Western Philosophy* (London: Routledge, 1993), viii.
2. Sandra Harding writes: "gendered social life is produced through three distinct processes: it is the result of assigning dualistic gender metaphors to various perceived dichotomies that rarely have anything to do with sex differences; it is the consequence of appealing to these gender dualisms to organize social activity, of dividing necessary social

activities between different groups of humans; it is a form of socially constructed individual identity only imperfectly correlated with either the 'reality' or the perception of sex differences." Harding, *The Science Question in Feminism* (Ithaca: Cornell University Press, 1986), 17–18.

3. She briefly offers a clarification in the introduction to the second edition to *The Man of Reason*, but this later article offers a more full development of her concept of metaphor.
4. Genevieve Lloyd, "Maleness, Metaphor, and the 'Crisis' of Reason," in *Feminist Social Thought: A Reader*, ed. Diana Tietjens Meyers (New York: Routledge, 1997), 289.
5. Lloyd, 290.
6. Lloyd, *The Man of Reason*, ix.
7. Lloyd, ix.
8. Lloyd, "Maleness, Metaphor," 290.
9. Lloyd, *The Man of Reason*, 2.
10. Lloyd, "Maleness, Metaphor," 300.
11. Alcoff, "Is the Feminist Critique of Reason Rational?," *Philosophic Exchange* 26 (1996): 59–79, 64.
12. Lloyd, *The Man of Reason*, 49.
13. For an illuminating treatment of that history, see Christine Fauré, *Democracy Without Women* (Bloomington: Indiana University Press, 1991).
14. Lloyd, *The Man of Reason*, 50.
15. Genevieve Lloyd, "History of Philosophy and the Critique of Reason," *Critical Philosophy* 1, no. 1 (1984): 18, emphasis mine. The quotation from *The Man of Reason* reads: "Philosophy reflects the characteristic preoccupations and self-perceptions of the kinds of people who have at any time had access to the activity. Philosophers have at different periods been churchmen, men of letters, university professors. But there is one thing they have had in common throughout the history of the activity; they have been predominantly male; and the absence of women from the philosophical tradition has meant that conceptualization of Reason has been done exclusively by men." Lloyd, *The Man of Reason*, 108.
16. Carole Pateman, review of *The Man of Reason: "Male" and "Female" in Western Philosophy*, by Genevieve Lloyd, *Political Theory* 14, no. 3 (August 1986): 509.
17. Diotima is treated in the section on Plato's conception of reason; Lloyd calls Diotima a "wise woman" and "Socrates' instructor in the art of love." Lloyd *Man of Reason*, 21. I'll discuss Lloyd's interpretation below.

Princess Elizabeth is mentioned in connection with Descartes to highlight what he said in correspondence to her (47). A discussion of Virginia Woolf's novel *Night and Day* serves as the introduction to the chapter "The Public and the Private" (74). Mary Wollstonecraft is mentioned as an exasperated critic of Rousseau (76).

18. The first English translator, H. M. Parshley, wrote: "Mlle de Beauvoir's book is, after all on women, not philosophy." Parshley, "Translator's Note," in *The Second Sex* (New York: Vintage, 1989), xxxviii.
19. Lloyd, *The Man of Reason*, 86–87.
20. Become "one of the boys," perhaps.
21. Tina Chanter, *Ethics of Eros: Irigaray's Re-Writing of the Philosophers* (New York: Routledge, 1995), 278.
22. I return to the importance of reading practices that analyze points of agreement and disagreements between philosophers as the result of work, rather than parroting or error in the chapter on Le Doeuff in the discussion of Harriet Taylor Mill and John Stuart Mill.
23. Chanter, *Ethics of Eros*, 52.
24. Chanter, 53.
25. Chanter, 78.
26. Chanter, 78.
27. Penelope Deutscher, *Yielding Gender* (London: Routledge, 1997), 7.
28. Lloyd, *The Man of Reason*, 50.
29. In the introduction to the second edition, Lloyd addresses her reading of Descartes on this point and suggests a more complex reading in conversation with Spinoza's transformation of Cartesian dualism (Lloyd, xii). Similarly, she gives a deconstructive reading of metaphors in Descartes in "Maleness, Metaphor, and the 'Crisis' of Reason." Her rethinking of Descartes still emphasizes that "his influential dualism has interacted with and reinforced the effects of the symbolic opposition between male and female" (Lloyd, *The Man of Reason*, xiv), rather than looking at the possibilities that are present, even if not victorious, in his writing.
30. See François Poullain de la Barre, *Three Cartesian Feminist Treatises*, trans. Vivien Bosley (Chicago: University of Chicago Press, 2002).
31. Lloyd, *The Man of Reason*, 21.
32. Lloyd, 21.
33. Lloyd, 22.
34. Lloyd, 3.
35. For a particularly illuminating discussion, see David Halperin, "Why Is Diotima a Woman?," in *One Hundred Years of Homosexuality, and Other Essays on Greek Love* (New York: Routledge, 1990), 113–151.

36. I recognize that a tempting answer to the last question is simply that women didn't practice philosophy in such a patriarchal context. But that answer doesn't satisfy in a couple of ways. First, it underscores the importance of Plato's use of a woman in this dialogue. In other words, if patriarchy is the answer to why there are so few women in Plato's dialogues, then we still need to grapple with why he introduced a woman in this dialogue. Second, if philosophers are gadflies, it seems they could be irritating on the question of patriarchy. So, why wasn't Plato or Socrates more irritating on this point? What work was the exclusion of femininity doing for philosophical thought?
37. Lloyd, *The Man of Reason*, 110.
38. Lloyd, 109.
39. Lloyd, 109.

3. RECLAMATION FROM ABSENCE

For this chapter, I have drawn freely on material published as "Reclamation from Absence?: Luce Irigaray and Women in the History of Philosophy," in *Hypatia* 28, no. 3 (Summer 2013): 483–498. Used with permission.

1. Penelope Deutscher's *Yielding Gender* offers an illuminating discussion of how Genevieve Lloyd, Karen Green, and Moira Gatens, among others, defend against feminism of difference in the work on the history of philosophy and fail to appreciate the resources in Irigaray for analyzing the role of women and the feminine in the history of philosophy. Deutscher, *Yielding Gender* (London: Routledge, 1997).
2. Heather Hadar Wright has asked: "Why are *feminist* thinkers so interested in arguing about the meaning of a relatively obscure figure in an ancient Greek text, a Platonic work which on the surface appears to be a discussion by men on the subject of male homosexuality?" Wright points to Luce Irigaray's essay "Sorcerer Love: A Reading of Plato, *Symposium*, 'Diotima's Speech.'" The essay first appeared in English translation in the issue of *Hypatia* from 1989 that preceded the issue in which the reviews of Waithe's work were printed. Irigaray's essay appeared with an introduction by Eleanor Kuykendall in which Kuykendall observes that "Sorcerer Love" both connects with the deconstructive work on Plato begun in *Speculum of the Other Woman* and sets up the positive ethical and ontological work of *Ethics of Sexual Difference*, in which the essay appears. Kuykendall connects Irigaray's essay to the ballet *El Amor Brujo/L'Amour Sorcier*, which, she observes, "culminates in a ritual fire dance." Eleanor H. Kuykendall, "Introduction to 'Sorcerer Love,' by Luce Irigaray," *Hypatia* 3, no. 3

(1989): 28–31, 29. Kuykendall makes the observation to underscore the magical or bewitching aspect of Irigaray's work, but does not speculate further about Irigaray's choice of title.

3. In "La Mystérique" (in Irigaray, *Speculum of the Other Woman*, trans. Gillian C. Gill [Ithaca: Cornell University Press, 1985], 191–202), Irigaray explores the role of the female mystic. Reclamationists have done important work engaging the writings of mystics. Thus, it seems that La Mystérique might also be an important resource for reclamation. It is—in a sense. Irigaray exposes the contradictions of the mystic's role, the countervailing excesses of the only opportunity for woman to speak and to speak publicly. That exposure can help us to lovingly engage the thinking of mystics, but it is not the direct modeling of reclamation that occurs in "Sorcerer Love."
4. Luce Irigaray, *I Love to You: Sketch of a Possible Felicity in History*, trans. Alison Martin (New York: Routledge, 1996), 12.
5. In *Socrates and Diotima: Sexuality, Religion, and the Nature of Divinity*, Nye reads Diotima's speech for an alternative spiritual tradition, the loss of which she traces through the reception of Plato's work. Interestingly, Nye uses historical contextualization throughout the book to make her argument, but her book's project receives a certain license from the doubt about historical accuracy we must have about Plato's rendering of Socrates's conversations: "If there can be no hard truth in memoranda of long past conversations—no certainty . . . that a visiting priestess named Diotima instructed the young Socrates in exactly the terms recalled by Socrates and passed on by Apollodorus—there is something better. What Plato's dialogues preserve is not a doctrine or theory, dead words that cannot answer back, but ideas sown in fertile minds where thoughts, as Socrates puts it in the *Phaedrus*, 'contain seeds from which other ideas can grow up' (277a–2)." Andrea Nye, *Socrates and Diotima: Sexuality, Religion, and the Nature of Divinity* (New York: Palgrave Macmillan, 2015), 5.
6. Judith Butler, *Gender Trouble* (New York: Routledge, 2006), 18.
7. Elizabeth Grosz, "Feminist Theory and the Challenge to Knowledges," *Women Studies International Forum* 10, no. 5 (1987): 477.
8. Margaret Whitford, *Luce Irigaray: Philosophy in the Feminine* (New York: Routledge, 1991), 58.
9. Whitford, 58.
10. Luce Irigaray, *This Sex Which Is Not One*, trans. C. Porter (Ithaca: Cornell University Press, 1985), 78.
11. Irigaray, 78.

12. Irigaray, 69.
13. Irigaray, 73.
14. Irigaray, 74.
15. Irigaray, 74.
16. Irigaray, 68.
17. Irigaray, 68.
18. Irigaray, *Speculum of the Other Woman*, 112.
19. Irigaray, *This Sex Which Is Not One*, 134.
20. And certainly Irigaray's willingness to play with language presents difficulties for her readers, but those difficulties are often part of the project.
21. Irigaray, *This Sex Which Is Not One*, 76.
22. Irigaray, 76.
23. Irigaray, *Speculum of the Other Woman*, 142.
24. Elizabeth Weed, "The Question of Style," in *Engaging with Irigaray: Feminist Philosophy and Modern European Thought*, ed. Carolyn Burke, Naomi Schor, and Margaret Whitford (New York: Columbia University Press, 1994), 79.
25. Weed, 101.
26. Irigaray, *This Sex Which Is Not One*, 74.
27. Irigaray, *An Ethics of Sexual Difference*, trans. Carolyn Burke and Gillian C. Gill (Ithaca: Cornell University Press, 1993), 32.
28. Irigaray, 23.
29. Irigaray, 21.
30. Irigaray, 24.
31. Irigaray, 25–26.
32. Irigaray, 27.
33. Somer Brodribb, *Nothing Mat(t)ers: A Feminist Critique of Postmodernism* (North Melbourne: Spinifex, 1992), 106. Brodribb discusses Diotima in the context of presenting Irigaray's views on procreation. While Brodribb is critical of Irigaray's work, particularly the role of the heterosexual couple in it, Brodribb does not critique or endorse Irigaray's use of Diotima.
34. Irigaray, *An Ethics of Sexual Difference*, 30.
35. Irigaray, 27.
36. Carolyn Burke, "Translation Modified: Irigaray in English," in *Engaging with Irigaray: Feminist Philosophy and Modern European Thought*, ed. Carolyn Burke et al. (New York: Columbia University Press, 1994), 255.
37. Irigaray, *An Ethics of Sexual Difference*, 129.
38. Irigaray, 129.

39. Irigaray, 127.
40. Irigaray, 24.
41. Irigaray, 75.
42. Penelope Deutscher, *A Politics of Impossible Difference: The Later Works of Luce Irigaray* (Ithaca: Cornell University Press, 2002), 5–6.
43. Andrea Nye, "The Hidden Host: Irigaray and Diotima at Plato's Symposium," *Hypatia* 3, no. 3 (1989): 47.
44. Nye, 47.
45. Nye, 49.
46. Margaret Whitford is very generous on the issue of *écriture féminine*, offering accounts of why Irigaray's writing may be associated with this concept (see Whitford, *Luce Irigaray*, 4), but also quite helpfully observes: "It is interesting that, although Irigaray has often been associated with *écriture féminine*, women's writing, in fact the terms which she privileges are not about writing at all: *parler-femme* and *la sexuation du discours* (translated by Catherine Porter and Carolyn Burke in *This Sex Which Is Not One* as 'speaking (as) woman' and the 'sexualization of discourse'). As far as I know, she does not use the term *écriture feminine* at all; it is a label which has been attached to her by others." Whitford, *Luce Irigaray*, 38.

    In Nye's case, she may have been guided by Kuykendall's judgment, appearing in the same issue of *Hypatia* as "Hidden Host," that Irigaray experiments with *écriture feminine*. Kuykendall, "Introduction to 'Sorcerer Love,' by Luce Irigaray," 28. That is only speculation on my part, but it is bolstered by the fact that Kuykendall provided the translation of "Sorcerer Love" that appears with the Nye essay.
47. Nye, "Hidden Host," 52.
48. Nye, 53.
49. Nye, 53.
50. Nye, 45.
51. Nye, 57.
52. This notion of "overreading" comes from David Kazanjian's "Freedom's Surprise: Two Paths Through Slavery's Archives," *History of the Present* 6, no. 2 (2016): 133–145, 143, which I discuss at greater length in chapter 5.
53. Irigaray, *An Ethics of Sexual Difference*, 69.
54. Deutscher, *A Politics of Impossible Difference*, 6.
55. Butler, *Gender Trouble*, 18. Penelope Deutscher's *A Politics of Impossible Difference* grapples with this problem and offers an intertwined

reading of Irigaray and Gayatri Spivak's critical work in which she notes, "But in the practice of Irigaray's writing, the scope of subjects remembered and discussed by her, particularly as reflects on multiculturalism, is limited" (184).

56. Irigaray, *This Sex Which Is Not One*, 78.
57. Deutscher, *A Politics of Impossible Difference*, 169.
58. See especially "Effacement Redoubled? *Between East and West*," in Deutscher, *A Politics of Impossible Difference*.
59. See, for instance, Irigaray, *Between East and West: From Singularity to Community* (New York: Columbia University Press, 2002).
60. Lisa Guenther, "Other Fecundities: Proust and Irigaray on Sexual Difference," *differences* 21, no. 2 (2010): 27.
61. See, for instance, Mariana Ortega, "Being Lovingly, Knowingly Ignorant: White Feminism and Women of Color," *Hypatia* 21, no. 3 (Summer 2006): 56–74.

4. INSULTS AND THEIR POSSIBILITIES

1. Michèle Le Doeuff, "Ants and Women, or Philosophy Without Borders," in *Contemporary French Philosophy*, ed. A. Phillips Griffiths (Cambridge: Cambridge University Press, 1987), 51.
2. Michèle Le Doeuff, *The Philosophical Imaginary* (London: Continuum, 2002), 107.
3. Le Doeuff, 126.
4. I will refer to Harriet Taylor Mill as Taylor throughout this chapter. Jo Ellen Jacobs has observed, "The difficulty in characterizing Harriet Taylor Mill begins with her name." Jacobs, ed., *The Complete Works of Harriet Taylor Mill* (Bloomington: Indiana University Press, 1998), xii. "Taylor" was her first husband's last name, Mill her second's. Harriet Hardy, her given or *maiden* name, was also her mother's name. Jacobs goes on to note: "Using only her first name, 'Harriet,' hardly seems to present her as an important intellectual figure in the history of philosophy. . . . But perhaps the history of philosophy would be approached differently if students studied Immanuel, René, and Baruch instead of Kant, Descartes, and Spinoza." Jacobs, *The Complete Works*, xii. Deutscher uses "Taylor Mill." Ultimately, and perhaps unsatisfactorily, I follow Le Doeuff's practice, as it was *The Sex of Knowing* that introduced me to Harriet Taylor Mill. Le Doeuff, *The Sex of Knowing* (New York: Routledge, 2003).

5. Tina Chanter, *Ethics of Eros: Irigaray's Re-Writing of the Philosophers* (New York: Routledge, 1995), 78.
6. Chanter, 55.
7. Michèle Le Doeuff, *Hipparchia's Choice: An Essay Concerning Women, Philosophy, Etc.* (Oxford: Blackwell, 2007), 162.
8. In *The Oxford Companion to Philosophy*, Jane O'Grady describes the complex this way: "Diagnosed by Michèle Le Doeuff, this is the tendency of women in philosophy to idolize either a male colleague or teacher (as did Héloïse and Beauvoir), or a 'great' living or dead philosopher whose banner they carry (as do contemporary women seeking the best male exponent of feminism, and becoming 'Lacanian,' 'Foucauldian,' even 'Nietzschean' feminists). This situation benefits the man, destroys the woman—removing her intellectual independence and need to create philosophy herself. De Beauvoir, however, escaped the Héloïse complex sufficiently to produce philosophy 'unawares.'" Jane O'Grady, "Heloise Complex," in *The Oxford Companion to Philosophy*, ed. Ted Honderich (Oxford: Oxford University Press, 1995), 350–351. The second edition of the *Companion*, published in 2005, which was published after Le Doeuff's modification of the concept, does not offer an update to the conception. Hence, in describing Le Doeuff's concept, the *Companion* reinforces the idea that women have not produced philosophy, except perhaps accidentally.

   Also worth noting, it is not clear where in Le Doeuff's works O'Grady finds the condemnation of Lacanian, Foucauldian, or even Nietzschean feminists. Certainly, Le Doeuff is scrupulous about avoiding claims of allegiance to any one thinker.
9. Le Doeuff, *Hipparchia's Choice*, 164.
10. The word Le Doeuff uses in French is "rédhibitoire." Michèle Le Doeuff, *L'Étude et le Rouet* (Paris: Éditions du Seuil, 1989), 185. This could be translated as "damning," but I think such a translation would paper over the connotations of ableism in the metaphor. At least in this sentence, Le Doeuff is metaphorizing her reclamationist practice as an overcoming of disability. That is unfortunate, since Le Doeuff's point is not that women's lack of philosophical authority is a disability that individual women need to overcome. Rather, her point is that the structures of philosophy disempower women as a mode of substantiating the discipline and therefore need to change. In other words, the metaphor is marginalizing and inaccurate. See Schalk, "Metaphorically Speaking: Ableist Metaphors in Feminist Writing," *Disability Studies Quarterly* 33, no. 4 (2013): 1–21.

11. Le Doeuff, *Hipparchia's Choice*, 165.
12. In the French original, Le Doeuff uses "aveugle," an adjective used metaphorically and literally to mean "blindness." Le Doueff, *L'Étude et le Rouet*, 188. Here, Le Doeuff's meaning is that we are not incapable of being accountable to philosophy's origins and its practices. We can and should understand where our practices come from through philosophical engagement with philosophical history. Thus, the metaphor problematically relies on an association of blind embodiment with being unaccountable, marginalizing people with disabilities while not making the point that the *practices* of philosophy are at issue. The metaphor is both ableist and ineffective at elaborating Le Doeuff's point. See Schalk, "Metaphorically Speaking."
13. Le Doueff, *L'Étude et le Rouet*, 168.
14. Another implication of this delinking is that texts by recognized philosophers that have previously been deemed nonphilosophical need reconsideration.
15. Le Doeuff, *The Sex Knowing*, 217.
16. Margaret Simons's "The Silencing of Simone de Beauvoir: Guess What's Missing from *The Second Sex*" (*Women's Studies International Forum* 6, no. 5 [1983]: 559–564) offers a succinct recap of how H. M. Parshley's English translation severely and somewhat arbitrarily abridged Beauvoir's discussions of history.
17. Le Doeuff, *Hipparchia's Choice*, 216.
18. Le Doeuff, 218. While economic dependence is clearly an important element in intimate partner abuse, Le Doeuff problematically reinforces the notion that married heterosexual women are (basically) the only people who experience this form of violence.
19. Le Doeuff, 217.
20. Le Doeuff, 217.
21. For a thorough (and disheartening) review of the phases and fads of scholarship dismissing Harriet Taylor Mill, see Jo Ellen Jacobs, "'The Lot of Gifted Ladies Is Hard': A Study of Harriet Taylor Mill Criticism," *Hypatia* 9, no. 3 (1994): 132–162.
22. Le Doeuff defines a methodological approach to reclamation that shares some of the features of the approach Chanter used in her reading of Beauvoir.
23. Nor do I think that the image of the independent thinker is ever meant to be an isolated figure in Le Doeuff's work. The influence of the Seneca Falls convention and the women's movement in the United States—as well as women petitioners in Sheffield, who seemed also to

have impressed Taylor (Le Doeuff, *The Sex of Knowing*, 205)—is part of a larger story often touched on in Le Doeuff's work about the power that women's collective work has to shift thinking. See Le Doeuff, "Ants and Women, or Philosophy Without Borders."

24. Briefly, on July 19 and 20, 1848, a crowd of around three hundred people instigated a mass movement for women's rights in the United States. The *Declaration of Sentiments* and resolutions to the problems it outlined were adopted and circulated with the signatures of one hundred of the participants. I explore the *Declaration* and resolutions more fully in chapter 6.
25. Le Doeuff, *The Sex of Knowing*, 205.
26. Le Doeuff, 205.
27. Le Doeuff, 206.
28. Le Doeuff, 208.
29. Le Doeuff, 215.
30. Penelope Deutscher, "When Feminism Is 'High' and Ignorance Is 'Low': Harriet Taylor Mill on the Progress of the Species," *Hypatia* 21, no. 3 (2006): 143, emphasis mine.
31. Deutscher, 146. It is interesting to note that the hierarchies shared by Mill and Taylor are present in philosophical discourse within Mill's work. Thus, Deutscher's critique of Taylor also makes a potential contribution to Mill scholarship, but only by contesting the dismissal of Taylor's importance that Le Doeuff and Jo Ellen Jacobs have shown to shape the discourse on Mill. By exposing these hierarchies, Deutscher has also made the points of agreement between Taylor and Mill possible sites of motivation for Taylor's reclamation.
32. Deutscher, 147. Deutscher, like Alcoff in a quotation in the first chapter, uses the metaphor of blindness, although in a seeing eye, to indicate something undesirable. In this case, the metaphor implies that the blind part of the seeing eye may be necessary but is lamentable. That is, the seeing eye has a structure of failure necessary to its functioning that may symbolize the structure of thinking. From a deconstructive angle, it is not surprising to find that a dominant term is actually dependent upon a subordinated term for its functioning. However, the ethical move of deconstruction is not an affirmation or vindication of the dominant term—seeing will save us, for example. Rather, it seems that the project of mastery needs displacement. Thinking cannot fully account for itself, and so we must always critically reflect on what makes thinking possible. Again, this ableist metaphor fails to do the critical work it was intended to do. See Schalk, "Metaphorically Speaking."

33. Le Doeuff, *The Sex of Knowing*, 190.
34. Le Doeuff, "Ants and Women, or Philosophy Without Borders," 51.
35. Le Doeuff, *The Sex of Knowing*, 57.
36. Michèle Le Doeuff, "Women and Philosophy," in *French Feminist Thought: A Reader*, ed. Toril Moi (Oxford: Basil Blackwell, 1987), 196.
37. Payne calls the essay he is responding to "Women in Philosophy." That is a rather more hopeful title than Le Doeuff's argument would allow, I think. It may be that Payne was directed in his usage by Le Doeuff's use of the title "Women in Philosophy" in her essay "Women in Dialogue and in Solitude," published in 2005 and based on a lecture from 2004. Payne cites *Radical Philosophy* as his source, however, and there the essay in question is titled "Women and Philosophy."
38. Michael Payne, review of *Selected Writings*, by Sarah Kofman, ed. Thomas Albrecht, *College Literature* 35, no. 3 (2008): 203.
39. See David Kazanjian, "Freedom's Surprise: Two Paths Through Slavery's Archives," *History of the Present* 6, no. 2 (2016): 133–145.

5. FROM EXCLUSION TO RECLAMATION

1. Indeed, we have mention of Diotima, and the works of many white women, from cultures of highly restricted literacy, while the violent massive erasures of chattel slavery happened during the burgeoning of literate cultures around the world.
2. See Kristie Dotson's work, especially "How Is This Paper Philosophy?," *Comparative Philosophy* 3, no. 1 (2013): 3–29.
3. Dancy, "On *A History of Women Philosophers*, Vol. I," review of *A History of Women Philosophers*, vol. 1, Mary Ellen Waithe, *Hypatia* 4, no. 1 (March 1989): 160–171, 166.
4. As I will explore below, part of Kazanjian's response to Hartman is to pluralize the archives of slavery, looking beyond, for instance, the genre of autobiography. Kazanjian, *The Brink of Freedom*, 136.
5. Saidiya Hartman, "Venus in Two Acts," *Small Axe* 12, no. 2 (2008): 1.
6. Hartman, 2.
7. Hartman, 10.
8. Spillers, "Interstices: A Small Drama of Words," in *Black, White, and in Color: Essays on American Literature and Culture*, 152–175 (Chicago: University of Chicago Press, 2003), 156.
9. Hartman, "Venus in Two Acts," 11–12.
10. Hartman, 2.
11. Hartman, 2.

12. Hartman, 2.
13. Spillers, "Interstices," 156.
14. Hartman, "Venus in Two Acts," 4.
15. Hartman, 4.
16. Hartman, 13.
17. Again, Kristie Dotson's work offers a particularly helpful guide to identifying and responding to these modes of philosophical practice.
18. Hartman, "Venus in Two Acts," 6.
19. Kazanjian, "Freedom's Surprise: Two Paths Through Slavery's Archives," *History of the Present* 6, no. 2 (2016): 133–145, 140.
20. David Kazanjian, "Scenes of Speculation," *Social Text* 33, no. 4 (125) (2015): 80.
21. Kazanjian, "Freedom's Surprise," 143.
22. Kazanjian, "Scenes of Speculation," 82.
23. Michelle Walker, "Silence and Reason: Woman's Voice in Philosophy," *Australasian Journal of Philosophy* 71, no. 4 (December 1993): 400.
24. Lloyd, "Maleness, Metaphor, and the 'Crisis' of Reason," in *Feminist Social Thought: A Reader*, ed. Diana Tietjens Meyers, 286–301 (New York: Routledge, 1997), 291.
25. Lloyd, 292. She then states, "And the operations of the symbolism in turn affect the constitution of sexual difference" (292). Though this statement makes clear that sexual difference is mutable, there is still a direct causal link between symbolism and sexual difference.
26. Lloyd, 289.
27. Eileen O'Neill, "Early Modern Women Philosophers and the History of Philosophy," *Hypatia* 20, no. 3 (Summer 2005): 190.
28. In her helpful review of how editors have justified excluding women from the canon of political theory, Penny Weiss observes: "'Reasons' will be used to defend this inequality as they are useful, not because they are valid." Weiss, *Canon Fodder: Historical Women Political Thinkers* (University Park: Pennsylvania State University Press, 2009), 5. She then debunks the most common reasons given. O'Neill shows that even when women are included, the reasons for their inclusion are not necessarily carefully considered.
29. O'Neill, "Early Modern Women Philosophers," 194.
30. O'Neill, 194.
31. Meaghan Morris, *The Pirates Fiancée: Feminism, Reading, Postmodernism* (London: Verso, 1988), 99.
32. Elizabeth Grosz, *Sexual Subversions: Three French Feminists* (Sydney: Allen and Unwin, 1989), 212.

33. Michelle Walker, "Silence and Reason: Woman's Voice in Philosophy," *Australasian Journal of Philosophy* 71, no. 4 (December 1993): 423. Steven Maras, in "Translating Michèle Le Doeuff's Analytics," gives a careful analysis of the concept of "l'imagier" in Le Doeuff's work and, in so doing, critiques Morris's and Grosz's readings. While I don't follow his critique here, it was Maras's attention to the concept (explained as having "less to do with the image or the imaginary as an autonomous site than with the conditions of rationality, and the tension between philosophy and the *socius* as they impact on the function of imagery") that helped me develop the critique of Morris and Grosz, as well as Walker, that I present here. Maras, "Translating Michèle Le Doeuff's Analytics," in *Michèle Le Doeuff: Operative Philosophy and Imaginary Practice*, ed. Max Deutscher, 83–104 (New York: Humanity, 2000), 93.
34. Le Doeuff, "Women, Reason, Etc.," *differences: A Journal of Feminist Cultural Studies* 2, no. 3 (1990): 1–13, 29.
35. Grosz, *Sexual Subversions*, 212.
36. Elizabeth Grosz, *Jacques Lacan: A Feminist Introduction* (London: Routledge, 1990), 150.
37. Penelope Deutscher, "'Imperfect Discretion': Interventions Into the History of Philosophy by Twentieth-Century French Women Philosophers," *Hypatia* 15, no. 2 (Spring 2000): 164.
38. Le Doeuff, *The Sex of Knowing* (New York: Routledge, 2003), 136.
39. Le Doeuff, 136.
40. Michèle Le Doeuff, "Long Hair, Short Ideas," in *The Philosophical Imaginary* (London: Continuum, 2002), 100.

6. INJURIES AND USURPATIONS

1. Judith Wellman, *The Road to Seneca Falls: Elizabeth Cady Stanton and the First Woman's Rights Convention* (Urbana: University of Illinois Press, 2004), 189. There are disagreements among sources about how many people attended the convention. Wellman, for instance, states there were one hundred (10). Angela Davis gives three hundred, as does Bonnie Mani. Angela Y. Davis, *Women, Race, and Class* (New York: Vintage, 1983), 51; Bonnie Mani, *Women, Power, and Political Change* (Lanham, MD: Lexington, 2007), 62. Scholars mainly agree there were 100 signatories, though many later recanted in the face of widespread disgust at the cause of women's enfranchisement. Wellman, *The Road to Seneca Falls*, 279. Some of the disagreement about the number of attendees may be due to the fact that the first day of the

meeting was reserved for women only to meet and the second day was open to men and women.

2. Wellman, *The Road to Seneca Falls*, 192. Hereafter I will refer to the *Declaration of Sentiments* and its resolutions as the *Declaration of Sentiments* or just the *Declaration*, rather than continuing to refer to the resolutions separately.
3. Elizabeth Cady Stanton, Susan Brownell Anthony, Matilda Joslyn Gage, and Ida Husted Harper, *A History of Woman Suffrage*, vol. 1 (Salem: Ayer, 1985), 70.
4. For the reliance of mainstream feminism on the carceral state, see Maria Bevacqua, *Rape on the Public Agenda: Feminism and the Politics of Sexual Assault* (Boston: Northeastern University Press, 2000); Marie Gottschalk, *The Prison and the Gallows: The Politics of Mass Incarceration in America* (New York: Cambridge University Press, 2006); Mimi Kim, *Dancing the Carceral Creep: The Anti-Domestic Violence Movement and the Paradoxical Pursuit of Criminalization, 1973–1986* (University of California, Berkeley: Institute for the Study of Societal Issues, 2015); Beth Richie, *Arrested Justice: Black Women, Violence, and America's Prison Nation* (New York: New York University Press, 2012). There is a huge literature on the racial bias of incarceration, as well as a growing literature on prisons as a mechanism of state racism. For incarceration as mechanism of state racism, see especially Angela Davis, *Are Prisons Obsolete* (New York: Seven Stories, 2003); and Natalie Cisneros, "Resisting 'Massive Elimination,'" in *Active Intolerance: Michel Foucault, the Prisons Information Group, and the Future of Abolition*, ed. Perry Zurn and Andrew Dilts, 241–257 (New York: Palgrave Macmillan, 2016), which connects practices of incarcerating immigrants and deportation to state carceral practices more broadly.
5. In "Feminism Is Back in France—Or Is It?," Le Doeuff refers to "our Seneca Falls grandmothers" (*Hypatia* 15, no. 4 [Fall 2000]: 253). The article is based on a lecture given after the publication of *Le Sexe du savoir.*
6. "Whereas, the great precept of nature is conceded to be that 'man shall pursue his own true and substantial happiness.' Blackstone in his Commentaries remarks that this law of nature, being coeval with mankind and dictated by God himself, is, of course, superior in obligation to any other. It is binding over all the globe, in all countries and at all times; no human laws are of any validity if contrary to this, and such of them as are valid derive all their force, and all their validity,

and all their authority, mediately and immediately, from this original; therefore, Resolved, that such laws as conflict, in any way, with the true and substantial happiness of woman, are contrary to the great precept of nature and of no validity, for this is 'superior in obligation to any other.'" Stanton et al., *A History of Woman Suffrage*, 71–72.

7. Le Doeuff, "Harsh Times," *New Left Review* 1, no. 199 (May-June 1993): 132.
8. Le Doeuff, 132.
9. In the second notebook of *Hipparchia's Choice*, in a section titled "Ascetical Attitudes," Le Doeuff discusses happiness as a theme in *The Second Sex*, observing: "it is a frightening book, not because it calls on us to give up a happiness we have, but because it does not promise the happiness we lack." Michèle Le Doeuff, *Hipparchia's Choice: An Essay Concerning Women, Philosophy, Etc.* (Oxford: Blackwell, 2007), 115. She then observes that the seduction of Irigaray's work is in its promise of bliss.
10. Deutscher, "When Feminism Is 'High' and Ignorance Is 'Low': Harriet Taylor Mill on the Progress of the Species," *Hypatia* 21, no. 3 (2006): 136–150, 143.
11. Le Doeuff, "Harsh Times," 132.
12. Stanton et al., *A History of Woman Suffrage*, 70.
13. Stanton et al., 70.
14. Stanton et al., 70.
15. Stanton et al., 70.
16. Stanton et al., 70.
17. Although the Twitter hashtag #repealthe19th had its moment during the 2016 presidential election, after the website fivethirtyeight.com speculated that Donald Trump would win the election if only men voted, and while this was disheartening, the discussion did not amount to robust debate (www.nydailynews.com/news/national/trump-supporters-repeal-19th-amendment-article-1.2828571). It is also worth noting that the handle quickly came to be used for critical comments.
18. Introducing a mass of new voters with unknown voting habits and no cultivation by local, state, or federal political machines was, of course, a pressing worry for politicians and political bodies right up until the passage of the Nineteenth Amendment.
19. Thanks to Carl Tyson for spending an evening speculating with me about what might have happened if the Compromise of 1850 had not taken place.

20. Antisuffrage thinkers were concerned about women's reproductive capacities explicitly in the mid-nineteenth century. As Sue Davis reports, for instance: "In an editorial, [James Gordon] Bennett asked his readers to consider how funny it would be if Lucy Stone, in the midst of arguing a case in court, were suddenly to be taken by the pangs of childbirth and give 'birth to a fine bouncing boy in court.' How ridiculous would it be, such comments suggested, for females to attempt to function in the public space that was appropriate only for males." Davis, *The Political Thought of Elizabeth Cady Stanton: Women's Rights and the American Political Traditions* (New York: New York University Press, 2008), 96. Not only how funny, I might add, but, with Carole Pateman in mind, how utterly disorderly.
21. Louise Michele Newman, *White Women's Rights: The Racial Origins of Feminism in the United States* (New York: Oxford University Press, 1999) is particularly illuminating about elite white women's willingness to forgo demands of racial justice to advance their own interests.
22. Stanton et al., *A History of Woman Suffrage*, 72.
23. I am not arguing here that enfranchisement was not the most contentious. As Angela Davis notes, it was the point in the document that caused disagreement among the conventioneers and Frederick Douglass was essential to having it adopted as part of the Seneca Falls agenda. Davis, *Women, Race, and Class*, 50–51. Lucretia Mott's initial reaction to Stanton's proposal seems to have been: "Lizzie, thou will make the convention ridiculous" (Wellman, *The Road to Seneca Falls*, 195). Stanton's husband refused to attend the convention and reportedly said to his wife: "You will turn the proceedings into a farce" (193). Further, the history Stanton, Anthony, Gage, and Harper produced was called *History of Woman Suffrage*. My point is that enfranchisement was only part of the radical agenda and, as one we now tend to consider addressed, perhaps the point on which the *Declaration* can be most easily dismissed as old news.
24. Stanton et al., *A History of Woman Suffrage*, 72.
25. The Equal Rights Amendment (ERA) reads:

> *Section 1.* Equality of rights under the law shall not be denied or abridged by the United States or by any state on account of sex.
> *Section 2.* The Congress shall have the power to enforce, by appropriate legislation, the provisions of this article.
> *Section 3.* This amendment shall take effect two years after the date of ratification.

Phyllis Schlafly was instrumental to defeating the bid for its ratification in the 1970s (www.equalrightsamendment.org/history.htm).

26. Stanton et al., *A History of Woman Suffrage*, 70.
27. Marital rape is an issue that Le Doeuff connects to what she argues is the larger problem that in marriage, "whatever the mode, the woman comes under a man's authority and hand, and there is something identifiable as marital authority." Le Doeuff, "Each Man in His Cave," in *Women's Voices, Women's Rights: Oxford Amnesty Lectures 1996*, ed. Alison Jeffries (Boulder: Westview, 1999), 109. Le Doeuff further argues that violence in marriage requires institutions to sustain it and that work to change that institutional support and organization of men's violence against women was only able to gain real ground with the establishment of reproductive rights.
28. "State Law Chart," http://ncmdr.org/state_law_chart.html.
29. Stanton et al., *A History of Woman Suffrage*, 70.
30. Stanton et al., 70.
31. Newman, *White Women's Rights*, 34–35.
32. Newman, 34–35.
33. The fifth resolution reads: "Resolved, that inasmuch as man, while claiming for himself intellectual superiority, does accord to woman moral superiority, it is preeminently his duty to encourage her to speak and teach, as she has an opportunity, in all religious assemblies." Stanton et al., *A History of Woman Suffrage*, 72.
34. Grievance 13 supports such an interpretation. It reads: "He has created a false public sentiment by giving to the world a different code of morals for men and women, by which moral delinquencies which exclude women from society are not only tolerated but deemed of little account in man" (Stanton et al., 71). Although they resolve that men ought to be held to the same standards as women, they don't seem to think the standards women are currently held to, even leaving aside the contradictory ones, are worthy of endorsement.
35. Issues covered explicitly in grievances 6, 9, 10, 11, 12, 14 and resolutions 7, 8, 11, 12, as well as in the preamble and transitional sections.
36. It has often been argued, including by the authors of *History of Woman Suffrage*, that the barring of Lucretia Mott and Elizabeth Cady Stanton from participation in the World Anti-Slavery Convention in 1840—"they found themselves excluded by majority vote, 'fenced off behind a bar and a curtain similar to those used in churches to screen the choir from public gaze'" (Davis, *Women, Race, and Class*, 46–47, quoting Stanton et al.)—was *the* event that gave birth to the women's

rights movement in the United States. Angela Davis has convincingly argued that this legend of the movement's birth obscures the greater complexity of how Stanton and Mott were differently radicalized, as well as the ongoing struggle by women in the abolitionist movement to be treated as equals. See especially "Race and Class in the Woman Suffrage Movement," in *Women, Race, and Class*.

37. Lisa Cochran Higgins, "Adulterous Individualism, Socialism, and Free Love in Nineteenth-Century Anti-Suffrage Writing," *Legacy* 21, no. 2 (2004), 197.
38. Stanton et al., *A History of Woman Suffrage*, 72.
39. Undoubtedly the 2016 presidential election offers fecund examples, but 2008 offered a particularly telling set of contrasts between three high-profile women.
40. Clinton's speech after the New Hampshire primary in which she claims to have found her voice can be seen at www.youtube.com/watch?v=-Gsovyf3u5U.
41. For Fox News Network's mid-campaign discussion of media coverage depicting Michelle Obama as angry, see www.youtube.com/watch?v=9a5DBDHQmtQ.
42. National Public Radio, for instance, has segment from September 7, 2008, titled "Sarah Palin: New Face of Feminism?," www.youtube.com/watch?v=9a5DBDHQmtQ. *The Daily Show with Jon Stewart* juxtaposed Palin's different answers to the question of her feminism on its show on October 27, 2008, www.thedailyshow.com/watch/mon-october-27-2008/moment-of-zen—is-sarah-palin-a-feminist-.
43. A comparison of the *Declaration of Sentiments* and Olympe de Gouges's *Declaration of the Rights of Women* must be done. The repetition of strategy is startling. The differences between French and U.S. feminist histories and theories would be well illuminated by such an undertaking. Also, the differences between a collective undertaking and an individual rewriting bear analysis. The drafters of the *Declaration of Sentiments* do not, to my knowledge, credit or cite de Gouges's work. It is doubtful they knew of it. None of the sources I consulted, including *The Second Sex* or Le Doeuff, connects these documents.
44. Stanton et al., *A History of Woman Suffrage*, 71.
45. Stanton et al., 70.
46. Davis, *Women, Race, and Class*, 53–54.
47. Davis, 57.
48. Sally Roesch Wagner, "The Indigenous Roots of United States Feminism," in *Feminist Politics, Activism, and Vision: Local and Global*

Challenges, ed. Luciana Ricciutelli, Angela Miles, and Margaret McFadden (Toronto: Inanna, 2004), 267.

49. Wagner, 279.
50. Wagner, 279. Joslyn Gage argues that the abridgement of native sovereignty represented by the vote and the denial of rights to women through the denial of the vote both expose problems with the United States republic (279). In other words, she recognizes how forced belonging and forced exclusion are evidence of problems with the government of the United States.
51. Indeed, it is unclear how this document could incorporate or recognize indigenous women's demands, since the *Declaration* assumed (albeit critically) and sought to strengthen the existence of the United States. For critiques of the existence of settler colonial states from indigenous perspectives, see, for instance, Glen Sean Coulthard, *Red Skin, White Masks* (Minneapolis: University of Minnesota Press, 2014); Leanne Simpson, *Dancing on Our Turtle's Back* (Winnipeg: Arbeiter Ring, 2011); and Eve Tuck and K. Wayne Yang, "Decolonization Is Not a Metaphor," *Decolonization: Indigeneity, Education, and Society* 1, no. 1 (2012): 1–40.
52. Stanton et al., *A History of Woman Suffrage*, 71.
53. There is much more to be said on this point and the complex development of race and voting rights. Barring people from voting based explicitly on gender and race was a later development in most states, for instance. Each state had different laws for who could vote and property qualifications were common. Women could vote, for instance, in New Jersey prior to 1807, if they met the property qualifications. Wellman, *The Road to Seneca Falls*, 138.
54. Davis, *Women, Race, and Class*, 54–58.
55. Clinton used this term to describe kids involved in gangs in a speech at Keene State College in New Hampshire in 1996 about the progress being made due to the Violent Crime Control and Law Enforcement Act of 1994 (which also contained the first version of the Violence Against Women Act). For a clip of the speech in which she uses the term: www.youtube.com/watch?v=jouCrA7ePno. For an overview of the comment and its role in the 2016 election, see www.politifact.com/truth-o-meter/statements/2016/aug/28/reince-priebus/did-hillary-clinton-call-african-american-youth-su/.
56. Roseann M. Mandziuk and Suzanne Pullon Fitch, "The Rhetorical Construction of Sojourner Truth," *Southern Journal of Communication* 66, no. 2 (2001): 120–138. Critical claims can be found throughout the

scholarship on Truth: for instance, her treatment as a symbol (Painter, especially *Sojourner Truth: A Life, A Symbol* [New York: Norton, 1996]), as an icon (John Ernest, "The Floating Icon and the Fluid Text: Rereading the Narrative of Sojourner Truth," *American Literature* 78, no. 3 [2006]: 460); a trickster figure (Donna Haraway, "Ecce Homo, Ain't [Ar'n't] I a Woman, and Inappropriate/d Others: The Human in a Post-Humanist Landscape," in *Feminists Theorize the Political*, ed. Judith Butler and Joan Scott [New York: Routledge, 1992]: 98); a proxy (Teresa C. Zackodnik, "'I Don't Know How You Will Feel When I Get Through': Racial Difference, Woman's Rights, and Sojourner Truth," *Feminist Studies* 30, no. 1 [2004]: 57); a synecdoche (Mandziuk and Fitch, "The Rhetorical Construction," Carla L. Peterson, *"Doers of the Word": African-American Speakers and Writers in the North, 1830–1880* [New Jersey: Rutgers University Press, 1995], 122); a symbol (Naomi Greyser, "Affective Geographies: Sojourner Truth's Narrative, Feminism, and the Ethical Bind of Sentimentalism," *American Literature* 79, no. 2 [2007]: 291); a myth (Katrine Smiet, "Post/Secular Truths: Sojourner Truth and the Intersections of Gender, Race and Religion," *European Journal of Women's Studies* 22, no. 1 [2015]: 8); and property (Cheryl Harris, "Finding Sojourner's Truth: Race, Gender, and the Institution of Property," *Cardozo Law Review* 18 [November 1996]: 309). My focus on Mandziuk and Fitch's claim that Truth has been turned into a metonym is in part driven by the resonance of this claim with Painter's, discussed below, that Truth has been used as a metonym for historical black women. Nell Irvin Painter, "Representing Truth: Sojourner Truth's Knowing and Becoming Known," *Journal of American History* 81, no. 2 (1994): 464. I also focus on this particular characterization because of its resonance with Spillers's charge that feminism engages in "a deadly metonymic playfulness" when it pursues a dominate position for white women while purporting to seek the liberation of all women. Spillers, "Interstices: A Small Drama of Words," in *Black, White, and in Color: Essays on American Literature and Culture*, 152–175 (Chicago: University of Chicago Press, 2003), 158.

57. Mandziuk and Fitch, "The Rhetorical Construction," 130.
58. Spillers, "Interstices," 158.
59. "Although she never distanced herself from the texts through which Gilbert and Gage portrayed her, she attempted to correct Stowe's article within three months of its publication, protesting in a letter to the *Boston Commonwealth* that she was not African and that she never called people 'honey.'" Painter, "Representing," 481.

60. Ernest, "The Floating Icon," 460.
61. In her argument about the ethical and appropriative uses of sentimentalism, Naomi Greyser in particular has done important work to understand the relationship between the speech and the larger *Narrative*. Greyser, "Affective Geographies," 275–305.
62. Painter, "Representing Truth," 464.
63. Ibid.
64. Ernest, while critiquing how Stowe and Gage portrayed Truth, at the same time reinforces the idea that what Truth knew was an effect of slavery and innate understanding: "Gage and Stowe separate Truth's power, her embodied experience and her native wisdom, from authority over the causes she served." Ernest, "The Floating Icon," 471. *Pace* this view of Truth, Painter argues that Truth employed practices of knowing common to those who cannot read. Painter, "Representing Truth," 465–470. Painter thus attributes to Truth ongoing practices of knowing that aided her in developing her authority, even within the constraints not just of white supremacist patriarchy, but within a culture that equates illiteracy with ignorance (465).
65. Davis, *Women, Race, and Class*, 64.
66. Carleton Mabee and Susan Mabee Newhouse, *Sojourner Truth: Slave, Prophet, Legend* (New York: New York University Press, 1995), 76.
67. Mabee and Mabee Newhouse, 76.
68. Mabee and Mabee Newhouse, 76.
69. Mabee and Mabee Newhouse, 77.
70. Davis, *Women, Race, and Class*, 60.
71. Mabee and Mabee Newhouse, *Sojourner Truth*, 71.
72. Mabee and Mabee Newhouse, 79.
73. Painter, *Sojourner Truth*, 169.
74. Mabee and Mabee Newhouse, *Sojourner Truth*, 80.
75. Mabee and Mabee Newhouse, 68.
76. Mabee and Mabee Newhouse, 68.
77. Painter points out that when Truth was a child, it was not illegal in New York state for slaves to learn to read. However, learning to read requires some help, which Truth did not have access to. Painter, "Representing Truth," 465. Mabee and Mabee Newhouse devote a chapter to speculating on why Truth never learned to read in which they explore many of the ways in which she negotiated white supremacy and was shaped by it. Mabee and Mabee Newhouse, "Why Did She Never Learn to Read?," in *Sojourner Truth*, 60–66.
78. Harris, "Finding Sojourner's Truth," 354.

79. Spillers, "Interstices," 156.
80. bell hooks, *"Ain't I a Woman?": Black Women and Feminism* (New York: Routledge, 2015).
81. Painter, *Sojourner Truth*, 287.
82. Painter, 285.
83. Painter could, of course, be wrong about why her audience cannot hear her argument. Aside from the compelling evidence Painter gives for her own account, the critical literature on Truth's reception well establishes a longstanding investment in mythological renderings of her. Particularly helpful is Mandziuk and Fitch's study of the "transformations" and "transfigurations" of Truth ("Rhetorical Construction"). Thus, even if Painter is wrong about why she, in particular, is not believed, her analysis helps us understand the staying power of a mythical version of Truth that renders hackneyed and anodyne not just her own words and actions, but those of black women throughout U.S. history.
84. Painter, *Sojourner Truth*, 285.
85. Harris, "Finding Sojourner's Truth," 355.
86. Saidiya Hartman, "Venus in Two Acts," *Small Axe* 12, no. 2 (2008): 4.
87. Painter, *Sojourner Truth*, 126.
88. Paralysis here seems to be meant to reinforce the idea of indecision. The implication is that one who cannot move is one who cannot decide to move. This implication not only denies important phenomenological features of paralysis that undermine a metaphysics of mind over matter, but it also leads away from the imperilment the image is meant to invoke. Not only are white men caught in a situation that could produce indecision, but one in which, whether they make a decision or not, they are caught between powerful and threatening forces. The metaphor is thus both ableist and works against Peterson's point. See Schalk, "Metaphorically Speaking: Ableist Metaphors in Feminist Writing," *Disability Studies Quarterly* 33, no. 4 (2013): 1–21.
89. Peterson, *"Doers of the Word,"* 54.
90. Sojourner Truth, *Narrative of Sojourner Truth* (New York: Penguin, 1998), 93. Peterson suggests that with this image, "Gage has in fact placed black women in the same structural position as those men who help white women into carriages and lift them over ditches." Peterson, *"Doers of the Word,"* 53.
91. Zackodnik, "'I Don't Know,'" 56.
92. Greyser, "Affective Geographies," 283.
93. Greyser's reading carefully traces how sentimentalism can be used to produce intimacy to different ends, some ethical, some co-opting.

94. Truth was also part of religious movements and was renowned as a preacher. Katrine Smiet's "Post/Secular Truths" draws attention to the importance of religious themes for feminist reception of Truth's work.
95. Kazanjian, *The Brink of Freedom: Improvising Life in the Nineteenth-Century Atlantic World* (Durham: Duke University Press, 2016), 123; David Kazanjian, "Hegel, Liberia," review of *Hegel, Haiti, and Universal History*, by Susan Buck-Morss, *diacritics* 40, no. 1 (2012): 25. In "Hegel, Liberia" (parts of which are incorporated into chapter 2 of *The Brink of Freedom*), Kazanjian is reviewing Susan Buck-Morss's *Hegel, Haiti, and Universal History*. It is clear from the exchange between Kazanjian and Buck-Morss that he is at pains to shift our focus from "great men" to texts written by people never recognized as such (33). Painter, in a critique of historical inheritance, calls Truth "an invented great." Painter, "Representing Truth," 462. While "great men" and "invented greats" are not the same thing, it still seems I may be erring to bring Kazanjian's points to one so apparently well remembered. My hope is that by contributing to the destabilization of Truth's "greatness," I am contributing to speculative reading of her work.
96. Painter, *Sojourner Truth*, 125.
97. Kazanjian, *Brink of Freedom*, 122–123; Kazanjian, "Hegel, Liberia," 24.
98. Kazanjian, *Brink of Freedom*, 125; Kazanjian, "Hegel, Liberia," 26.
99. Harris, "Finding Sojourner's Truth," 355.
100. Audre Lorde, "The Master's Tools Will Never Dismantle the Master's House," in *Sister Outsider: Essays and Speeches by Audre Lorde* (Freedom: Crossing, 1984), 112.
101. Ida B. Wells-Barnett, "Crusader for Justice," in *Let Nobody Turn Us Around: Voices of Resistance, Reform, and Renewal: An Anthology*, 2nd ed., ed. Manning Marable and Leith Mullings (Lanham, MD: Rowman and Littlefield, 2009), 192.
102. Crystal N. Feimster, *Southern Horrors: Women and the Politics of Rape and Lynching* (Cambridge, MA: Harvard University Press, 2009), 109.
103. Painter, "Representing Truth," 488. See also "Truth in Photographs," in Painter, *Sojourner Truth*, 185–199.
104. Painter, "Representing Truth," 462. Even in her earliest work on Truth, Painter connects the difficulties the archive presents for Truth to larger issues of telling history: "The obstructions in the way of Sojourner Truth's biography are commonplace and lie between the biographer and most of her female, poor, and/or non-white subjects. If Sojourner Truth, who is at least very famous, poses such challenges to biographers, there are scores—hundreds?— of other, less-known

but worthy subjects who pose exactly the same problems. The Sojourner Truth biographical problem becomes a larger question of how to deal with people who are in History but who have not left the kinds of sources to which historians and biographers ordinarily turn. In order not to cede biography to subjects who had resources enough to secure the educations that would allow them to leave the usual sources for the usual kind of biographies, we need to construct new biographical approaches." Nell Irvin Painter, "Sojourner Truth in Life and Memory: Writing the Biography of an American Exotic," *Gender and History* 2, no. 1 (Spring 1990): 14.

105. Sarah Jane Cervenak offers a reading of Truth as philosophically authoritative, but concludes her reading with the following: "if we really believe in Truth's philosophical intervention, then maybe it's best to leave the 'deeper pattern' of her philosophical desire alone." Cervenak, *Wandering: Philosophical Performances of Racial and Sexual Freedom* (Durham: Duke University Press, 2014). Such a conclusion seems to contradict what Cervenak's otherwise perspicacious reading indicates. That is, Cervenak's reading seems to indicate there is a lot of reason to read Truth's words philosophically rather than leaving them alone. Cervenak's point, I believe, is to warn us against thinking we have made Truth transparent to ourselves through a philosophical reading, but I worry that in a context where the philosophical authority of Truth is already a tenuous thing, any license to dismiss her will be welcome.
106. Ladelle McWhorter, "The Abolition of Philosophy," in *Active Intolerance: Michel Foucault, the Prisons Information Group, and the Future of Abolition*, ed. Perry Zurn and Andrew Dilts (New York: Palgrave Macmillan, 2016), 36.
107. McWhorter, 36.

CONCLUSION

1. Deutscher, "When Feminism Is 'High' and Ignorance Is 'Low': Harriet Taylor Mill on the Progress of the Species," *Hypatia* 21, no. 3 (2006): 136–150, 147.
2. See "Kansas," chapter 24 in Painter, *Sojourner Truth: A Life, A Symbol* (New York: Norton, 1996).
3. Painter, *Sojourner Truth*, 236.
4. For an overview of how the dominion over occupied land was and is conceived of as European (and later U.S. American), see Patrick Wolfe,

"Settler Colonialism and the Elminiation of the Native," *Journal of Genocide Research* 8, no. 4 (2006): 387–406.

5. Tuck and Yang, "Decolonization Is Not a Metaphor," *Decolonization: Indigeneity, Education, and Society* 1, no. 1 (2012): 1–40, 5.
6. As Tuck and Yang write, "The abolition of slavery often presumes the expansion of settlers who own Native land and life via inclusion of emancipated slaves and prisoners into the settler nation-state." Tuck and Yang, 29.
7. Tuck and Yang offer a helpful visual in the form of maps showing snapshots of settler invasions at different historical moments, 1850, 1865, 1880, and 1990, and proposing a decolonial reversal of that timeline.
8. Tuck and Yang, 3.
9. Tuck and Yang, 26.
10. Deutscher, "When Feminism Is 'High,'" 143.
11. Kazanjian, *The Brink of Freedom: Improvising Life in the Nineteenth-Century Atlantic World* (Durham: Duke University Press, 2016), 123; Kazanjian, "Hegel, Liberia," review of *Hegel, Haiti, and Universal History*, by Susan Buck-Morss, *diacritics* 40, no. 1 (2012): 25.
12. Sarah Deer, *The Beginning and End of Rape: Confronting Sexual Violence in Native America* (Minneapolis: University of Minnesota Press, 2015), 16.
13. Deer, 20.
14. Deer, 17–18.
15. Deer, 30.
16. Tuck and Yang, "Decolonization Is Not a Metaphor," 21.
17. Tuck and Yang, 21.
18. Tuck and Yang, 19.
19. See especially Taiaiake Alfred, *Peace, Power, and Righteousness: An Indigenous Manifesto* (Oxford: Oxford University Press, 1999); Glen Sean Coulthard, *Red Skin, White Masks: Rejecting the Colonial Politics of Recognition* (Minneapolis: University of Minnesota Press, 2014); Audra Simpson, *Mohawk Interruptus: Political Life Across the Borders of Settler States* (Durham: Duke University Press, 2014); and Leanne Simpson, *Dancing on Our Turtle's Back: Stories of Nishnaabeg Re-Creation, Resurgence and a New Emergence* (Winnipeg: Arbeiter Ring, 2011).
20. Tuck and Yang, "Decolonization Is Not a Metaphor," 35.
21. "Having encountered what they understand as chaos, the empowered need not name further, since chaos is sufficient naming within itself."

Spillers, "Interstices: A Small Drama of Words," in *Black, White, and in Color: Essays on American Literature and Culture*, 152–175 (Chicago: University of Chicago Press, 2003), 156.

APPENDIX B

1. Carleton Mabee and Susan Mabee Newhouse, *Sojourner Truth: Slave, Prophet, Legend* (New York: New York University Press, 1995), 81–82; and Nell Irvin Painter, *Sojourner Truth: A Life, a Symbol* (New York: Norton, 1996), 125–126.
2. Sojourner Truth, *Narrative of Sojourner Truth* (New York: Penguin, 1998), 131–135.

BIBLIOGRAPHY

Alanen, Lilli, and Charlotte Witt, eds. "Feminist History of Philosophy." In *Feminist Reflections on the History of Philosophy*. Dordrecht: Kluwer Academic, 2004.

Alcoff, Linda. "Is the Feminist Critique of Reason Rational." *Philosophic Exchange* 26 (1996): 59–79.

Alfred, Taiaiake. *Peace, Power, and Righteousness: An Indigenous Manifesto*. Oxford: Oxford University Press, 1999.

Arnal, Stella Gonzalez. Review of *Women Philosophers*, by Mary Warnock. *British Journal for the History of Philosophy* 6, no. 2 (1998): 306–308.

Bevacqua, Maria. *Rape on the Public Agenda: Feminism and the Politics of Sexual Assault*. Boston: Northeastern University Press, 2000.

Blair, Elena Duverges. "Women: The Unrecognized Teachers of the Platonic Socrates." *Ancient Philosophy* 16 (1996): 333–350.

Broad, Jacqueline. *Women Philosophers of the Seventeenth Century*. Cambridge: Cambridge University Press, 2002.

Brodribb, Somer. *Nothing Mat(t)ers: A Feminist Critique of Postmodernism*. North Melbourne: Spinifex, 1992.

Brown, Wendy. "'Supposing Truth Were a Woman . . .': Plato's Subversion of Masculine Discourse." In *Feminist Interpretations of Plato*, edited by Nancy Tuana, 157–180. University Park: Pennsylvania State University Press, 1994.

Burke, Carolyn. "Translation Modified: Irigaray in English." In *Engaging with Irigaray: Feminist Philosophy and Modern European Thought*, edited by Carolyn Burke, Naomi Schor, and Margaret Whitford, 249–262. New York: Columbia University Press, 1994.

Butler, Judith. "Against Proper Objects. *Introduction*." *differences: A Journal of Feminist Cultural Studies* 6, nos. 2–3 (1994): 1–26.

——. *Gender Trouble*. New York: Routledge, 2006.

Cervenak, Sarah Jane. *Wandering: Philosophical Performances of Racial and Sexual Freedom*. Durham: Duke University Press, 2014.

Chanter, Tina. *Ethics of Eros: Irigaray's Re-Writing of the Philosophers*. New York: Routledge, 1995.

Cisneros, Natalie. "Resisting 'Massive Elimination.'" In *Active Intolerance: Michel Foucault, the Prisons Information Group, and the Future of Abolition*, edited by Perry Zurn and Andrew Dilts, 241–257. New York: Palgrave Macmillan, 2015.

Coulthard, Glen Sean. *Red Skin, White Masks: Rejecting the Colonial Politics of Recognition*. Minneapolis: University of Minnesota Press, 2014.

Craig, Maxine Leeds. *Ain't I a Beauty Queen? Black Women, Beauty, and the Politics of Race*. Oxford: Oxford University Press, 2002.

Dancy, R. M. "On *A History of Women Philosophers*, Vol. I." Review of *A History of Women Philosophers*, vol. 1, Mary Ellen Waithe. *Hypatia* 4, no. 1 (March 1989): 160–171.

Davis, Angela Y. *Are Prisons Obsolete?* New York: Seven Stories, 2003.

——. *Women, Race, and Class*. New York: Vintage, 1983.

Davis, Sue. *The Political Thought of Elizabeth Cady Stanton: Women's Rights and the American Political Traditions*. New York: New York University Press, 2008.

de Botton, Alain. *The Consolations of Philosophy*. New York: Vintage, 2000.

Deer, Sarah. *The Beginning and End of Rape: Confronting Sexual Violence in Native America*. Minneapolis: University of Minnesota Press, 2015.

De Gournay, Marie le Jars. "The Equality of Men and Women." In *The Neglected Canon: Nine Women Philosophers First to the Twentieth Century*, edited by Therese Boos Dykeman, 89–100. Dordrecht: Kluwer Academic, 1999.

DesAutels, Peggy. "Is the Climate Any Warmer for Women in Philosophy?" *APA Newsletter for Feminism and Philosophy* 11, no. 1 (2011): 4–7.

Deutscher, Penelope. "'Imperfect Discretion': Interventions Into the History of Philosophy by Twentieth-Century French Women Philosophers." *Hypatia* 15, no. 2 (Spring 2000): 160–180.

——. *A Politics of Impossible Difference: The Later Works of Luce Irigaray*. Ithaca: Cornell University Press, 2002.

——. "When Feminism Is 'High' and Ignorance Is 'Low': Harriet Taylor Mill on the Progress of the Species." *Hypatia* 21, no. 3 (2006): 136–150.

——. *Yielding Gender*. London: Routledge, 1997.

Dotson, Kristie. "Conceptualizing Epistemic Oppression." *Social Epistemology: A Journal of Knowledge, Culture, and Policy* 28, no. 2 (2014): 115–138.

——. "How Is This Paper Philosophy?" *Comparative Philosophy* 3, no. 1 (2013): 3–29.

Duran, Jane. *Eight Women Philosophers: Theory, Politics, and Feminism.* Urbana: University of Illinois Press, 2006.

Dykeman, Therese Boos. "Introduction: Philosophy in a Feminist Voice?" In *Philosophy in a Feminist Voice: Critiques and Reconstructions*, edited by Therese Boos Dykeman, 3–17. Princeton: Princeton University Press, 1998.

Ernest, John. "The Floating Icon and the Fluid Text: Rereading the Narrative of Sojourner Truth." *American Literature* 78, no. 3 (2006): 459–486.

Evans, Nancy. "Diotima and Demeter as Mystagogues in Plato's *Symposium*." *Hypatia* 21, no. 2 (Spring 2006): 1–27.

Fauré, Christine. *Democracy Without Women: Feminism and the Rise of Liberal Individualism in France.* Bloomington: Indiana University Press, 1991.

Feimster, Crystal N. *Southern Horrors: Women and the Politics of Rape and Lynching.* Cambridge, MA: Harvard University Press, 2009.

Gardner, Catherine Villaneuva. *Historical Dictionary of Feminist Philosophy.* Lanham, MD: Scarecrow, 2006.

——. *Rediscovering Women Philosophers: Philosophical Genre and the Boundaries of Philosophy.* Boulder: Westview, 2000.

Garfield, Jay L., and Bryan W. Van Norden. "If Philosophy Won't Diversify, Let's Call It What It Really Is." *New York Times*, May 11, 2016. www.nytimes.com/2016/05/11/opinion/if-philosophy-wont-diversify-lets-call-it-what-it-really-is.html?mcubz=0&_r=0.

Gottschalk, Marie. *The Prison and the Gallows: The Politics of Mass Incarceration in America.* New York: Cambridge University Press, 2006.

Green, Karen. *The Woman of Reason: Feminism, Humanism, and Political Thought.* Cambridge: Polity, 1995.

Greyser, Naomi. "Affective Geographies: Sojourner Truth's Narrative, Feminism, and the Ethical Bind of Sentimentalism." *American Literature* 79, no. 2 (2007): 275–305.

Grosz, Elizabeth. "Feminist Theory and the Challenge to Knowledges." *Women Studies International Forum* 10, no. 5 (1987): 475–480.

——. *Jacques Lacan: A Feminist Introduction.* London: Routledge, 1990.

——. *Sexual Subversions: Three French Feminists.* Sydney: Allen and Unwin, 1989.

Guenther, Lisa. "Other Fecundities: Proust and Irigaray on Sexual Difference." *differences* 21, no. 2 (2010): 24–45.

Gurko, Miriam. *The Ladies of Seneca Falls: The Birth of the Woman's Rights Movement.* New York: Macmillan, 1974.

Hall, Kim Q. "Queerness, Disability, and *The Vagina Monologues*." *Hypatia* 20, no. 1 (2005): 99–119.

Halperin, David. "Why Is Diotima a Woman? Platonic Eros and the Figuration of Gender." In *Before Sexuality: The Construction of Erotic Experience in the Ancient Greek World*, edited by David Halperin, John Winkler, and Froma Zeitlin, 257–308. Princeton: Princeton University Press, 1990.

Haraway, Donna. "Ecce Homo, Ain't (Ar'n't) I a Woman, and Inappropriate/d Others: The Human in a Post-Humanist Landscape." In *Feminists Theorize the Political*, edited by Judith Butler and Joan Scott, 86–100. New York: Routledge, 1992.

Harding, Sandra. *The Science Question in Feminism*. Ithaca: Cornell University Press, 1986.

Harris, Cheryl. "Finding Sojourner's Truth: Race, Gender, and the Institution of Property." *Cardozo Law Review* 18 (November 1996): 309–408.

Hartman, Saidiya. "Venus in Two Acts." *Small Axe* 12, no. 2 (2008): 1–14.

Haslanger, Sally. "Changing the Ideology and Culture of Philosophy: Not by Reason (Alone)." *Hypatia* 23, no. 2 (2008): 210–223.

Higgins, Lisa Cochran. "Adulterous Individualism, Socialism, and Free Love in Nineteenth-Century Anti-Suffrage Writing." *Legacy* 21, no. 2 (2004): 193–209.

hooks, bell. *Ain't I a Woman? Black Women and Feminism*. New York: Routledge, 2015.

Hunter, Richard. *Plato's Symposium*. Oxford: Oxford University Press, 2004.

Irigaray, Luce. *Between East and West: From Singularity to Community*. New York: Columbia University Press, 2002.

——. *An Ethics of Sexual Difference*. Translated by Carolyn Burke and Gillian C. Gill. Ithaca: Cornell University Press, 1993.

——. *I Love to You: Sketch of a Possible Felicity in History*. Translate by Alison Martin. New York: Routledge, 1996.

——. *Speculum of the Other Woman*. Translated by Gillian C. Gill. Ithaca: Cornell University Press, 1985.

——. *This Sex Which Is Not One*. Translated by C. Porter. Ithaca: Cornell University Press, 1985.

Jacobs, Jo Ellen, ed. *The Complete Works of Harriet Taylor Mill*. Bloomington: Indiana University Press, 1998.

——. "'The Lot of Gifted Ladies Is Hard': A Study of Harriet Taylor Mill Criticism." *Hypatia* 9, no. 3 (1994): 132–162.

Jones, Rachel. *Irigaray: Towards a Sexuate Philosophy*. Cambridge: Polity, 2011.

Kazanjian, David. *The Brink of Freedom: Improvising Life in the Nineteenth-Century Atlantic World*. Durham: Duke University Press, 2016.

——. "Freedom's Surprise: Two Paths Through Slavery's Archives." *History of the Present* 6, no. 2 (2016): 133–145.

——. "Hegel, Liberia." Review of *Hegel, Haiti, and Universal History*, by Susan Buck-Morss. *Diacritics* 40, no. 1 (2012): 6–39.

——. "Scenes of Speculation." *Social Text* 33, no. 4 (125) (2015): 77–84.

Kersey, Ethel M. *Women Philosophers: A Bio-Critical Sourcebook*. New York: Greenwood, 1989.

Kim, Mimi. *Dancing the Carceral Creep: The Anti-Domestic Violence Movement and the Paradoxical Pursuit of Criminalization, 1973–1986*. University of California, Berkeley: Institute for the Study of Societal Issues, 2015.

Kittay, Eva Feder, and Linda Martín Alcoff. *The Blackwell Guide to Feminist Philosophy*. Malden, MA: Blackwell, 2006.

Kourany, Janet. "Philosophy in a Feminist Voice?" In *Philosophy in a Feminist Voice: Critiques and Reconstructions*, edited by Janet Kourany, 3–17. Princeton: Princeton University Press, 1998.

Kuykendall, Eleanor H. "Introduction to 'Sorcerer Love,' by Luce Irigaray." *Hypatia* 3, no. 3 (1989): 28–31.

Landau, Iddo. *Is Philosophy Andocentric?* University Park: Pennsylvania State University Press, 2006.

Le Doeuff, Michèle. "Ants and Women, or Philosophy Without Borders." In *Contemporary French Philosophy*, edited by A. Phillips Griffiths, 41–54. Cambridge: Cambridge University Press, 1987.

——. "Each Man in His Cave." In *Women's Voices, Women's Rights: Oxford Amnesty Lectures 1996*, edited by Alison Jeffries, 101–116. Boulder: Westview, 1999.

——. "Feminism Is Back in France: Or Is It?" *Hypatia* 15, no. 4 (Fall 2000): 243–255.

——. "Harsh Times." *New Left Review* 1, no. 199 (May-June 1993): 127–139.

——. *Hipparchia's Choice: An Essay Concerning Women, Philosophy, Etc.* Oxford: Blackwell, 2007.

——. *The Philosophical Imaginary*. London: Continuum, 2002.

——. *The Sex of Knowing*. New York: Routledge, 2003.

——. "Simone de Beauvoir and Existentialism." *Feminist Studies* 6, no. 2 (Summer 1980): 277–289.

——. "Women and Philosophy." In *French Feminist Thought: A Reader*, edited by Toril Moi, 181–209. Oxford: Basil Blackwell, 1987.

——. "Women, Reason, Etc." *differences: A Journal of Feminist Cultural Studies* 2, no. 3 (1990): 1–13.

Lloyd, Genevieve. *Feminism and the History of Philosophy*. Oxford: Oxford University Press, 2002.

——. "Feminism in the History of Philosophy: Appropriating the Past." In *The Cambridge Companion to Feminism in Philosophy*, edited by Miranda Fricker and Jennifer Hornsby, 245–263. Cambridge: Cambridge University Press, 2000.

——. "History of Philosophy and the Critique of Reason." *Critical Philosophy* 1, no. 1 (1984): 5–23.

——. "Maleness, Metaphor, and the 'Crisis' of Reason." In *Feminist Social Thought: A Reader*, edited by Diana Tietjens Meyers, 286–301. New York: Routledge, 1997.

——. *The Man of Reason: "Male" and "Female" in Western Philosophy*. London: Routledge, 1993.

Lorde, Audre. "The Master's Tools Will Never Dismantle the Master's House." In *Sister Outsider: Essays and Speeches by Audre Lorde*. Freedom: Crossing, 1984.

Mabee, Carleton, and Susan Mabee Newhouse. *Sojourner Truth: Slave, Prophet, Legend*. New York: New York University Press: 1995.

Mandziuk, Roseann M., and Suzanne Pullon Fitch. "The Rhetorical Construction of Sojourner Truth." *Southern Journal of Communication* 66, no. 2 (2001): 120–138.

Mani, Bonnie. *Women, Power, and Political Change*. Lanham, MD: Lexington, 2007.

Maras, Steven. "Translating Michèle Le Doeuff's Analytics." In *Michèle Le Doeuff: Operative Philosophy and Imaginary Practice*, edited by Max Deutscher, 83–104. New York: Humanity, 2000.

Martin, Biddy. "Sexualities Without Genders and Other Queer Utopias." *Diacritics* 24, nos. 2–3 (Summer-Autumn 1994): 104–121.

May, Vivian M., and Beth A. Ferri. "Fixated on Ability: Questioning Ableist Metaphors in Feminist Theories of Resistance." *Prose Studies* 27, nos. 1–2 (2005): 120–140.

McAllister, Linda Lopez. "On the Possibility of Feminist Philosophy." *Hypatia* 9, no. 2 (1994): 188–196.

McWhorter, Ladelle. "The Abolition of Philosophy." In *Active Intolerance: Michel Foucault, the Prisons Information Group, and the Future of Abolition*, edited by Perry Zurn and Andrew Dilts, 23–40. New York: Palgrave Macmillan, 2016.

Minnich, Elizabeth. *Transforming Knowledge*. Philadelphia: Temple University Press, 2005.

Morris, Meaghan. *The Pirates Fiancée: Feminism, Reading, Postmodernism*. London: Verso, 1988.

Navia, Luis E. *The Socratic Presence: A Study of the Sources*. New York: Garland, 1993.

Nussbaum, Martha. *The Fragility of Goodness: Luck and Ethics in Greek Tragedy and Philosophy*. Cambridge: Cambridge University Press, 2001.

Nye, Andrea. "The Hidden Host: Irigaray and Diotima at Plato's Symposium." *Hypatia* 3, no. 3 (1989): 45–61.

——. *Philosophia: The Thought of Rosa Luxemborg, Simone Weil, and Hannah Arendt*. New York: Routledge, 1994.

——. *Socrates and Diotima*. New York: Palgrave Macmillan, 2015.

O'Dwyer, Shaun. "The Unacknowledged Socrates in the Works of Luce Irigaray." *Hypatia* 21, no. 2 (Spring 2006): 28–44.

O'Grady, Jane. "Heloise Complex." In *The Oxford Companion to Philosophy*, edited by Ted Honderich, 350–351. Oxford: Oxford University Press, 1995.

O'Neill, Eileen. "Early Modern Women Philosophers and the History of Philosophy." *Hypatia* 20, no. 3 (Summer 2005): 185–197.

——. "Justifying the Inclusion of Women in Our Histories of Philosophy: The Case of Marie de Gournay." In *The Blackwell Guide to Feminist Philosophy*, edited by Linda Martín Alcoff and Eva Feder Kittay, 17–42. Malden, MA: Blackwell, 2007.

Painter, Nell Irvin. "Representing Truth: Sojourner Truth's Knowing and Becoming Known." *Journal of American History* 81, no. 2 (1994): 461–492.

——. *Sojourner Truth: A Life, a Symbol*. New York: Norton, 1996.

——. "Sojourner Truth in Life and Memory: Writing the Biography of an American Exotic." *Gender and History* 2, no. 1 (Spring 1990): 3–16.

Pateman, Carole. Review of *The Man of Reason: "Male" and "Female" in Western Philosophy* by Genevieve Lloyd. *Political Theory* 14, no. 3 (August 1986): 505–509.

Paxton, Molly, Carrie Figdor, and Valerie Tiberius. "Quantifying the Gender Gap: An Empirical Study of the Underrepresentation of Women in Philosophy." *Hypatia* 27, no. 4 (2012): 949–957.

Payne, Michael. Review of *Selected Writings*, by Sarah Kofman, edited by Thomas Albrecht. *College Literature* 35, no. 3 (2008): 201–206.

Peterson, Carla. *Doers of the Word: African American Women Speakers and Writers in the North (1830–1880)*. New Brunswick: Rutgers University Press, 1995.

Poullain de la Barre, François. *Three Cartesian Feminist Treatises*. Translated by Vivien Bosley. Chicago: University of Chicago Press, 2002.

Richie, Beth. *Arrested Justice: Black Women, Violence, and America's Prison Nation*. New York: New York University Press, 2012.

Riley, Denise. *"Am I That Name?": Feminism and the Category of "Women" in History*. Minneapolis: University of Minnesota Press, 1988.

Rogers, Dorothy. "The Other Philosophy Club: America's First Academic Women Philosophers." *Hypatia* 24, no. 2 (Spring 2009): 164–185.

Saul, Jennifer. "Implicit Bias, Stereotype Threat, and Women in Philosophy." In *Women in Philosophy: What Needs to Change*, edited by Katrina Hutchison and Fiona Jenkins, 39–60. Oxford: Oxford University Press, 2013.

Schalk, Sami. "Metaphorically Speaking: Ableist Metaphors in Feminist Writing." *Disability Studies Quarterly* 33, no. 4 (2013): 1–21.

Scott, Alan, and William A. Welton. *Erotic Wisdom: Philosophy and Intermediacy in Plato's Symposium*. Albany: State University of New York Press, 2008.

Scott, Joan Wallach. *Gender and the Politics of History*. New York: Columbia University Press, 1999.

Simons, Margaret A. "The Silencing of Simone de Beauvoir: Guess What's Missing from *The Second Sex*." *Women's Studies International Forum* 6, no. 5 (1983): 559–564.

Simpson, Audra. *Mohawk Interruptus: Political Life Across the Borders of Settler States*. Durham: Duke University Press, 2014.

Simpson, Leanne. *Dancing on our Turtle's Back: Stories of Nishnaabeg Re-Creation, Resurgence and a New Emergence*. Winnipeg: Arbeiter Ring, 2011.

Smiet, Katrine. "Post/Secular Truths: Sojourner Truth and the Intersections of Gender, Race and Religion." *European Journal of Women's Studies* 22, no. 1 (2015): 7–21.

Spillers, Hortense. "Interstices: A Small Drama of Words." In *Black, White, and in Color: Essays on American Literature and Culture*, 152–175. Chicago: University of Chicago Press, 2003.

Stanton, Elizabeth Cady, Susan Brownell Anthony, Matilda Joslyn Gage, and Ida Husted Harper. *A History of Woman Suffrage*. Vol. 1. Salem: Ayer, 1985.

Taylor, A. E. *Plato: The Man and His Work*. London: Methuen, 1969.

Truth, Sojourner, and Olive Gilbert. *Narrative of Sojourner Truth; A Bondswoman of Olden Time, with a History of Her Labors and Correspondence Drawn from Her "Book of Life."* New York: Penguin, 1998.

Tuck, Eve, and K. Wayne Yang. "Decolonization Is Not a Metaphor." *Decolonization: Indigeneity, Education, and Society* 1, no. 1 (2012): 1–40.

Vidali, Amy. "Seeing What We Know: Disability and Theories of Metaphor." *Journal of Literary and Cultural Disability Studies* 4, no. 1 (2010): 33–54.

Wagner, Sally Roesch. "The Indigenous Roots of United States Feminism." In *Feminist Politics, Activism, and Vision: Local and Global Challenges*, edited by Luciana Ricciutelli, Angela Miles, and Margaret McFadden, 267–284. Toronto: Inanna, 2004.

Waithe, Mary Ellen, ed. *A History of Women Philosophers*. Vol. 1. Dordrecht: Kluwer Academic, 1987.

Walker, Margaret Urban. "Diotima's Ghost: The Uncertain Place of Feminist Philosophy in Professional Philosophy." *Hypatia* 20, no. 3 (Summer 2005): 153–164.

Walker, Michelle. "Silence and Reason: Woman's Voice in Philosophy." *Australasian Journal of Philosophy* 71, no. 4 (December 1993): 400–424.

Warnock, Mary, Ed. *Women Philosophers*. London: Orion, 1996.

Warren, Karen J. *An Unconventional History of Western Philosophy: Conversations Between Men and Women Philosophers*. Lanham, MD: Rowman and Littlefield, 2009.

Warren, Mary Ann. "Feminist Archeology: Uncovering Women's Philosophical History." Review of *A History of Women Philosophers*, vol. 1, by Mary Ellen Waithe. *Hypatia* 4, no. 1 (March 1989): 155–159.

Weed, Elizabeth. "The Question of Style." In *Engaging with Irigaray: Feminist Philosophy and Modern European Thought*, edited by Carolyn Burke, Naomi Schor, and Margaret Whitford, 79–110. New York: Columbia University Press, 1994.

Weiss, Penny A. *Canon Fodder: Historical Women Political Thinkers*. University Park: Pennsylvania State University Press, 2009.

Wellman, Judith. *The Road to Seneca Falls: Elizabeth Cady Stanton and the First Woman's Rights Convention*. Urbana: University of Illinois Press, 2004.

Wells-Barnett, Ida B. "Crusader for Justice." In *Let Nobody Turn Us Around: Voices of Resistance, Reform, and Renewal: An Anthology*, 2nd ed., edited by Manning Marable and Leith Mullings, 191–195. Lanham, MD: Rowman and Littlefield, 2009.

Whitford, Margaret. *Luce Irigaray: Philosophy in the Feminine*. New York: Routledge, 1991.

Witt, Charlotte. "Feminist History of Philosophy." In *Feminist Reflections on the History of Philosophy*, edited by Lilli Alanen and Charlotte Witt, 1–17. Dordrecht: Kluwer Academic, 2004.

Wright, Heather Hadar. "Irigaray's Appropriation: *Sorcerer Love's* Flawed Reading of Plato's *Symposium*." Presentation at the Western Political Science Association Meeting, San Diego, CA, March 20–22, 2008. Used by permission of the author.

INDEX